PRACTICAL GARDENING
FOR AMATEURS

By the same author

The Amateur Gardener
Your New Garden
Your Garden Week by Week
Amateur Gardening Pocket Guide
Garden Pest Control
Utility Garden for Home Needs
Simple Rose Growing
The Encyclopaedia of Plant Portraits
The Encyclopaedia of Garden Work and Terms
Flowers in Colour
Garden Plants in Colour

SPRAYING ROSES WITH A USEFUL TYPE OF KNAPSACK MACHINE

PRACTICAL GARDENING

for Amateurs

A. G. L. HELLYER, F.L.S.

LONDON: W. H. & L. COLLINGRIDGE LTD
FLORIDA: TRANSATLANTIC ARTS

First Published in 1935
by W H & L Collingridge Limited
2-10 Tavistock Street London WC2
and in the United States of America
by Transatlantic Arts Incorporated
Hollywood-by-the-Sea Florida
Printed in Great Britain by
Billing & Sons Limited
Guildford and London

Fourth Edition
(Revised and reset) 1954

Sixth Impression 1958

Seventh Impression 1960

Foreword

THE fact that Practical Gardening for Amateurs has run through three editions and that a fourth is now called for suggests that it continues to fulfil its purpose. This was to provide an introduction to gardening; a simple summary of garden craft for the reader with little or no practical experience.

From time to time I have made slight alterations and additions to the book to keep it up-to-date but at no time have I thought it wise to depart from its basic plan. There is much that must remain unsaid when one tries to write about every aspect of gardening in a book of this length. Also, there must be an occasional tendency to over-simplify; to make statements that are, perhaps, a little too dogmatic and which in a larger work would be qualified with a few 'ifs' and 'buts'. That may not be a bad thing in a book intended for beginners who do not wish to be hedged around by too many uncertainties but rather seek plain guidance as to what they should do.

In each preceding edition I have added a footnote to my foreword telling readers that this is an *Amateur Gardening* book and that the service of that popular weekly paper is available to them. If there are any points about gardening that remain obscure to them after reading this book or if they meet any unexpected difficulties as they commence to garden, they have only to write to the 'Doubts and Difficulties' department of *Amateur Gardening* and our experts will give them all the help in their power. I repeat the added wish that they may find in gardening a hobby which will give them many hours of happiness and no causes for regret.

Rowfant, 1954   A. G. L. HELLYER

Contents

3. THE GREENHOUSE

4. THE FRUIT GARDEN

5. THE VEGETABLE GARDEN

Illustrations

9

LINE DRAWINGS

I

GENERAL GARDEN MANAGEMENT

CHAPTER ONE

The Selection of Tools

'NEITHER wise men nor fools can work without tools,' says the old jingle. The proverb certainly applies to gardening, and one is tempted to add 'good tools' into the bargain, for it is impossible to cultivate ground properly with inferior implements; yet thorough working of the soil is the secret of every garden success.

The beginner is often at a loss to know what best to purchase in the way of tools. Certain implements will be found absolutely necessary at the very beginning of gardening operations, while others which are used only a few times during the season may be dispensed with during the early and more expensive years of laying out a garden. It is, however, neither wise nor economical in the long run to try to cultivate ground without reasonably good equipment.

Spades Every gardener must have a spade, but even the selection of this is not so simple as the novice might think. If a spade is too small there will be much grumbling at the time it takes to dig a plot of ground, and if too large the work will prove too tiring to be pleasant. For most people a No. 2 size is big enough. The blade should always be the full length to ensure deep digging, and if a lighter spade is required for ladies or children it should be narrower rather than shorter. There is no economy in buying a low-priced spade, made of cheap, soft metal, with inadequate strengthening plates for the wooden haft.

Forks A four-pronged fork will be required not only for breaking up soil, but for digging potatoes, collecting refuse and moving dung. In one of the illustrations a broad flat-tined variety that is most serviceable for lifting artichokes, potatoes, etc., is shown, while in another a square-tined fork is shown for breaking up stiff, clay subsoils.

Hoes There are several kinds of hoe; the most important is the Dutch hoe. This should be the most used of all tools. A loose, open surface soil is essential for the successful growth of most flowers and vegetables, and this can best be obtained without risk of damage to the roots by using the Dutch hoe whenever conditions are suitable. As a weed-killer it is indispensable, and has the advantage that the ground worked with it is not walked on as with other hoes and therefore there is no chance of the weeds being trodden in again to make fresh roots. The draw hoe, of which a useful variety is illustrated, can also be used for aerating the soil and for weeding, but is especially serviceable for break-

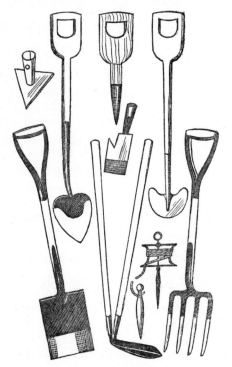

SOME USEFUL TOOLS

Top, left to right: triangular hoe, turf lifting iron, dibber, with daisy spud below, turfing iron. Below, left to right: spade, edging shears, two good lines, square tined fork.

ing down the surface of roughly dug ground and drawing up soil as in earthing up potatoes, leeks, etc. It can also be used for drawing deep seed drills. The three-cornered hoe also has many uses: such as chipping weedy and moss-grown pathways, breaking the hard-baked surface of soils that have 'caked' through being trodden on during rainy weather, and drawing shallow drills.

For soil that is being cultivated for the first time yet another hoe is invaluable. This is the Canterbury hoe, the blade of which is composed of three prongs like a fork.

Cultivator For very heavy soil a cultivator, such as that illustrated, may be necessary.

Rake A steel-toothed rake will be needed for preparing seed beds, but is a tool that is generally used too much by beginners with detrimental results. One 12 inches in width is most suitable.

Trowel and Hand Fork A small garden trowel will be needed to transplant almost every kind of small plant, for there are few that plant well with a dibber. A small hand fork is better than a trowel for lifting

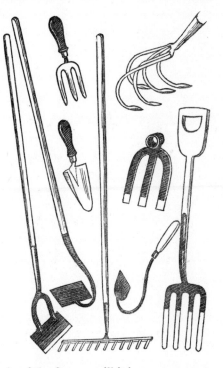

A FURTHER SELECTION
Left: Dutch hoe and swan-necked hoe. Left top: hand fork, with trowel below. Centre: rake. Right top: hand cultivator with Canterbury hoe below. Extreme right: flat tined potato fork. Right of centre: hand cultivator.

seedling plants, for the sharp blade of the former will injure many roots if thrust into a crowded seed box or bed.

Lawn Tools Wherever there is a lawn other tools become necessary. These include a good mowing machine if the area is of any size, together with a roller if the lawn is to be used regularly for sports. For a purely ornamental lawn, not subject to much hard wear, a roller is not essential. An edging iron is a great convenience for keeping the edges neat, and some kind of shears will be needed to trim the grass at the margin. These shears may be specially made for the task, in which case they will have long handles to prevent stooping. Where the length of edge to be cut is not excessive it is quite possible to use short-handled hedging shears for this purpose. These latter are, of course, necessary for the proper maintenance of a formally trimmed hedge. For a semi-wild hedge a bill-hook is more useful, and for hedges of large-leaved or flowering shrubs pruning sécateurs are essential.

To keep a lawn free from creeping weeds and moss and generally in a healthy condition a spring-toothed steel grass rake is a great asset. Used regularly it will enable the surface to be kept quite even without the use of a roller. Other tools for the lawn, the need for which will vary with the circumstances, are a daisy weeder, a turfing iron (for lifting turf), and a besom for removing fallen leaves and worm casts.

For marking the edges to beds and lawns and for ensuring straight

PRUNING AND TRIMMING
Left: A tree pruner or long handled shears with sécateurs below. Centre: a good pruning saw. Right: two different kinds of shears; the lower is used with one hand only and so is useful for awkward corners.

seed drills a garden line is used. For this two stout sticks and a good length of stout cord are all that is necessary, though a revolving metal spool is a useful refinement.

Pruning Tools For pruning fruit trees, roses, and ornamental trees and shrubs generally, and for cutting off dead stems in the herbaceous border, a good, modern pair of pruning sécateurs is undoubtedly the most useful tool. By the expert a pruning knife may be favoured, but this requires a skilled and steady hand for its successful use, while modern sécateurs have none of the disadvantages of their primitive predecessors and may be used with safety by the beginner. For tall trees a standard tree pruner with an eight- or ten-foot handle is necessary.

Watering Can A watering can will be needed all the year round if a greenhouse or frame is available, and in any case for the greater part of the summer. It is worth while obtaining a galvanized one, as these are much less liable to rust. The rose should have small holes, or the can might as well be used without one. For use in greenhouses and for watering plants in frames it is advisable to have a can which holds only a gallon, for plants in pots and seedlings in boxes need very careful watering, which process is rendered exceptionally difficult by the weight of a heavy can, especially if frame lights have to be supported with the other hand. For watering large areas a hose may be necessary, but in all but very exceptional conditions a system of mulching and top-dressing can be followed which will make much outdoor watering unnecessary.

A USEFUL SPRAYER
Pressure is raised in the cylinder by means of the hand pump, the sprayer then put on the back and spray released by depressing the trigger.

Syringe For spraying against pests and diseases some form of syringe or sprayer is needed. The type selected will depend largely upon the area to be covered and the money available, but the best quality only should be purchased, for cheap metal will soon corrode with the action of the many different chemicals used in this type of work. A nozzle capable of producing a mist-like spray is necessary, and an extension for reaching the underside of bushes and up into tall trees makes for more thorough cleansing.

Wheelbarrow For moving soil, manure, stone and rubbish a wheelbarrow is essential on all but the smallest plots. This should be strongly made and so balanced that the lifting weight is not excessive. A pneumatic tyre will be found to make for easier running on soft and uneven ground, and will do less damage to grass and paths than the old-fashioned iron wheel.

Accessories Among the accessories are a mattock for breaking up very hard ground and for removing tree stumps, a light border fork for use among the plants in an herbaceous border, a bulb trowel or planter for naturalizing bulbs in grass, a tub for making liquid manure, and such small things as a budding knife for propagating roses, a hammer and wall nails, layering pins for strawberries, carnations, etc., and bamboo canes of various lengths, squared deal stakes, tarred twine, raffia and labels for frames and greenhouses, seed boxes and pans and flower pots of all sizes.

Care of the Tools There is, of course, no need to purchase all the tools at once, for there are few periods during the first years when all will be required. Once acquired it is well worth while to take care of all tools. Ideally they should be housed in a dry shed, as many as possible being hung up on the walls in specially assigned places, as this prevents them from becoming mislaid and broken. All keen-edged tools should be kept sharp, the finer knives on an oil-stone and the coarser ones on an ordinary grindstone. After use all tools should be cleaned thoroughly and, when quite dry, oiled well. It is much easier to work with bright, sharp tools than rusty ones, and the work will be of far better quality. The blades of a mowing machine should be ground all together in a special machine to ensure that they all meet the fixed knife evenly throughout their lengths. It is almost impossible to do the work properly if each blade is ground separately with a stone or file.

CHAPTER TWO

Soils: Their Nature and Improvement

I N order to make the maximum use of the existing soil on any piece of ground it is necessary to discover something of both its chemical and physical nature and also to know what plants in general and in particular require in the way of nourishment. Knowing this, it is possible to set about the cultivation and improvement of the ground in the most economical manner, as regards both labour and expenditure on manures.

Now the majority of plants use the soil for two things—to obtain a firm root-hold and to get the water and mineral salts necessary for growth. Plants can only take in their food supplies in the form of certain quite definite chemicals, all of which are soluble in water; therefore, water supply is very important. Roots, however, do not grow healthily if soaked continuously in water, but need air, and thus do not do well in waterlogged soil. Drainage is most essential.

Types of Soil On examination of soils it is found that they can be grouped roughly into six main classes—sands, clays, chalks, loams, peats and marls.

Sandy soils are gritty to the touch, allow water to drain through them very rapidly, and therefore soon get washed bare of food materials, and become dried out and very hot in summer. They are easy to dig.

Clay soils are composed of much finer particles, which stick together when wetted to form a slippery mass which 'cakes' and cracks when dried in the sun. Such soil quickly becomes waterlogged, and therefore readily sours, is cold by reason of the water that it holds, and is hard to dig. Many plants find such a soil too firm for easy penetration by their roots, while a sandy soil offers inadequate support. Clay soils are usually rich in such necessary foods as potash and magnesium salts, while sandy soils are frequently lacking in almost all plant foods.

Soil containing a large amount of chalk or limestone is almost as porous as sand, tends to get hot in the summer, and, though not sticky, is fairly hard to dig. It is often whitish in colour.

Loam is an intimate mixture of sand and clay, with or without a

23

certain amount of lime. Good loam is also characterized by the large amount of roots and decaying vegetable matter that it contains. From this fact it will be realized that loam is the most suitable soil for the majority of plants. It is moderately easy to work, drains reasonably well without drying out rapidly, and has a pleasant, almost velvety touch to the hand. The fully decayed organic material found particularly in this type of soil and in peat is known as humus. Humus is valuable for several reasons. It holds water, but at the same time, being partly fibrous and springy, keeps the soil particles apart sufficiently to prevent waterlogging. This is particularly true of peat, which is composed of the partially decayed remains of such small, rather woody plants as ling, bilberries, bracken, and other plants commonly found on heaths. The dark colour of humus is also an asset, for dark soil absorbs, rather than reflects, the sun's rays, and thus remains warm at night, at which time sand and chalk lose heat rapidly. Useful bacteria thrive in humus and liberate plant foods locked in the soil.

Pure peaty and sandy soils are generally deficient in lime, but this is not always so with clay soils or loams. These may be tested for free lime by adding a few drops of spirits of salts (hydrochloric acid) to a little of the moistened soil. If free lime is present to any extent the soil will be seen to froth or bubble (effervesce). This test must be done with great care, as the acid will burn holes in any wood or clothing on which it is dropped. Should any touch the hands, they should be washed in running water immediately.

The addition of lime to clay soils, in the form of chalk, limestone, or slaked lime, causes the fine particles of the clay to cling together into small granules, and thereby makes the soil more porous. On all soils it corrects acidity, so maintaining useful bacterial activity and assisting in the release of plant foods in the soil. The chemical improvements of soils will be dealt with in the following chapter. Marl is a natural mixture of clay and lime.

It will therefore be seen that a waterlogged soil can be improved by any method that will render drainage more effective, such as digging in lime or sand or fibrous plant refuse. The very act of digging improves drainage by opening up large spaces down which water can run. Therefore the deeper a bed is dug the better will it be drained, but ground must not be dug while it is waterlogged, or it will cake badly. The soil should not stick to the spade when dug.

Cultivation All types of cultivation, such as digging, trenching, hoeing, forking, raking, etc., which are methods of breaking down the soil into

a well-drained, well-aerated mass of small pieces, are said to produce a
fine 'tilth.' The finest tilth is needed on seed beds. Deep cultivation has a
great advantage over shallow digging, for soil which is merely forked
over superficially for several years rapidly forms a hard pan just below
the surface. This holds up water, causing the soil to become waterlogged in wet weather and to dry out equally rapidly in dry weather, as
the subsoil water cannot rise through it. Every part of the vegetable
garden should be trenched once in three years, and all herbaceous
borders and flower beds should be trenched when made, after which
they may be merely forked over for several years.

Digging When soil is turned over to the depth of the spade's blade it is
said to be 'dug.' When this layer or 'spit' of soil is removed and the one
below it dug in turn the ground is said to be 'bastard' or 'half trenched.'
And when yet a third layer is dug the term 'trenching' is used.

To dig a plot of land, remove the first line of spadefuls of soil to the
other end of the plot, so as to leave a trench. When digging the second

SOIL AND SUBSOIL
*The illustration shows
clearly the relation of
the fertile upper soil to
the comparatively stony
and infertile subsoil.*

row, face this trench and turn the soil into it, leaving a new trench to
take the next row of soil. Proceed in this way backwards down the plot
until the soil is all turned over, then shovel the first soil dug out into
the last trench made. The work is most easily and effectually accom-
plished if the correct art of digging is learnt at the start. The spade
should be held upright, not sloping, and pushed in to the top of the
blade. The handle is then forced downwards and backwards by the
right hand at the top of the handle while the left hand slips down towards the blade and lifts. With practice the whole series of movements
will become rhythmical and work will proceed faster. If the ground is
being broken up for the first time, it may be found necessary to cut

the turf at the side of each spadeful by a sharp downward cut before lifting the soil, or the grass will drag. Each spadeful should be thrown so that the grass side falls downwards, where it will soon rot. In this way all weeds will be buried. Whenever ground is dug in the autumn (which is the best time) the clods should not be broken up, but allowed to lie as they fall, as the roughness of the surface improves its drainage, and frost will do much to break up the lumps.

Indeed, frost has such a very beneficial effect in breaking up heavy soil that it is always wise to dig vacant ground early in the winter. In order to expose as large an area as possible to the action of frost, the soil on unplanted plots, whether it has already been dug or awaits such treatment, may be thrown into a series of ridges as shown in one of the illustrations.

Half trenching For half trenching it is necessary to take out a wider trench of soil to start off with. Three feet makes for ease in working. Thus all the soil, including the loose pieces, is dug from the top spit of soil along a 3 feet strip at one end of the plot and wheeled to the other end. With a strong fork the spit below is broken up. The fork should be handled in a similar manner to the spade, but it will be found easiest to dig this second spit sideways, across the trench, instead of along the length of it. The second spit forked over, the top spit of the next 18 inches is dug forward on top of it, making a new trench to be forked up. To do this may need two or three rows of digging, according to the amount that can be conveniently lifted each time. At the end of the plot the soil removed at the beginning will be returned to the last trench as before. In this manner the two layers of soil will be dug over and thus broken up and aerated, but the soils of the two layers will not be mixed. This is important, for the lower down the layer of soil, the poorer it will be in quality, for it will not contain so much humus as the upper layer, on which leaves, etc., are frequently falling, and in which there are more earthworms and useful insects and bacteria.

Trenching For this reason even greater pains have to be taken to keep the three layers of soil apart in full trenching. For this deep trenching proceed as before, digging out a strip 2 feet wide. Having wheeled this first layer of soil to the other end of the plot, dig out a second layer and wheel that down to the further end, but do not put it in the same pile with the first. The third spit down can now be forked over sideways. The top spit from the second trench must not be placed on top of this forked lower layer, or subsoil, as it is called, or the layers would get in their wrong order. It too must be dug off and wheeled to the other end of the bed, then the second spit can be dug on to the forked-up soil in the first trench and the third layer forked over in this trench. Next the top soil from the third strip has to be thrown across on to the top of the first strip dug, and the second layer into the second trench dug, and its bottom layer has to be forked in turn. Four feet may seem a good way to have to throw soil, but narrower trenches are difficult to work in.

When digging or trenching a large piece of ground it is frequently an economy of labour first to divide the plot into two longitudinally. Each half is then dug separately. Instead of wheeling the soil removed from the first trench to the far end of the plot, it is wheeled or thrown

TRENCHING
The second spit of soil is being dug out.

to one side so that it lies at the foot of the second half of the plot along-side the starting-point. When the first half has been finished, the second half is worked in the opposite direction, the soil from the first trench on the second half being used to fill the last trench of the first half.

During trenching, lime or manure may be incorporated, according to the requirements of the soil. Stones, except when very excessive in number, should not be removed, especially from the lower layers of soil, as they do not heat up as quickly as the rest of the soil and, being cooler, cause water to condense on their surfaces. Plants send masses of roots out round these stones in search of water. This must not be held to be a contradiction of the statement that humus is good for the soil, as it darkens it and thereby makes it warmer, for where the soil is uniformly cold the roots will grow but slowly and water will accumulate equally in all parts.

Drainage Stones also make for good drainage. In fact, where the natural drainage of a plot is very poor it is advisable to lay land drains surrounded by clinkers or stones in the bottoms of specially cut trenches 15 to 20 feet apart. These pipes should lead either to some existing drain or to a large pit or soak-away, which should be constructed at

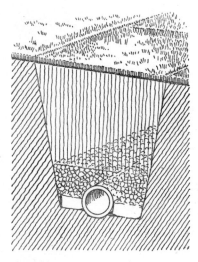

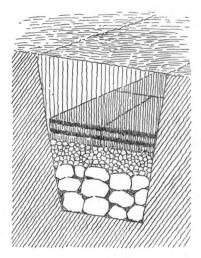

A PIPE DRAIN
Earthenware land-drain pipes are laid in rough rubble.

A STONE DRAIN
Large stones take the place of the pipes shown on the left.

the lowest point convenient on sloping land. Where the land is perfectly flat the trenches will have to be cut out in such a way that they all slope down to the soak-away. In a small garden this can take the form of a sunken tub. The stored drainage water can then be used for watering where necessary.

The trouble with sandy soil is not that the drainage is poor, but that it is too good. What water does fall on the land rushes away so fast that the plants are unable to use any quantity of it. Any materials that tend to hold up water should therefore be dug in freely. These include strawy manure, dead leaves (or leaf-mould, as it is called), peat, spent hops, the scrapings from tanyards, shoddy and general garden refuse—provided this is free from disease. During the summer it is necessary to keep as much water in the soil as possible. If a bed in the garden is left untouched for some weeks and the soil is examined when no rain has fallen for several days, it will be found that the soil just below the surface is quite moist. This water has come from the great supplies of underground water deep down in the soil. At the surface it is evaporated into the air and thus is lost to the plants. The distance down at which such moisture can be found will, of course, vary with the supply of water in the deeper layers, but also with the type of soil. Water rises higher through a finely grained soil such as clay than through sand, for the fine particles stick together and form narrow channels up which the water can travel. The narrower the channel, the higher the water rises. Thus the loose, coarse grains of sand do not form good channels.

Hoeing and Mulching To keep the water round the roots of the plants in summer and yet to prevent it from being lost to the hot air is the problem which is solved by hoeing or mulching. The blade of the hoe is pushed or pulled through the soil (according to the variety of hoe) in such a manner that the top inch of soil only is disturbed. This top layer is cut through so that the water-conducting channels are broken across, with the result that the top layer dries out, forming what is known as a dust mulch. Under this the soil will keep moist and lose little of its water to the air. To be really effective hoeing should be done as soon after rain as the water has had a chance to soak in, and right through the summer. Ground should not be hoed while the water is still standing about on the surface, any more than it should be dug in this condition, or the soil will stick to the blade of the hoe.

It is equally possible to trap the water in the soil without hoeing the surface, by covering it with a layer of loose littery material, such as strawy manure, dry grass clippings, or dry leaves or peat dust—in fact, with any material that is dry and traps air. Grass clippings to be effective must be dry. If wet, the leaves stick together and the tiny channels in the soil are continued upwards and water is lost as before. Mulches therefore need drying or renewing after rain and can be improved by being shaken up occasionally with a fork.

To prevent the loss of water from a lawn, which can neither be hoed nor protected with a mulch, a top-dressing of peat dust, finely sifted leaf-mould, and sharp sand can be applied, and grass clippings can be left unswept. This application should only be about $\frac{1}{4}$ inch thick and should be left quite loose. If the top-dressing is rolled in, its value as a mulch will be nil. It is necessary that the sand should be of a sharp variety, as the soft sands used by builders contain fine particles which stick together when wetted and form a hard cake when dry. The loose layer on the top of a lawn can be kept in good condition for a considerable period, considering its comparative shallowness, by regular use of the spring-toothed grass rake, which keeps the top-dressing from settling down and yet does not hurt the grass. The drainage of the lawn can be improved by the gradual accumulation of such small dressings, applied once every six or eight weeks during the summer, and by piercing the turf during the winter. This method is illustrated in Chapter Nine.

CHAPTER THREE

The Use of Manures and Fertilizers

To increase the fertility of the soil has been the aim of every
gardener since the land was first tilled. Alas, how many novices
have come to grief over that very laudable endeavour! In olden times,
perhaps, there were not so many pitfalls, for soil manures were few
in number and for the most part safe in action, consisting mainly of
the dung of domestic animals. But now that science has arrived to take
a part in every detail of our existence it behoves the gardener to 'tread
delicately.' True, the research worker and experimentalist have made it
possible to stimulate growth in a manner that would have been quite
impossible under the old régime, but in the very power of the fertilizers
which they have discovered lies their danger, for an overdose or an
unwise application may prove fatal.

Supplying Humus One most important point which the beginner must
realize at the outset is that to improve the fertility of the soil is a complicated process and includes not only the application of chemicals
essential for plant growth, but also the addition of humus to improve
the porosity and tilth of the soil generally. For this latter purpose such
bulky organic manures as stable and farmyard manure, spent hops,
decaying leaves and other vegetable refuse, seaweed, and such materials
as the scrapings from skins prepared in tanyards, shoddy, and wool and
cotton waste are excellent. All these substances hold water like a
sponge and therefore prevent the rapid drying out of light sandy soil;
they also separate closely sticking particles of clay and make channels
through which superfluous water can pass. They therefore improve the
water content of both very wet and very dry soils. Some manures are
naturally better suited to one kind of soil than others. Thus strawy
stable manure is more valuable on heavy clay soil than on sandy ground,
as it does not readily become sodden. Sticky substances, such as cow
and pig dung, are of most use on light land.

Organic Manures Organic manures—that is, those substances which
owe their origin to plants or animals—are all very complex in their
chemical composition, and therefore the food materials that they

31

contain are not available for immediate absorption by plants, for these can only take in very simple chemicals, all of which are soluble in water. In the soil are innumerable minute organisms, known as bacteria, which cause the decomposition of complex manures into the desirable simple substances. These bacteria are only active in well-aerated ground. When the soil is waterlogged other harmful bacteria thrive. These turn the manures into unwanted acids that cause souring of the soil.

To make the most of organic manures they should be dug well into the ground in the autumn before the crop is planted. They are useless for summer feeding of quick-growing crops. Land that has been given a good application of stable or farmyard manure or bone or fish meal will have a supply of food materials for approximately two years (depending upon the amount applied, the soil conditions, and the crop), for the bacteria cannot change the whole bulk of the material into available food all at once.

The majority of organic manures are particularly rich in nitrogenous food supplies, and for this reason should not be applied at the same time as a dressing of lime, which may liberate nitrogen in the form of ammonia. This is given off into the air for the most part and is thus lost to the plant. Nitrogen is necessary for the formation of green, leafy growth, and is therefore invaluable for 'green crops' such as cabbage, Brussels sprouts, and spinach. All dungs contain other important plant foods, such as phosphates and potash, and, therefore, are of more value as general manures than horn parings, dried blood, tanyard scrapings and shoddy, which must be supplemented for most crops, or they will cause rank, sappy growth with an absence of flowers and fruit. Fish and bonemeals are rich in phosphorus and tend to harden and ripen growth.

All dung, especially stable manure, is improved by keeping in a dry place for a few weeks before being applied to the ground. This is particularly necessary if it is to be applied to land already containing plants. During the early period of decay dung tends to form acids which sour the soil and are very injurious to young roots. Bulky manure should never be placed in direct contact with roots, but should for preference be some inches lower down in the soil so that the plants can send their roots down to it.

Inorganic Fertilizers Of the inorganic or purely chemical fertilizers there are two which are not quick acting, and should therefore be applied, like organic manures, during the autumn or winter. These are basic slag and kainit. Basic slag is most suitable for heavy or medium

Left: Plain digging. A spadeful of soil is being marked out with a downward chop.
Right: The spade is thrust vertically and to its full depth into the soil.

Left: The spadeful of soil is turned right over and thrown well forward. *Right:* Manure
is spread in the bottom of the completed trench.

Left: The correct way to make a joint between earthenware land drains.　*Right:* Breaking down the surface of a roughly dug plot by swinging blows with a fork.

Ridging land. Two ridges have been completed and a third has been marked out.

soils and is rich in phosphorus. It also contains a certain percentage of lime. Kainit, on the other hand, is more suitable for light or medium soils and is rich in potassium.

Phosphorus and potassium are essential for the production of flowers and fruit and aid the ripening of the shoots which is so necessary for successful over-wintering of roses and other flowering shrubs. Their application checks the coarse growth encouraged by a plentiful supply of nitrogen, and to ensure good all-round growth purely nitrogenous manures should be followed at short intervals by fertilizers rich in these food materials.

Town gardeners who are unable to obtain bulky organic manures will find that chemical fertilizers are essential, and they are equally valuable for top-dressing growing crops when an additional stimulant that will

THE INCINERATOR
A useful brick incinerator for burning all garden rubbish. The ashes make an excellent manure and are rich in potash.

act immediately is needed. If employed as the only food material, peat or some other bulky organic material should be used to supply humus.

For supplying nitrogen, Nitro-chalk, sulphate of ammonia, and nitrate of soda are most frequently used. These are very strong, quick-acting fertilizers and must therefore be used sparingly and be applied evenly. As top-dressings for lawns sulphate of ammonia is invaluable. Applied in excess to large-leaved weeds in the lawn, it will burn these out. This fact illustrates the danger of applying pure chemicals in large quantities, for equally strong solutions in contact with the roots of the plants will shrivel them up. When used for top-dressing salad beds, care should be taken not to spill any of the fertilizer on the leaves of the plants, for young lettuce leaves are soon ruined.

Potassium can be applied in the form of one of its salts, such as sulphate of potash, muriate of potash, phosphate of potash, or nitrate

C

of potash. Sulphate of potash is the most generally useful, as it is reasonable in price and not liable to cause injury to roots or leaves. Phosphate of potash also supplies phosphorus, while nitrate of potash adds nitrogen. Wood ashes contain considerable quantities of potassium salts, and therefore potash may be supplied to the soil by digging in the ashes from the garden bonfire. The charcoal contained in these is also of value, as it keeps the soil sweet.

Lime Another great soil sweetener is lime, which combines with the acids that might otherwise cause souring and puts them out of action. Lime is seldom necessary as a fertilizer as the small amount required is almost always present. But it is valuable on heavy clay soils, as it liberates the potash and magnesium locked up in the clay. Additionally as previously recorded, it causes the fine particles of clay to cling together and thereby improves aeration and drainage. Thus the growth of harmful bacteria is checked, and the sweetening action of lime is twofold. On light sandy soils chalk should be used instead of lime, as it sweetens the soil and at the same time helps it to retain moisture.

Superphosphate The great source of phosphorus is superphosphate of lime. It is also present in bones, but unless these are very finely divided, as in steamed bone flour, their action is delayed. Peruvian guano combines phosphorus with nitrogen and small quantities of potash. Phosphate of ammonia, phosphate of potash, and phosphate of soda can all be used instead of the cheaper superphosphate of lime if so desired.

Soot Soot can be used as a fertilizer and also as a soil fumigant. When fresh it contains noxious compounds of sulphur which make it valuable as a sterilizer of vacant ground, but fatal to plants. If applied with lime and dug in immediately, this fumigating effect is increased, as the nitrogen which the soot contains is liberated as ammonia. Its value as a fertilizer is then lost. To use soot as a fertilizer it must be stored for three months under cover, but exposed to the air. The sulphurous fumes will then disperse. If exposed to rain, the nitrogenous materials, which are soluble, will be washed out. Soot is also of value on light-coloured soils, as it darkens them and so helps them to retain the sun's heat, as already explained in the case of humus.

Applying Fertilizers Fertilizers used during the spring and summer may be applied as top-dressings or in liquid form. Alternatively such fertilizers may be raked or forked in immediately prior to sowing or planting. They should not be applied to any plant which is looking unhealthy, unless it has been definitely proved that this condition is due to lack of a particular food material.

Top-dressings to lawns are most easily applied if the chemical in finely divided form is intimately mixed with its own bulk of sharp sand. This makes it easier to distribute correctly, for ½ ounce per square yard of sulphate of ammonia is the maximum dose that should be given, and it is difficult to spread this evenly without something to increase bulk. To facilitate distribution it is wise to mark out the lawn into square yards, by means of strings stretched across temporarily, and to apply the correct amount over each small area.

When applying a top-dressing to a bed the fertilizer should be sprinkled lightly between the plants and subsequently watered or hoed in. It is unwise to place the fertilizer close against the stems of plants. A flour dredger will be found useful for sprinkling.

The maximum dose of any fertilizer should never be exceeded. Especially is this true with compound fertilizers obtained ready mixed, the constituents of which it is difficult to discover. Fertilizers com-

A FERTILIZER MIXING CHART

Fertilizers connected by a thick black line should never be mixed, while those joined by double lines must only be mixed when for immediate use. Those connected by dotted lines can be mixed quite safely.

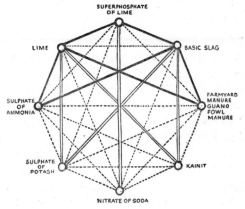

pounded by skilled manufacturers to meet the needs of special plants should always be applied exactly as recommended. They have the advantage for the novice that, made by a reliable firm, they avoid the dangers of an unbalanced diet.

Liquid Manures Liquid manures are most valuable for pot plants, for it is very difficult to incorporate the necessary amount of organic food in the small quantity of soil without souring it, and top-dressing is not very easy. Such liquid fertilizers are most easily prepared by suspending dung in a sack in a tub of rain water. The bag should be squeezed periodically between two sticks to obtain the maximum yield. This strong liquor should on no account be applied to the plants. For use it must be diluted to the colour of pale straw. One peck of horse, cow, or pig's dung will require about 36 gallons of water, but only one-quarter of this amount of poultry droppings is required for the same volume of water, as these are very much richer in plant foods.

Quantities of Fertilizers The exact quantities of the fertilizers that should be used are incorporated in the table on page 37 for ease of reference. Plants should be given a change of liquid fertilizer as often as possible. The soil must always be moist at the time of application, and, if this is not the case, must be watered with clear water first. A sufficiently large volume of liquid manure should then be given at each application to soak right through the soil. Applications may be made as frequently as once a week if the solution is dilute enough. If only a small volume of liquid is applied, the roots of the plant will tend to come to the surface to obtain the food, and will be liable to severe burning and scorching when the surface dries out. To prevent waste a shallow trench may be made round the plant and the liquid poured into this.

Mixing Fertilizers It is unwise to mix any two fertilizers without a thorough knowledge of their properties. Thus, where possible, lime and manure should not be applied at the same season. If it is desired to use the two together for any reason, the manure should be dug into the second spit when trenching and the lime applied as a top-dressing. Land does not generally need manuring more than once in two years, nor is lime necessary more frequently. They are often given in alternate years, though an application of lime once in three years is usually sufficient on all but heavy clay soils. Some plants resent the presence of lime. Notable among these are many members of the heath family (Ericaceae), such as the heathers, rhododendrons, andromedas, pieris, and vacciniums. Some choice alpine plants also appear to resent lime strongly. *Gentiana Farreri*, *G. sino-ornata*, lithospermum, and most varieties of meconopsis are familiar examples. It is wise to make enquiry when ordering rock plants and shrubs from nurserymen as to whether any of those supplied are likely to require lime-free soil.

LIQUID MANURES AND FERTILIZERS

Manure or Fertilizer	Quantities	Effect upon Growth
Ammonia, sulphate of	½ oz. per gal.	Encourages growth of foliage
Blood, dried	1 oz. per gal.	Encourages growth of foliage
Cow dung	1 pk. to 36 gal.	**Promotes** healthy growth generally
Fowl droppings	½ gal. to 36 gal.	An all-round fertilizer
Guano, Peruvian	1 oz. per gal.	An all-round plant food
Horse dung	1 pk. to 36 gal.	Promotes healthy growth generally
Pig dung	1 pk. to 36 gal.	Promotes healthy growth generally
Potash, nitrate of	1 oz. per 3 gal.	Promotes growth and fruiting
Potash, phosphate of	½ oz. per gal.	Encourages fruiting and ripening of growth
Potash, sulphate of	½ oz. per gal.	Encourages fruiting and ripening of growth
Sheep dung	1 gal. to 36 gal.	Promotes healthy growth generally
Soot	1 gal. to 36 gal.	Encourages growth of foliage

MANURES AND FERTILIZERS FOR USE DRY

Manure or Fertilizer	Class	Quantities Per Sq. Yd	When to Apply	Soil
Ammonia, phosphate of	N. & P.	1 oz.	Summer	Light
Ammonia, sulphate of	N.	½ oz.	Spring or summer	All except lime-free soils
Basic slag	P.	4 oz.	Autumn	Heavy or medium
Blood, dried	N.	2 oz.	Spring or summer	All soils
Bonemeal	P.	3 oz.	Spring or autumn	All soils
Bones, dissolved	P.	2-3 oz.	Spring	All soils
Chalk, ground	—	1-2 lb.	Autumn or winter	Sandy
Cow dung	G.M.	7-14 lb.	Autumn or winter	Light or sandy
Fish meal	P.	2 oz.	Autumn or spring	All soils
Guano, Peruvian	N. & P.	2 oz.	Spring or summer	All soils
Hops, brewers' spent	G.M.	7-14 lb.	Winter	All soils
Hop manure	G.M.	4-6 oz.	Spring or summer	All soils
Horse dung	G.M.	7-14 lb.	Autumn or winter	Heavy
Kainit	Pot.	3 oz.	Autumn or winter	Light or medium
Leaf-mould	G.M.	5-7 lb.	Winter or spring	All soils
Lime, hydrated	—	6-12 oz.	Any time	All soils
Lime, nitrate of	N.	1 oz.	Spring or summer	All soils
Night soil	G.M.	1 lb.	Autumn or winter	All soils
Nitro-chalk	N.	1-2 oz.	Spring or summer	All soils
Nitrolim	N.	1 oz.	Spring	Heavy
Peat moss	G.M.	5-7 lb.	Autumn or winter	All soils
Pig dung	G.M.	7-14 lb.	Autumn or winter	Light or sandy
Potash, nitrate of	N. & pot.	1 oz.	Spring or summer	All soils
Potash, phosphate of	P. & pot.	1 oz.	Summer	All soils
Potash, sulphate of	Pot.	1 oz.	Spring or summer	All soils
Poultry dung (fresh)	G.M.	3-4 lb.	Spring or summer	Light or medium
Salt	—	1 oz.	Spring	Heavy
Seaweed (wet)	G.M.	10-20 lb.	Autumn or winter	All soils
Sheep's dung	G.M.	7 lb.	Autumn or winter	All soils
Soda, nitrate of	N.	½ oz.	Spring or summer	Medium and light
Soot	N.	8 oz.	Spring or summer	All soils
Superphosphate	P.	2-3 oz.	Spring	All soils
Vegetable refuse	G.M.	10-20 lb.	Autumn or winter	All soils
Wood ashes	Pot.	8 oz.	Autumn or spring	All soils

Abbreviations: G.M. = General Manure.   N. = Nitrogen.   P. = Phosphorus.   Pot. = Potassium

A few useful fertilizers for special purposes are as follows:

FOR REVITALIZING WEAK LAWNS

Sulphate of potash	2 parts
Sulphate of ammonia	1 part
Dried blood	2 parts
Sharp sand	20 parts

Apply at the rate of 6 oz. per square yard twice in the spring.

FOR FEEDING POT PLANTS

John Innes Liquid Feed

Ammonium Sulphate	15 parts
Potassium nitrate	$2\frac{3}{4}$ parts
Mon-ammonium phosphate	$2\frac{1}{4}$ parts

Dissolved in water at the rate of $\frac{1}{2}$–1 oz. per gallon and used once a week during the period of growth.

GENERAL GARDEN FERTILIZER

Superphosphate of lime	3 parts
Sulphate of ammonia	2 parts
Sulphate of potash	1 part

Applied in spring or early summer at the rate of 2 to 4 oz. per square yard, or dissolved in water at the rate of $\frac{1}{2}$ oz. per gallon and applied about once a week.

All parts by weight, not by bulk.

CHAPTER FOUR

Successful Planting

PLANTING is not a task to be undertaken carelessly. It is true that there are plants which can be literally torn from the soil, thrust back roughly in almost any kind of hole, and yet will survive. But they are very few in number, and for the majority of garden plants anything approaching this treatment would prove fatal. In this chapter general principles are dealt with, peculiarities of certain plants being relegated to the special chapters set apart for them.

Preparation of the Soil Two golden rules to be borne in mind in all transplanting are: First, to damage the roots as little as possible, and, second, to bring them into close contact with the new soil. This involves, among other things, thorough preparation of the ground. It is impossible to plant properly in soil that is lumpy or very wet. It must be in that fine crumbly condition known to the gardener as 'friable.' Planting should be discontinued during very wet weather, as the soil readily becomes 'puddled' and subsequently caked if worked at this time. Occasional showers do no harm; indeed, they are beneficial in that they help to keep the plants from flagging. Even so, surface stickiness should be allowed to dry out first.

Correct soil condition is more important than the exact date of transplanting; and a calendar of times of planting should be used solely as a rough guide to the season at which the plants are least likely to suffer harm through moving. Any attempt to keep too slavishly to a preconceived calendar must result in much disappointment, weather being the deciding factor as to the advisability of proceeding with the work.

Planting Holes Holes must in all cases be made sufficiently large to accommodate all the roots in a natural position. This is most important advice and can hardly be repeated too frequently. Planting in either too narrow or too shallow a hole may spell disaster. Nor must roots be planted too deeply. With trees and shrubs the point to which the soil reached previously can usually be detected by an alteration of the colour of the stem. It is a safe general rule to replant just a trifle more deeply than this. Good holes cannot be made with a dibber—it is a lazy man's tool. A trowel or spade is essential.

Replacing the Soil Rough clods and coarse pieces of turf and manure should not be thrown into direct contact with the roots, as large air spaces are bound to be left, and new roots will only form where the main ones are in direct contact with the soil. The smaller the plant being transplanted, the finer the soil should be broken, but even with comparatively large trees and shrubs the soil should not contain too many large lumps, or the plants will be a long while in resuming growth.

When small plants are being established on heavy clay soils it is an excellent plan to have a large box or wheelbarrow of specially prepared, finely broken compost ready to hand. A trowelful can then be placed round the roots of each plant. It is an advantage if some can also be mixed with the surrounding soil, as this encourages the roots to grow out into the main mass of soil. If the change is too marked between the types of soil the roots sometimes tend to grow only in the finer compost, in which they form a tight ball.

Planting Pot-grown Plants Such unnatural restriction of root growth may also occur if the roots of a pot-grown plant are not loosened gently from the close ball of soil from the pot. These roots will often be tightly coiled round and must be carefully unwound and spread out properly in the hole. If a plant that has had the tips of its roots curled up in order to make them all go into too small a hole is dug up six or eight months after planting, it will be found that these tips have died back for a considerable distance and that all the fresh roots have been formed further back. This is necessarily a set-back to the plant, and shows the folly of slovenly planting.

Small Plants Very small plants should have their roots kept moist throughout the whole of the time that they are out of the ground; and roots of all trees and shrubs must be afforded adequate protection against drying winds and hot sun. Any roots that have been damaged in lifting the plant should be cut back to above the injury, as they will die below it.

Firming No plants, with the exception of ferns, make good growth in loose soil, and for this reason it is important that the roots should be firmed in properly. In addition to making fewer roots in loose soil, the plants are liable to be disturbed during windy weather and to be injured by the greater penetration of frost or the more rapid drying out of the soil in sun and wind. For all but the smallest and tenderest of plants firming can be done with the foot. When planting large trees and shrubs the soil should be trodden down little by little as it is put in, or they will suffer through being firm only at soil level. Loose soil may also be rammed between the roots with a stout piece of wood, but care must be taken not to damage the roots.

Though firming is so desirable, it is a mistake to leave the surface of the soil beaten down and hard. This encourages drying out of the surface in summer and puddling in winter. The surface should be covered with a little light soil after firming; this will act as a mulch, which may be maintained by hoeing round the plants occasionally after planting. Care must be taken not to push the hoe in too deeply.

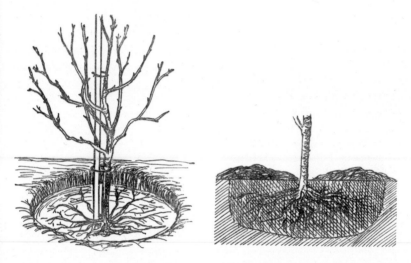

PLANTING AND STAKING

A half standard fruit tree. Note stake driven into position before filling in the hole; also the 'mulch,' or extra covering of loose soil applied to the surface.

Half an inch will be sufficient, and more will tend to loosen the plants as well as the soil.

Staking Standard trees and large bushes and plants should be securely staked at the time of planting. Nothing is more detrimental to freshly planted trees that have not yet got a good hold on the soil than to be blown this way and that by the wind, for as fast as the delicate new roots are formed they are snapped or rubbed off by the movement. To avoid injuring the roots it is wisest to drive the stake into the empty hole and then plant the tree with its roots round it. The stem must then be fastened to the stake in such a way that it cannot rub against the support, and the tie must be of such a kind that it does not cut into the plant.

Planting Evergreens Evergreen trees and shrubs should not be moved during the winter, for these plants lose water from their leaves at all seasons of the year, and during cold weather are unable to replace this water easily from the soil. If, therefore, they are temporarily cut off from their water supply, while unable to form new roots in the cold soil, they will die. These plants may be moved in the autumn while the soil is still warm or, better still, as soon as they show new growth in the spring, for at that time the trees are making new roots actively.

Deciduous Trees and Shrubs Deciduous trees and shrubs—that is, kinds which lose their leaves in the autumn—may be moved at any time while they are leafless, always provided that the soil conditions are suitable. It is a good plan to get them planted as early as possible, however, as they are then often able to form some new roots and make contact with the soil before the depths of winter. This is particularly true of roses, which transplant best early in November. If such plants are lifted in January or February they will usually be found to have made plenty of new, hair-like roots.

Herbaceous Plants All perennial plants of a herbaceous character cannot be treated alike. September or October planting appears to suit many, but those with succulent shoots are less likely to be killed by frost if left undisturbed till the spring. This also applies to many tuberous-rooted plants, and is particularly true if the soil into which they are to be planted is at all liable to become waterlogged. On balance, therefore, spring is the safer season when in doubt, though a drawback is that flowers may be few or lacking the first year.

With a few summer-flowering plants the foliage of which does not die down completely during the winter it is most satisfactory to transplant immediately after flowering. It will be found that new roots are formed at this period. This advice applies in particular to all the flag irises and to *Lilium candidum*, the Madonna lily; but it is equally true of heleniums, pyrethrums, and moon daisies. This is a very useful method where the plants can be given individual attention and be watered for the first week or two.

Bulbous Plants Almost all bulbous-rooted plants have a definite season of rest—that is to say, there is a period when they show little or no outward signs of growth. In many of them all leaves die down, familiar examples being the tulip, narcissus, and hyacinth, all of which go to rest a little after midsummer and may remain dormant for three or four months. It is during this period that most bulbs or corms can be transplanted most successfully. If they are somewhat tender, for example gladioli and choice montbretias, planting is delayed till March or April in order that growth may not be exposed to frost. Further details will be found in Chapter Seventeen.

Heeling-in If early frosts occur, all autumn planting should be delayed for a few days until the weather becomes milder. If plants are received from a nurseryman during such a frosty period or during snow or heavy rain, they must be 'heeled' into a trench until they can be dealt with. To do this it is merely necessary to cut out a slanting trench, lay the plants in this at an angle, and cover the roots well with soil. This will provide adequate protection against frost and wind.

Planting Ferns The planting of ferns differs from that of other perennials only in the matter of firming. Ferns thrive most successfully if planted in a rather fine, loose compost. Although the plants should not have the soil packed down against the roots by pressure, this does not mean that the surrounding soil should be full of large air spaces.

Exceptions to the Rule Flag irises and eremuruses provide two other exceptions to general rules, as for both of these very shallow planting is necessary, with the roots spread out horizontally. Indeed, the fleshy rhizomes of irises will soon work themselves right out of the soil. No attempt should be made to prevent this natural habit.

The planting of climbers, in so far as this differs from the planting of shrubs, is dealt with in detail in Chapter Thirteen.

CHAPTER FIVE

Raising Plants from Seed

UNTIL the garden owner has tried his—or her—hand at raising plants from seed, and has experienced the thrill of watching the tiny seedlings struggle through the soil, has followed their subsequent career with all a parent's fears and hopes, and has finally known the joy of realized expectation, he has missed the most enthralling enterprise on which he might embark, and is, indeed, scarcely worthy of the honourable name 'gardener.'

Seeds afford the most economical method of raising large numbers of plants, such as are frequently required for summer bedding and greenhouse display, and are therefore especially welcome to the average amateur faced with the problem of stocking a new garden. Additionally the raising of seedlings is a fascinating occupation which greatly enlarges the gardener's knowledge of individual plants by bringing him in contact with their requirements from the very start. It is the only way of propagating annuals and biennials—that is, plants which flower and die in one or two years. Plant breeders also realize the value of plants raised from seed, for by carefully selecting the parents they are able to obtain many fascinating new varieties.

Harvesting and Storing Seeds Seeds form a resting stage in the life of a plant, during which the rate of living is very slow indeed. Nevertheless, seeds are alive when they are harvested from the parent plants, and for this reason should be kept in an airy place, not in a tightly closed tin. The place chosen for storage must not be subject to great changes of temperature and should be frostproof.

Seed harvested at home should be carefully cleaned of all dust and pieces of seed pod before being stored, for dead fragments are liable to be attacked by fungi, which, if they once obtain a hold, may damage the seeds too. If the seeds are large the chaff may be blown gently from them, or they may be picked out individually, but this is difficult to do with small seeds.

Smooth small seeds, such as those of the poppy, can be cleaned by allowing the seeds and chaff to roll down the slope of a moderately steeply inclined board, the surface of which has been covered with some new flannelette. The chaff, being proportionately lighter and of uneven shape, catches on the fine hairs of the material, and the seeds can be collected at the base. In large quantities seeds are cleaned by centrifugal force.

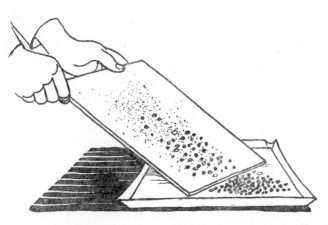

CLEANING SEED BEFORE STORING

Small pieces of husk and also dust can be removed by gently rolling the seeds down a board covered with fairly smooth cloth. The clean seeds can be collected at the bottom.

The Longevity of Seeds Seeds do not retain their life indefinitely, for chemical changes take place within them which result in their death. Hard-coated seeds appear to live the longest. It is not easy to tell from the outside whether a seed is alive or dead, and therefore when buying seeds it is worth while to purchase them from reliable firms. If a seed is dead it will not grow or germinate. Good firms test the ability of their seeds to germinate before selling them by trying out a sample. A simple home test can be made by placing a known number of seeds on a piece of damp flannel in a saucer, standing this in a warm place and calculating the percentage of seeds which germinate. Seeds that are below a satisfactory standard, as shown by the sample, should be discarded.

Good seed will only have been saved from healthy plants and will have been allowed to ripen thoroughly before being gathered. In wet summers it is difficult to ripen seed properly in this country except under glass, and therefore most of the seed sold here has been grown specially in such warm countries as Italy and California. Thus in the spring following a wet season it is especially wise to buy seeds rather than use home-saved ones.

The seeds of many plants germinate best almost immediately after they are ripe; others require a period of rest in the soil before they will grow at all. The individual requirements of different kinds of seeds can only be discovered by experiment or consultation with an experienced gardener, but beginners are safe in following the directions printed on the seed packet.

Covering the Seeds The size of seeds differs tremendously, some being almost dustlike, and others large, like the beans. Small seeds contain very little stored food material and are therefore harder to grow than the large ones, which will produce big seedlings, much better able to fend for themselves. Soil preparation for the tiny seeds must therefore receive very careful attention. Wherever the seeds are to be sown, the

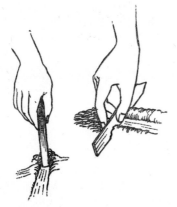

MAKING A SEED DRILL
A useful method of drawing and covering a shallow seed drill with a wooden tally. This is particularly useful where seeds are sown in a frame.

surface soil will have to be reduced to a very fine tilth, or the seeds will fall down between the lumps and be lost, for the tiny plants are unable to penetrate through any great depth. In fact, it should be a general rule not to cover any seed with much more than twice its own depth of soil.

The Advantages of Sowing Under Glass Obviously it is not easy to obtain and maintain a high degree of tilth in a seed bed in the open, and therefore wherever possible seeds should be sown in a seed box or pan in the shelter of a frame or greenhouse. An additional advantage accrues when the house or frame can be heated (with pipes, sunken electric cable, or hotbed—see Chapter Thirty-one), for it is found that the majority of seeds germinate most successfully in a temperature slightly higher than that in which the plants are afterwards to be grown. Thus seeds of hardy and half-hardy plants that are wanted for summer

bedding can be germinated in February in a warm greenhouse, whereas
late March is the earliest time outdoors in sheltered gardens, and May
is the normal month in many places for the soil to become sufficiently
warm. By this latter date many people will be requiring plants of sufficient size for bedding out, not tiny seedlings. Therefore where a frame or
greenhouse is not available hardy bedding plants should be raised from
seed sown in July or August. This seed will produce plants which will
flower early the following year. Half-hardy plants cannot be raised in
this manner, however, unless some protection can be given them during
the cold weather, for they will only survive the very mildest of winters
without protection.

Preparing a Seed Bed To prepare a seed bed out of doors the surface
of the selected plot, which should be in a sheltered position, must be

DRAWING A DRILL
*The back of the hoe can be used to draw
out a shallow drill along a garden line.*

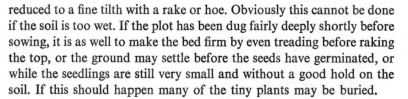

reduced to a fine tilth with a rake or hoe. Obviously this cannot be done
if the soil is too wet. If the plot has been dug fairly deeply shortly before
sowing, it is as well to make the bed firm by even treading before raking
the top, or the ground may settle before the seeds have germinated, or
while the seedlings are still very small and without a good hold on the
soil. If this should happen many of the tiny plants may be buried.

Sowing Seeds Out-doors Seeds may be sown broadcast or in drills.
If the plants are to remain in the positions in which they germinate, it
may be an advantage to have the seedlings spaced unevenly, but the
irregular scattering of seeds has very little else to recommend it. If
this method is employed it is very difficult to keep the surface of the soil
cultivated, for there is no means of telling where it is safe to hoe until

all the seeds have grown. This may not be important with quickly growing annuals which germinate in ten days or so, but is another matter if
the seeds take many months to appear above ground, as some plants do.

Seeds sown in rows can be clearly marked, and the intervening soil
cultivated even before the seeds germinate. Weeds are more readily
distinguishable from the seedlings and soon hoed up. When sowing in
rows there is no necessity to make drills unless the seeds are sufficiently
large to require fairly deep burying. The position of the row can be
marked out by pressing a cane lightly on to the surface soil, and the
seeds covered with a sprinkling of fine soil.

To ensure that small seeds are sown thinly and evenly they should
be mixed with dry sand. This mixing must be thorough. The mixture
can then be shaken from the corner of the seed packet or from a folded
piece of paper. It is unwise to sow 'pinches' of fine seeds unless the seed
coats are very hard, for many seeds, such as carnations, are damaged
very easily.

The more space that can be left between the seedlings the better,
within reason, for this will ensure freedom from disease and delay
transplanting or thinning.

Sowing Seeds in Boxes Where seeds are to be sown in boxes or pans
the receptacles must be well drained. The compost may vary slightly

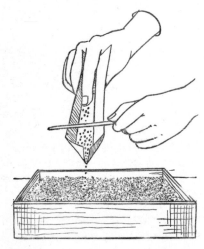

SOWING SMALL SEEDS
*A small 'chute' of stiff paper holds the
seeds and makes it an easy matter to
tap them out evenly.*

with the kind of seed to be sown, but a good mixture for almost all
seeds can be made by using two parts of good fibrous loam, one part
of sharp sand and one part of granulated peat. For all but the quickest-

Top: Scattering fertilizer in a frame being prepared for a seed bed. *Centre:* The fertilizer is forked into the surface soil. *Bottom:* The soil is trodden firmly and evenly throughout the frame.

Top: The surface is raked as fine and level as possible. *Centre:* A drill is made by pressing the rake handle into the soil. *Bottom:* Seed is sprinkled evenly in the bottom of the drill.

Sowing seed broadcast. This method is particularly suitable when informal groups of flowers are required to grow where sown.

The broadcasted seed is covered with a little fine soil scattered through a seive.

germinating seeds it is an advantage if the loam can be sterilized before use. This is almost a necessity if seeds which take many months to germinate are sown, for otherwise the soil becomes mossed over. It can easily be done in small quantities by filling a pail with the compost and standing it in a copper of boiling water for fully half an hour. The water should not be allowed to splash into the soil, and seed sowing must not take place until the soil is cold again.

The compost should be made flat in the receptacle and the seeds sown on the surface and then covered. Seeds can be sown more thickly in pans and boxes than in the open ground, but should not be very close together unless it is certain that time will be available to prick them out, as the first transplanting of seedlings is called, as soon as this is neces-sary. If left too close together seedlings rapidly become drawn—that is, long and spindly with pale weak growth—and, apart from the fact that they can never become really strong and healthy after this has

SOWING SEEDS
IN A POT
Note the ample layer of crocks to provide good drainage.

happened, they are very subject to damping off disease in this condition. This disease is caused by a fungus which attacks the tiny plants at soil level, with the result that they fall over at this point. Once a seedling is recognizably infected with the disease there is little hope of saving it. Surrounding plants can be protected by watering with a weak solution of permanganate of potash or with Cheshunt compound. Details of the treatment and quantities are to be found in Chapter Thirty-four.

Watering It is easier to water the prepared seed pan thoroughly before sowing, and when this is done, to cover the surface with a sheet of glass to prevent rapid evaporation, than to attempt to water the newly planted seeds, especially if these are small. Every morning any moisture that has collected on the under-surface of the glass during the night must be wiped off, or the drops may either fall, splashing up tiny seeds, or act as lenses or burning glasses during the day, causing scorching of the first leaves by concentration of the sun's rays.

Seed boxes and pans must never be allowed to dry right out. If the soil needs water, this can be applied from above by means of a watering can with a very fine rose, or, better still, from below, by holding the pan in a bath or pail of water. The pan should be held so that the level of the water outside is just below that of the soil. In this position the water will soak right through the compost, but the tiny seeds will remain undisturbed. If the surrounding level is higher than the soil surface, even if there is no danger of a sudden inrush of water over the rim, small seeds will be floated up out of the soil.

Germinating in the Dark Many seeds germinate most rapidly in the dark, though this is by no means always true. The thin layer of soil does not compensate for the shade which would normally be afforded by surrounding plants, but this may be remedied by placing a sheet of

WATERING BY PARTIAL IMMERSION

An excellent method with tiny seeds. The pans are held in water to their rims for a few moments until the surface darkens with rising moisture.

brown paper below the glass. This must be removed as soon as the majority of the seeds have started to germinate, or the most rapidly growing ones will soon become drawn and weakly. The glass must also be tilted up at the edge at this time to allow air to reach the growing plants, and should be removed entirely in a few days. After this the seedlings must be kept close to the glass of the greenhouse or frame to allow them as much light as possible. They must be well ventilated, but should not stand in a draught, or they may succumb to disease.

Pricking Out Pricking out should be done as soon as it becomes necessary. This will vary with the spacing of the seeds and the rapidity of their growth, but will generally be necessary when the first true leaves are formed. The earliest structures produced are usually simple in shape and are the 'seed leaves,' or cotyledons, which have grown above ground. The true leaves can generally be easily distinguished by their more complicated shape, and sometimes by their hairiness. Where germination of a pan of seeds is very irregular it may be necessary to remove the seedlings singly, as they become large enough, without disturbing the remaining ones. This is a task requiring care and patience.

Usually the first pricking out will take place when the seedlings are so small that they can be irreparably damaged by anything like rough handling. Such tiny plants are often most easily moved with the aid of an ivory-tipped pair of forceps, after they have been dug from the seed pan with a small pointed stick. The end of a small wooden tally makes a

PRICKING OUT SEEDLINGS

Tiny seedlings can be lifted from seed pots with a forked stick, as soon as they are big enough to handle, and pricked out in rows. Take care to firm the soil round the roots.

useful miniature trowel. The box into which the seedlings are to be moved must be ready to hand and the plants put in immediately, as only a few minutes' exposure to dry air will kill them. The soil should be similar to that used in the seed pans, but the loam can be slightly coarser beneath, and must be well drained. It is best to water the compost an hour or two before it will be used and to keep the box in the greenhouse for that period so that the tiny roots avoid the additional shock of cold soil. The quickest method of planting the uprooted seedling is to make a hole in the compost with the stick used to lift it, and to drop the roots into this and press the soil firmly round them with the point of the stick, which thus acts as a little dibber. The distance apart that the seedlings are placed will naturally depend upon their size and the length of time that it is proposed to grow them in that particular box. Two inches space each way is necessary for all but the smallest.

Transplanting When the leaves of the seedlings touch in the boxes they require transplanting, to either the open ground, pots, or larger boxes. Plants intended for the open ground must be thoroughly hardened off before they are planted out. This is easily done if the boxes can be placed in a frame from which the lights are taken for the greater part of each day at least.

Planting out of seedlings is similar to the methods of planting already dealt with in the previous chapter, and note should be taken of the procedure. The necessity for pricking out and further transplanting from a box, with all the root disturbance that these processes necessarily involve, can be avoided if the seeds are sown singly, or in small numbers and later thinned to one, in the special seed containers that are now obtainable. The container and the young seedling can be placed directly into the soil, where the container will rot harmlessly away.

Thinning If the seeds sown out of doors are too close together when germinated they must be thinned to suitable distances apart or else transplanted. In thinning, all unwanted seedlings are pulled up. This must be done with great care, or the surrounding plants which it is desired to keep will have their roots damaged. The best method is to press two fingers on the soil, one on each side of the plant to be removed, and to pull with the other hand. This prevents the soil from being pulled up with the plant. If any soil has become loosened in spite of this precaution, it must be made firm at once, and in any case the bed should be watered after thinning to give the remaining plants a good chance of settling into the soil. It is a mistake to pull up all the tiny seedlings when thinning a seed bed in which the plants are likely to vary in colour or other similar character, for it is found that often the slowest growing, least vigorous-looking plants turn out to be the choicest in other respects.

CHAPTER SIX

Propagation Simply Explained

A T the outset the novice will doubtless be satisfied to purchase from a nurseryman most of the trees and plants that he requires to stock his garden. But sooner or later, if he is worthy of his salt, the desire to produce at least a proportion of his own stock, if only to have some spare plants to exchange with other enthusiasts, is bound to grow. New varieties are necessarily expensive to purchase, and there is considerable saving if it is only necessary to purchase a few plants on account of the skill which one has developed at 'propagation.' This, by the way, is the term used to include all methods of raising new plants; but in this chapter only what is termed 'vegetative propagation'—that is to say, the production of plants by any means other than seeds—is dealt with. These methods include such very different processes as division of existing plants, the rooting of various kinds of cuttings and layers, and budding and grafting. Seed raising has already been dealt with fully in the preceding chapter.

Propagation by Division Of the various vegetative means, division is the simplest and most widely applicable. Anyone who has ever grown a plant of phlox, Michaelmas daisies, heleniums, or iris, to name but a few of the innumerable herbaceous perennials to which division may be applied, must have been struck with the rate at which the size of the clump has increased. Instead of the single stem originally planted there soon appears a whole thicket of stems. In fact, in four of five years these positively choke one another. If such a large clump is dug up in the spring, which process will often be attended with much difficulty and mean little short of excavation, it will be found to consist of large numbers of young shoots coming from a woody rootstock. Most of the shoots will be rooted at their base. The soil should be shaken gently from these to facilitate division. It is the most healthy of these rooted portions that will make the best divisions.If the clump is not too big and the shoots are merely intertwined, as in Michaelmas daisy clumps, the division may be done by hand, but for most plants it is necessary to use two forks. The prongs of these should be embedded in the centre of the clump back to back and touching; they can then be levered apart by outward pressure on the two handles. In this way great force can be applied

without injuring the plant to any appreciable extent. A spade should not
be used, as this is bound to part many of the intertwining roots from
their shoots. If the centre of the clump is hard and woody, as often
happens with phloxes and some ferns, it may be necessary to cut the
clump into pieces with a sharp knife, which should only be used to
sever the tough part. The roots should be shaken out gently. The hard
part must be broken off as far as possible and not replanted, as the best
plants are always formed from the young outer growths. The actual size
of the divisions will depend on the kind of plant, but the majority will
have one or two shoots only. To ensure a good display in the first year
after planting, several such divisions may be arranged to form a group.

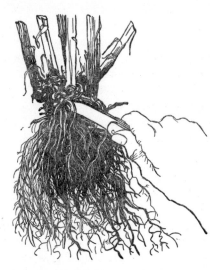

**DIVIDING AN HERBACEOUS
PLANT**

*Strong clumps with plenty of roots
attached are pulled or cut apart,
taking care that each division has
its fair share of roots.*

The method of division is by no means confined to perennials in the
herbaceous border, but applies equally to tiny alpine plants and to
bulbs and corms, such as daffodils and crocuses. Single bulbs soon
increase to form clumps if left undisturbed, and should be lifted and
divided periodically, as they cannot obtain enough food when crowded
together.

Rooting Runners Some plants, such as strawberries and violets, send
out long horizontal shoots or runners, which, if left to themselves, will
usually form roots from the underside of the stem, and thus make new
plants. The roots grow where leaves join the stem, which place is known
as a node. To ensure that the runners root properly it is advisable to peg
down the stem close to one of these nodes. The peg may consist of a

piece of wire bent like a hairpin, and known as a layering pin, or a forked twig or smooth stone. Once the stem has rooted well at the node the new plant that grows at this point may be severed from the parent and subsequently moved to a new position. To facilitate moving, it is a good plan to sink a small flower pot full of sandy compost flush with the surface of the soil wherever it is intended to root a runner. The young plant can then be moved in the pot and will suffer much less from root disturbance. To ensure strong new plants, the number of runners formed by the plant should be limited, and no runner must be allowed to root more than once.

Propagation by Layering It is a very easy step from rooting a runner to layering a stem. In this case the plant would not be so likely to root unaided, and therefore it is induced to do so by burying a part of the

**LAYERING
A LOGANBERRY**
If the tips of young canes are pegged into the soil as shown they will soon form roots and can be detached from the parent plant.

stem in the soil. Prior to this the stem is usually injured in some way at the point to be covered. This injury generally takes the form of a cut, but may consist in ringing the stem. The object is to draw sap to the part and thereby induce the formation of roots. The method is simplicity itself. A fairly young shoot is taken, thin and supple enough to bend down to ground level. Then, at the part to be buried, a long cut is made in an upward direction through a joint or node. The growth should not be entirely severed; the knife must pass only about halfway through it. When bent this cut portion will project; it is known as a 'heel.' Some gardeners, especially when layering carnations, recommend that this portion should be removed entirely. The cut portion of the stem, if the layering is successful, will heal over—that is, form a callus— and from this callused surface roots will grow. To induce callus and root formation it is necessary for the part to be in direct contact with the soil, as in planting, and therefore if the ground surrounding the plant is lumpy it is wise to scoop out a hole and fill it with fine sandy compost and peg the stem into this. The cut section of the stem is kept in position in the soil by means of a layering pin, and where the plant is a rose or other shrub the portion of the stem beyond this point should be firmly staked in an upright position. This staking not only prevents the wind from uprooting the layer, but by keeping the shoot upright encourages a more rapid flow of sap and consequent speedy rooting. When such a layer is well rooted it may be severed from the parent plant. By that time layers of roses, honeysuckles, and similar plants will have formed new shoots at the base where the roots have also been growing. This does not happen so readily in more hard-wooded shrubs. In no instance should the shoot taken be very woody, and the sap must

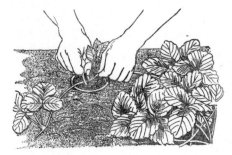

PEGGING DOWN STRAWBERRY RUNNERS

Plantlets are pegged into small pots of prepared compost, plunged rim deep into the strawberry bed. The runners are pegged down to hold the young plants in position until they have made good roots.

always be flowing freely; thus shrubs may be layered from the end of April onwards and carnations and violets in July. A special kind of layering is used for blackberries, loganberries and other brambles. The tips of strong canes are pegged to the soil in August without special preparation. They root freely, soon make new growths and may generally be transplanted by the following November.

Sometimes it is desirable to layer shoots which cannot be made to reach the soil. In these plants layering may be effected by enclosing the cut or ringed section of the stem in a flower pot full of sandy compost. The pot must be split in halves and the parts placed round the stem, the weight of the pot being completely and firmly supported, and the soil kept moist. After rooting, the stem is cut below the pot.

Propagation by Cuttings It is possible to root stems which have been entirely removed from the parent plant. These are called stem cuttings. Pieces of roots of other subjects will likewise produce new shoots, and even leaves of some will yield new plants. These are known as root and leaf cuttings respectively.

Stem Cuttings These may be made from young, unripened shoots, when they are called soft-wooded cuttings, from well-grown but not fully ripened summer shoots, in which case they are known as summer or half-ripe cuttings, or from ripened twigs a season old, when they are designated hard-wooded.

Soft-wooded Cuttings Plants regularly propagated from young growth include chrysanthemums, pelargoniums, violas, and perpetual-flowering carnations. To form a cutting of this kind a young shoot from 2 to

TAKING A PELARGONIUM CUTTING
A young shoot, without flower buds, is severed just below the leaf.

4 inches in length, according to the size of the plant, is removed and cut off squarely beneath a joint. The leaves are carefully cut, not ripped, from the bottom two or three nodes, and the cutting is ready for insertion. Although it is possible to root soft cuttings of some plants in the open border, it is more usual to insert them in pots, boxes, or special beds in a frame or greenhouse. The reason for this is that the conditions in a frame or greenhouse are under the control of the gardener, who is then able to maintain the necessary damp atmosphere which prevents the cut stems from losing all their moisture and dying before they can form roots.

Rooting Media Silver sand is often used as a rooting medium. It encourages rapid rooting, but dries out quickly, so needs frequent watering. Horticultural grade vermiculite is equally good for quick rooting and holds moisture much better. Neither of these materials contains any plant food, so cuttings that have rooted should be removed to an ordinary potting compost as soon as possible. Alternatively,

PREPARING A PELARGONIUM CUTTING

The cut should be made just below the leaf joint at the mark shown on the right. Cut with a sharp knife and trim off the lower leaves as shown on the left.

a mixture of 3 parts of sharp sand, 2 parts of sphagnum peat, and 1 part of medium loam may be used as a compost in which to insert cuttings. They may be a little slower forming roots in this, but they will not starve so rapidly, as the mixture will contain a good deal of plant food.

The Use of Hormones Certain chemicals, known as plant hormones, have the power of encouraging root formation if applied to the base of cuttings in very small quantities. That most commonly used is a form of naphthaleneacetic acid which is sold under various trade names. It can be purchased as either a liquid or a powder. The former must be diluted with water at a strength determined by the nature of the cuttings. In general, hard-wooded or autumn and winter cuttings need a stronger solution than soft-wooded or spring and summer cuttings. Manufacturers usually supply detailed instructions on these matters. About $\frac{1}{2}$ inch of the dilute fluid is then placed in a jar, and the cuttings are placed with their prepared lower ends in this and left to stand for from 12 to 18 hours, after which they are washed in clean water and inserted in the ordinary way.

The powder hormone is really more convenient to use, as it is only necessary to dip the base of the cutting in it and then place in the cutting bed. As a rule three different strengths of powder are offered, one for soft cuttings, one for half-ripe or midsummer cuttings, and one for hard-wooded cuttings. All are ready for use as purchased.

All pots or boxes, and also beds of soil made up on the greenhouse staging or in a frame, must be well drained by having a layer of rubble or broken crocks in the bottom. The sand must be prevented from blocking this up by covering it with a layer of coarse fibrous material, such as rough leaf-mould.

Inserting the Cuttings Cuttings are most easily inserted by means of a small dibber. Holding this in the right hand and the cutting in the left, make a hole deep enough to cover one-third of the cutting. Drop the latter into the hole, making certain that the bottom of the cutting rests at the base of the hole and is not held up halfway with a space beneath it. Then press the soil round the base of the shoot by means of the dibber. Cuttings inserted in a pot should be placed round the edge rather than in the centre. They will usually be found to root more rapidly round the edge of the pot, and are disturbed much less when transplanted. Cuttings in beds and boxes can be placed quite close together in the rows, an inch apart being sufficient for chrysanthemums.

After-treatment After insertion the cuttings should be kept in a close atmosphere—that is to say, ventilation should practically cease. This

A SIMPLE PROPAGATING BOX
The box should be placed over the hot water pipes in the greenhouse and the glazed lid made to fit as closely as possible.

keeps the air damp and therefore prevents loss of water from the shoots. If the days are sunny the cuttings must be shaded. A little air may be given when the cuttings commence to make new growth, but ventilation must not reach the normal for the time of the year until the cuttings are well rooted. They should then be carefully transplanted into small pots filled with compost which is still rather sandy, but contains some food in the form of well-decayed leaf-mould or a little peat moss litter and, perhaps, a sprinkling of bone flour. Immediately after potting it is necessary to keep the plants in a close atmosphere again for a day or so until they recover from the move. The loss of water from soft cuttings is rapid in dry weather, and, as they are unable fully to make good this loss until they have rooted into the new compost, these precautions are essential to success. If the cuttings show sign of flagging after the first few days they may be sprayed overhead very lightly with clear water, but care must be taken not to disturb the soil. The water must be at the same temperature as the soil, not cold from the main.

Half-ripe Cuttings Half-ripe cuttings of shrubs may be made in a different manner from that described above. Instead of cutting off the young shoot and trimming it below a node, it is pulled from the branch in a downward direction so that a strip or heel of the older wood comes away. The heel is trimmed neatly into shape, the lower leaves are removed, and the cutting is inserted as before. Roots will be found to form on the heel, which provides a larger surface for rooting than the tiny stem cut squarely. Additionally, the woody nature of the lower portion enables the cutting to remain healthy in the soil for a longer period. Evergreen shrubs respond well to this method, but it is not suitable for a few exceptional plants which root better between the nodes instead of at them, nor are such good results obtained with plants which root readily from half-ripened wood if inserted during July.

Hard-wooded Cuttings Hard-wooded cuttings are used for currants and gooseberries, and also for many deciduous trees and shrubs, including rambler roses and rose species. They are often known as 'naked cuttings' because they are taken at about the time when the plants are shedding their leaves in the autumn. These cuttings are prepared from firm, well-ripened young wood formed during the previous summer. They are usually from 9 to 15 inches in length and are inserted 4 or 5 inches deep in trenches nicked out with a spade in a bed or border outdoors, preferably in a sheltered position. Frequently no protection is given, though where choice shrubs are concerned a handlight placed over the cuttings will facilitate rooting. It is also an excellent plan to scatter a little sharp sand at the bottom of the shallow trench before lining the cuttings out. Then finely broken soil is returned round the cuttings and made thoroughly firm by foot pressure.

Root Cuttings Many plants with thick fleshy roots can be propagated from portions of the roots, but even some fibrous-rooted plants, such as summer-flowering phloxes, gaillardias, and *Morisia hypogaea*, may be treated similarly. Cuttings made from quite thin pieces of root will form new shoots in a comparatively short space of time. A plant of the desired subject is lifted at any time when not in active growth; any reasonably thick root is detached and cut into pieces about an inch in length. These may be laid fairly thickly in a pan of sandy soil and covered with ¼ inch of the same compost, if the roots are thin. If the plant is one with very fleshy roots, such as an anchusa, perennial statice, or Oriental poppy, the pieces should be cut in such a manner that it is possible afterwards to distinguish the top from the bottom. This is easy if the lower surface is cut on the slant and the top one square. These thick cuttings are then stood upright in a pot almost filled with sandy compost and more soil added until they are just covered. They must be made firm in the soil, or rooting will be delayed. The soil must be sandy and the receptacles well drained. After insertion the pots should be placed in a greenhouse or frame, and when they have been given a thorough watering from a fine rose the tops should be covered with pieces of slate or glass to prevent evaporation. As soon as shoots appear these sheets must be removed.

The pots may be watered carefully to prevent the soil from becoming too dry, but the compost must never become sodden with water, or the cuttings will soon rot.

Using a Propagating Box Soft stem cuttings, and also in one or two cases root cuttings, of tender subjects may also be made as already explained, but can only be induced to root if the pans are placed in a propagating box supplied with steady bottom heat. A simple propagating box may be made by standing a margarine or similar wooden box on the top of the greenhouse pipes. The interior of the box should be filled to within a few inches of the top with coconut fibre. This should be kept damp and will then prevent the loss of water by evaporation from the pans of root cuttings, which should be plunged in the fibre up to their rims. The temperature is also kept steadier by this method. The top of the box must be kept covered by a sheet or two of glass, and the soil should be maintained at a temperature of from 65° to 70°. Bottom heat can also be supplied by means of the soil-warming electrical cables which are now made by many manufacturers or by passing a low-voltage current through bare wires buried 6 to 8 inches below the surface of the soil.

Leaf Cuttings The leaves of begonias, gloxinias, streptocarpus, and several other warm-greenhouse subjects will root from the base of the leaf stalk if this portion of the leaf is buried in the sand of a propagating frame. The leaves should be fully formed, but not so old as to have become hard, if the best results are to be obtained. If kept close and given a certain amount of bottom heat, roots and then a tiny plant will be formed from the end of the stalk. Begonias of the Rex type will also

INSERTING
LEAF CUTTINGS
OF GLOXINIA
The leaf is simply slipped into a very peaty compost, pressed firm and kept in a close, humid atmosphere until tiny roots form.

root from the leaf blade, especially if this is wounded in the region of a main vein. To do this the veins may be cut across, one cut per vein. The veins will be seen to stand out clearly as ridges, if the leaf is turned over. Alternatively, the leaves may be pegged down to the sand by strips of metal, one end of which pierces the leaf at a vein. Whichever method is used the leaves must be laid with the under-surface on the sand. A tiny leaf will form wherever the cutting has rooted.

Budding In both grafting and its specialized form, budding, a piece of the plant it is desired to propagate is inserted in the shoot of an allied plant, which is known as the stock. Budding differs from grafting proper in that only a bud, not a shoot, is taken from the plant to be perpetuated, and also that the work is done during the growing season, not when the plants are dormant, as with grafting. Both result in the union of the living tissues of the scion, or part inserted, with those of the stock.

Budding is most useful for the propagation of roses and fruit trees. It must be done when the sap is rising in full vigour. Usually the end of June is early enough to start the budding of rose stocks and end of

July for most fruit stocks. The sure test that the stock is in the right condition is to insert a sharp knife in the stem and try to lift the bark away from the woody layer beneath. If the bark parts easily and the wood beneath is moist with sap, budding may start, but if the wood is dry and the bark only parts by tearing, the stocks should be left for another week or two. The buds or scions are obtained from half-ripened shoots of the current year's growth. Stems about 6 inches in length should be taken and the tip removed, as this will be insufficiently

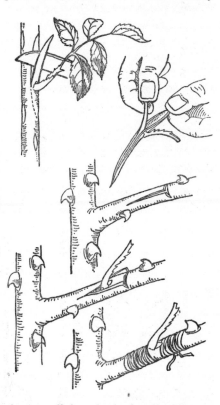

A LESSON IN BUDDING

At the top left a suitable bud is being removed with a sharp knife. At the top right the slip of wood behind the bud is being removed. The centre illustration shows the T-cut made in the stock to be budded. Below, on the left, the bud has been inserted and on the right it is shown tied in place with raffia. All these operations are described more fully on page 64.

ripe. The leaf blades should then be cut off, but the leaf stalks allowed to remain, as these are very convenient for holding the little bud in place. The scions prepared for use should be stood upright in a jar containing not more than $\frac{1}{2}$ inch of water. This will keep the shoots from withering, but will not soak the lower buds.

The budding knife must be very sharp, and if much work has to be done will need sharpening continually. The only other requirement is a supply of soft raffia. To prepare the bud for insertion, select a scion and insert the knife ¾ inch below one of the leaf stalks, in the axil of which lies a dormant bud. Draw the knife through the wood, bringing it out about ½ inch above the leaf stalk so as to sever it and its bud with a shield-shaped portion of bark just over an inch in length. Grip this by the leaf stalk, and with the point of the knife and the thumb grip the tiny slip of wood enclosed by the bark and smartly draw it out. If the work is done correctly the bud will be left intact in the bark ready for insertion in the stock. This latter is prepared by making a T-shaped incision on a straight portion of one-year-old wood. The flaps of this incision are then very carefully raised with the thin ivory blade at the end of the handle of a budding knife. It is a simple matter to slip the shield-shaped portion of bark containing the bud beneath these flaps so that the exposed surfaces of both stock and scion lie snugly together. Finally, the bud is bound firmly in position with pliable raffia.

No further attention is usually necessary until the following spring, when the whole of the growth of the stock should be removed just above the point at which the bud was inserted, and the tie is cut so that it shall not impede growth. If the stock is forming sucker shoots below the bud, these must also be removed.

Grafting Grafting is similar in effect to budding, but is carried out in March or April. There are many different systems, but only two need

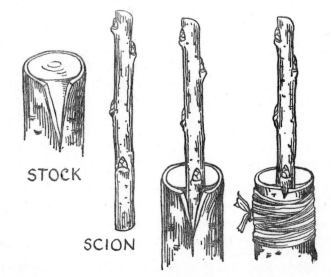

STOCK

SCION

RIND GRAFTING
The wedge-shaped scion is pushed beneath the bark and bound with raffia.

Left: Widening the drainage slit in the bottom of a wooden seed box. *Right:* Crocks and rough rubble placed in the bottom of the seed box to ensure good drainage.

Left: The soil in the seed box is pressed firmly with a smooth wooden block. *Right:* The seed is sown as evenly as possible on the level surface.

Examining seed boxes for signs of germination. Note that each box has been covered with a sheet of newspaper and a pane of glass to conserve moisture.

Pricking off seedlings into a rather deep seed box filled with a similar compost to that used for seed raising.

concern the beginner. One is known as whip grafting, or tongue grafting, and is used when stock and scion are nearly the same in diameter. The other is known as crown or rind grafting, and is used when the stock is much larger than the scion.

In either case well-ripened young shoots to provide scions must be removed during the winter from the bushes or trees it is intended to propagate. In the case of apples, pears, and many other fruit trees the ends of leaders and the thicker laterals removed when pruning are ideal. These should be carefully labelled, tied in small bundles, and heeled in in a shallow trench in a shady border. The stocks are cut hard back in winter.

To make a whip graft, a piece of scion from 3 to 4 inches in length is selected, and the lower half is cut on one side in the form of a wedge. Then a reverse slit is made about two-thirds from the bottom of the first cut to make a thin 'tongue' of wood. The stock is cut in a similar manner, as shown in the illustrations, and the two tongues are fitted together. The more closely the two cut surfaces coincide the better. Finally, scion and stock are bound firmly together with raffia and are protected from excessive evaporation by a generous covering of grafting wax.

Scions for rind grafting are prepared in a similar manner, but no tongue is cut. The bark of the stock is then slit down with a sharp knife, and the wedge-shaped end of the scion is inserted between it and the hard wood beneath. The scion is then pressed down until the cut surface is all lying snugly against the wood of the stock and is bound in position and covered with grafting wax.

II

THE ORNAMENTAL GARDEN

CHAPTER SEVEN

Laying Out the Garden

IN planning a pleasure garden it is necessary not only to consider the type of soil and aspect, but also such varied influences as the style of architecture of adjacent buildings, the proposed permanence of the garden, and the amount of money likely to be available for plants, paths, greenhouse, and other accessory features and for labour, both at the beginning and in the future. Thus a business man who has only his week-ends and summer evenings in which to attend to the garden will be wise to include such permanent features as shrub and herbaceous borders, which need comparatively little attention for many months of the year. Also, although he may realize that the initial outlay on a garden frame can readily be made good by the saving effected by raising bedding and other plants from seed instead of purchasing them, he must also consider the fact that more time is necessary for daily attention to the young seedlings.

The nature of the soil may have some influence on the types of garden that it is possible to construct on a plot of a given size. For example, although it is comparatively easy to improve a poor soil by good cultivation, it is a difficult and expensive matter to convert a large amount of stiff clay into a well-drained plot, and therefore on such land it will be wise to exclude such a feature as a sunken garden, which would almost certainly become waterlogged unless elaborately drained.

The amount of sun that the different parts of the garden will receive throughout the year must be taken into account when planning. It is not enough to know which way the plot faces if shadows from buildings, walls, and fences and large trees are temporarily forgotten. All slopes, corners, and passageways between buildings must be considered, for a bed on a slope dipping to the north will receive less sun than the northern end of a flat garden; tender plants may be grown in sheltered nooks, and an unanticipated and persistent draught down a suburban side entrance

66

may play havoc with all but the hardiest plants—and even these will require secure staking.

Beds and Borders Almost all gardens are planned with a certain amount of grass and a number of beds for flowers, whatever additional features they may incorporate. The size and position of beds will depend not only upon the available space and the aspect and slope of the plot, but also upon the type of plant intended to be grown in them.

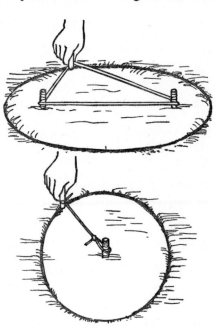

MARKING OUT OVAL
AND CIRCULAR BEDS
Oval beds can be marked out by driving two stakes into the ground, looping a piece of string over them and using a pointed stick inside the loop to draw a furrow. The distance between the stakes and the length of the loop determines the size and shape of the oval bed.
Circular beds are marked out as shown in the lower illustration, using a pointed stick looped with string to a centre stake. The length of the string determines the size of the circle.

Thus it is difficult to obtain anything but a seasonal display with beds narrower than 4 feet. Even bedding plants are more effective in wide than in narrow beds; and a narrow border should only be planned when it is desired to grow climbing plants on a wall or fence. Even then the bed should be at least 18 inches wide. Such a border will be found very useful in a long, narrow, enclosed villa garden, for such a plot produces its best blooms away from the fences. A single path can then be constructed near the boundary and a wide bed be made on the other side of it.

Paths In small gardens paths can often be dispensed with, but they play an important part in the laying out of larger areas. It is not necessary for a path to be straight, but it should lead directly to some

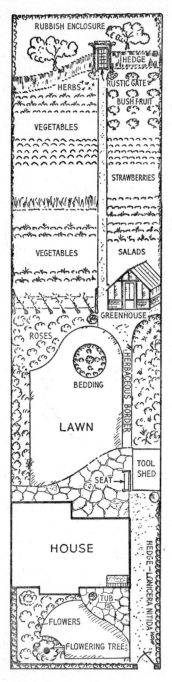

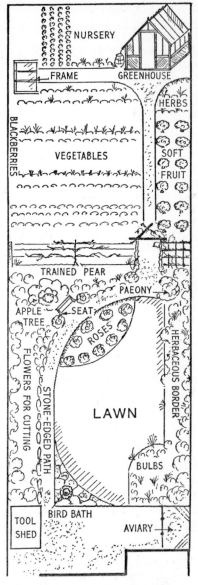

SUGGESTED PLANS FOR THE
LONG, NARROW PLOT

*Two garden plans including lawns,
flower borders and kitchen garden and
soft fruit are shown, both designed to
make maximum use of the space.*

important feature and not merely meander aimlessly. Paths are more expensive and difficult to make than beds, and should therefore be planned with even more care. Details of their construction are contained in the next chapter, but it may be mentioned here that the paths should be made of some material that is in keeping with the style of the house. Thus crazy paving is quite unsuitable in the vicinity of Georgian architecture, which is worthy of a more dignified medium, such as brick or rectangular flagstones. The style of the garden should also be in harmony with the house. With all but stone houses rock gardens are best well away from the buildings, and very formal gardens hardly blend with the average suburban villa. This need for thought applies even to small details such as garden ornaments. What bird is attracted to a bird bath placed within a few feet of a main road? And sundials are useless in the shade of buildings or trees.

The Garden Near the House Round the house the garden should be laid out in such a manner that it presents a pleasing front when viewed from each of the principal windows. This does not mean that the greater part of the plot should be visible from these windows or that the more important features of interest need be close to them, but merely that none of these views should lack interest. This is indeed more likely to be attained if all the garden is not visible from any one viewpoint, for curiosity as to the rest of the plot will be awakened. However small the garden, some effort should be made to break up a monotonous flat surface. This may be done by the judicious use of isolated shrubs and trees, sweeping shrub borders and ornamental hedges, or by altering the actual ground level with rock gardens. Sunken gardens and pools also relieve the surface, though they do not break the view.

There is no excuse for an ugly spot in any garden. Garage drives can be covered with pergolas, outhouses and bare walls and fences with wall trees and climbers. Even if the builder has made it impossible to plant these close to the wall, one can always grow ornamental trees in tubs. If the style of the house permits, these may take the form of topiary specimens, when they will look even more in place if the garden nearest to the house is planned on formal lines. There are, however, plenty of shrubs of less severe appearance suitable for inclusion in an informal garden. Wide borders and rambling creepers on the walls suit old houses with spacious gardens.

Planning for the Future A garden should be planned not only for the present, but also for the future, unless it be but a temporary possession. This necessitates a knowledge of the future needs of the plants. It is folly to plant a young tree in a site in which shade must not be allowed to increase, or to plant a hedge where it cannot expand in width. Trees should not be planted very close to boundary fences, for they will soon be growing into the neighbouring property, where their presence will possibly be resented, and where they may be lopped back with impunity.

Thorough Preparation is Necessary When making a new garden on a plot not previously cultivated, too much stress cannot be laid on the importance of thorough preparation of the ground for all such permanent features as lawns, shrub and herbaceous borders and hedges. Permanent weeds left in any of these will cause endless work. Therefore in the first year, with the permanent scheme in mind, the parts of the garden intended for such features should be sown with annuals or vegetables, after being well dug. The weeds can then be detected and removed without disturbing newly planted trees or grass. The temporary scheme need not look any less pleasing than the finished layout. There are any number of annuals, both brilliantly coloured and of the most delicate pastel shades, suitable for all kinds of soils and aspects, which are ideal for temporary schemes. Incidentally, this method of laying out a garden permits of a more even distribution of money, paths and other constructional features taking the giant's share in the first year, and shrubs and other planting stock following as the ground is worked into suitable condition.

CHAPTER EIGHT

Paths and Path Making

THE beginner need not shirk the task of path making. If carried out rightly, it is not more difficult than many other operations which every gardener, no matter how much of a novice, undertakes without hesitation, and there is considerable satisfaction to be derived from a knowledge that paths have been well made upon sound principles. Too frequently the professional jobber cares only for immediate effect, and does not put that honest workmanship into foundation work from which alone lasting satisfaction can result.

Preparing the Foundations No matter what the surfacing material may be, every garden path should have a substantial core of clinkers, broken brick ends, small stones, or similar hard rubble. In order to make room for this, the soil from the site of the path must be excavated to a depth of 9 inches or a foot. Each path should have a slight but definite slope in one direction, in order that surface water may be carried away. Sufficient foundation material is then placed in position to make the path up to within about 3 inches of the level of the finished surface. An inch-deep layer of sifted ashes is placed on top of this coarse rubble and raked perfectly even so as to form a smooth base for the surfacing material. When paths are to be set in concrete, it is as well to mix these ashes with a little cement—about one part of cement to six of ashes will be sufficient—in order that it may bind together and obtain a really firm hold upon the stones or clinkers.

Crazy Paving Crazy paving has increased immensely in popular favour of recent years. It has much to recommend it in gardens of moderate size, for, if well laid, its appearance is good and in keeping with the rough-cast finish of so many modern villas, while it is durable and easily set by the amateur. For paths that are not in constant use, crazy paving is best laid in ashes or sand. The slabs vary a good deal in thickness and are usually graded at the quarries into two types, thick and thin. Roughly one ton of the former will cover 8 or 9 square yards, while the same quantity of thin crazy will serve for 14 square yards.

Before commencing to lay the stone, it should be roughly spaced in heaps along the length of the path. Unless this precaution is taken there

71

will be a tendency to use up all the large slabs first, and be left with an assortment of small pieces for the end of the path. Do not attempt to make the stones fit accurately. Irregular fissures, so long as they do not exceed an inch or so in width, provide an admirable opportunity for establishing many trailing or creeping plants, which will add greatly to the beauty of the path. The best plan is to place the larger pieces in position first, leaving the filling of small gaps until last. Crazy paving may easily be broken with a hammer and cold chisel, but has an unfortunate knack of splitting in the wrong place in unskilled hands.

Frequently the slabs are coated with tenacious yellow clay. This

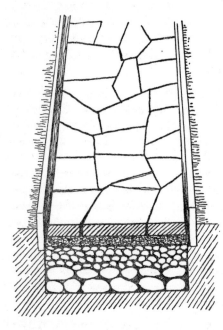

PATH CONSTRUCTION
Note the ample layer of drainage material and really sound foundations. A slight camber on the surface will also ensure good drainage.

should be removed from the lower side of each piece before setting it in position, or it will be found very difficult to make it lie flat. Should the stone vary much in thickness, the underlying layer of ashes or sand must be scraped away or added to. It is of the utmost importance that each slab should be evenly embedded in the foundation material, otherwise in time it will work loose and cause much trouble. The upper surface of the path must be quite free from bumps and unevenness. It should be tested from time to time as the work proceeds, with a plank having a straight edge. This should be placed across the stones in different directions and any irregularities rectified.

When the path is complete, finely sifted ashes, sand, or very sandy soil should be scattered over the surface and brushed this way and that, so as to fill up all the small crevices between the stones. After one or two heavy downpours of rain this will wash down and it will be necessary to brush a little more in.

When setting in concrete, the work proceeds in a similar manner, except that only a yard or so should be completed at a time. It is not possible to tread on the slabs after they have been placed in position until the concrete has hardened, so no alterations can be made once a section is finished. Subsequently the fissures between the stones should be pointed with cement and sand.

The concrete is made by mixing two parts of gravel, passed through a $\frac{1}{2}$-inch mesh sieve, and one part of sand, with one part of best Portland cement. These materials are first thoroughly mixed on a clean, hard base, and then water added until the whole is about the consistency of rather stiff porridge.

All main crazy paving paths that are subjected to constant and heavy wear should be laid in concrete. If this precaution is not taken it is practically inevitable that some of the blocks will, after a time, become loosened and the path be uncomfortable, and even dangerous, to walk on.

Yorkshire Paving Stones These are laid in a manner precisely similar to crazy pavement, and are even easier to handle, as their rectangular shape renders unnecessary a good deal of the fitting and scheming

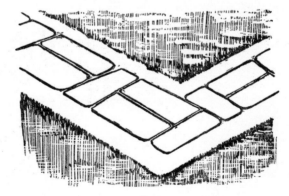

A FLAGGED PATH

A popular and durable surfacing material which can be set in sand or concrete.

needed when dealing with pieces of irregular outline. They are un-rivalled for formal designs, and are to be preferred to crazy in gardens adjoining houses of sedate or very solid architecture. The covering capacity of ordinary Yorkshire paving is a little greater than that of thick crazy pavement.

Gravel   Almost every locality has its own type of gravel, some of which is excellent for path making, while other samples are totally unsuited for the purpose. A gravel which binds down well and does not pick up during wet or frosty weather is ideal. Shingle from the seashore makes a clean, tidy path, but does not look particularly at home in the garden, and is most tiring to walk on. Limestone chippings have a limited use, being attractive in the alpine garden for surfacing winding tracks between the rocks.

All gravelled paths must have a porous yet solid foundation, made in the manner already described. If the gravel is placed directly on the soil, water will collect beneath it during the winter and cause much trouble in frosty weather. Incidentally, a considerable economy in the quantity of gravel required will be effected if a substantial core is constructed, for a 2-inch layer of gravel will be sufficient, which means that a cubic yard of gravel will cover from 15 to 18 square yards.

Asphalt   Although it makes a durable and clean path, asphalt is not to be recommended. Its dead black surface does not associate well with flowers, and a number of asphalt paths may easily spoil the appearance of an otherwise well-designed garden.

Brick or Tile   These paths look well if laid by an expert in suitable surroundings, but are not adapted to every garden. The bricks or tiles should form a regular pattern.

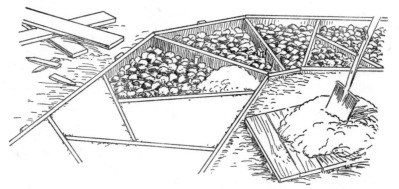

MAKING A CONCRETE PATH

Clinkers are put into the foundations of the path to ensure good drainage.
The concrete is mixed and laid in small quantities, filling only one section at
a time. The retaining boards are moved when the concrete has hardened.

Concrete This affords an easy and cheap method of paving yards or standing grounds outside greenhouses, but is not a pleasant-looking material. It is harsh and cold in appearance, and does not encourage that slight encroachment of creeping plants that is such a pleasant feature of a well-ordered path.

CHAPTER NINE

Lawns from Seed and Turf

A LAWN FROM SEED

THE preparation and seeding of a new lawn calls for more careful and painstaking work than the average amateur would imagine. Like every other plant, grass requires both cultivation and plant food, and, as the lawn cannot be dug over and manured at will, the preparation of the site must be both thorough and long-lasting in its effects.

Some soils are, in their natural state, well suited to the growth of grasses. Their preparation will be a more or less simple matter, but if extremes of clay or sand have to be dealt with, considerable improvements must be made before grass will thrive, and any newly made garden which has not been previously cultivated needs a season's preparation.

Preparing the Site For all new lawns trenching is advisable, and the opportunity should not be missed, while this work proceeds, to work in anything procurable which will improve the texture of the soil and remedy any physical defects. Heavy, tenacious clay is the most difficult soil to deal with, and failure is inevitable if grass seed is sown before it is brought into a friable condition. Grit, burnt earth, peat, moss, sand, ashes, crushed shells all help to open such soils, improving their porosity; but even with their aid, more than one season's cultivation is necessary to bring them into really suitable condition for the base of a lawn. That is why experienced gardeners so strongly advocate that, for the first season, a new garden on heavy ground should grow flowers and vegetables that may be cleared at the end of the season, enabling the whole to be dug a second time. If these temporary crops are well manured, the results so far as the grass is concerned, will be more beneficial than manuring shortly before sowing. The disadvantage of the latter course is that, as the manure decomposes, the soil sinks, causing irregularities in the lawn surface.

Another very important point is the cleaning of the site. The chance of ridding the soil of all weeds during its preparation is too valuable to be missed. The wisest policy again is to allow a summer season's growth to intervene between the first attempt at eradication of the weeds and the final effort before putting down to grass.

When to Sow There are two sowing seasons for grass, and it is a moot point which may be the better. The fact is it depends entirely on the weather that follows sowing. In the ordinary way, if the ground surface is workable any time from the middle of March to the latter end of April, it will do well for sowing, and, if April showers are frequent, germination will be rapid, but a severe drought will punish the young grass. Autumn sowing is calculated to escape the ill-effects of drought, but, with favourable conditions at any time from the last days of August to the end of September, sowing should be safe. Even October sowing is all right if there are no hard frosts before Christmas.

Making a Good Seed Bed Prior to sowing, the soil should be forked and raked until it is reduced to a fine even tilth. It is then a good plan to run over the ground with a light roller, but do not roll to a firm,

A SEED-SOWING HINT

When sowing seed it is an excellent plan to mark out the plot into squares and sow these one at a time, measuring out just enough seed for each.

impervious mass, through which no seedling growth can penetrate. The purpose is simply to enable the soil to retain sufficient moisture to germinate the seed, and, if overdone, rolling will prove a serious handicap to the growth of the young grass. Just before sowing, top-dress the whole area with some finely sifted loam, firm it with the roller, and then rake lightly.

Sowing the Seed Do not attempt to broadcast the seed. Mark off the whole area to be sown with strings running down and across and a yard apart. To each of the squares so formed allow 2 ounces of seed, and sow this as evenly as possible. After sowing, rake the seed lightly into the ground and roll lightly.

Protection from Birds Birds are sometimes a trouble, or, perhaps, it may be said they are expected so to be, for, if the seed is lightly covered with soil by careful raking or in the case of small areas by scattering fine soil over evenly, few seeds will be visible, and it is only these that the birds collect. As a matter of fact, under ordinary circumstances enough seeds are left behind to make a good sward, even if the birds seem at first to be having a good time. Where protection is desired it can be secured by covering the lawn site with fruit tree netting, supported on sticks 6 inches or so above the surface. Failing this, insert sticks, as before, and carry black cotton from one to another in criss-cross fashion. Or use the new scarers advertised.

After-treatment Do not walk over the lawn after it is sown and protected, nor when the new grass is in a young and growing state. No stimulant is needed, though, should May prove to be a very dry month, a gentle hosing or the use of a lawn sprinkler thoroughly to moisten the soil will be helpful. One such watering should suffice. The question of cutting will arise, but this should not be attempted till the grass is 4 or 5 inches tall. Where the tool is to hand, the scythe is best used for the first cutting, but, failing this, hedge shears may be used on small lawns, the grass being cut to about 3 inches tall. On larger areas use the lawn mower set high.

A LAWN FROM TURF

When a lawn must be walked or played on within a month or so of making, turves should be used in preference to seed. Preparation of the site is the same in both cases, so need not be repeated. October and March are the two best months for the actual laying of the turf.

Buying the Turves Great caution should be exercised when purchasing turves. Endless labour will be avoided if a sample can be obtained reasonably free from perennial weeds. Creeping buttercup, plantains, yarrow, and daisies are among the worst pests likely to be introduced with meadow turf, though sometimes coarse grasses, such as Yorkshire fog and cocksfoot, give a lot of trouble. The grasses should be fine and close, and the turves, when cut, should be so full of fibrous roots that they can be handled readily without breaking.

Cutting and Trimming Usually turves are cut in strips 1 foot wide, 3 feet long, and 2 inches in thickness. These are rolled up for convenience of handling. Far better are turves cut in 1-foot squares. These can be cut to a much more even thickness, are easier to lay, and do not need to be rolled up—a point of some importance, as much damage is often done to the turves when rolling and unrolling them. They are also easier to handle.

Much time and labour will be saved if a shallow wooden trough is made, the size and depth of one of the turves, and open at one end. The turves can then be placed in this, one at a time, face downwards, and the bottom trimmed to an absolutely even thickness with a large kitchen knife. At the same time any large weed roots that are noted can be cut out.

Laying the Turves For the actual laying the beginner must provide himself with a couple of stout planks to walk and kneel on, and a turf

LAYING TURVES
Note the staggered arrangement to avoid all joins coming together; also the wooden beater used for settling the turves.

beater, made by nailing a handle to a heavy block of wood some 9 inches square.

If the edge of the lawn is to be curved, mark out a straight line a few feet back and lay the first row of turves against this, filling in the end afterwards. On no account should a curved line of turves be laid at the commencement. Always use whole turves at the edge, placing smaller pieces behind to fill in any gaps.

The next row is laid in the same way, save that first a half-turf is placed down at one end. In this way the joins between the turves will not all meet together, but will be staggered like the bricks in the various courses of a wall. The beater is now brought into operation. This is not to be used to even out irregularities by hammering them down. That would only be to lay up trouble for the future. Difference in the firmness of the soil will mean irregular settling and uneven growth of the grass. Any such irregularities must be rectified by lifting the offending turf and adding or removing some of the soil. The beater is solely for the purpose of settling the turves together and to the soil beneath. It must be used evenly all over with slow, rather sustained strokes. Great care must be used to strike with the whole surface of the beater, and not to twist it slightly so that one edge tends to produce grooves in the surface.

When the two lots of turf have been settled evenly all over, another couple of rows can be laid in the same staggered manner as before (first a row starting with a whole turf, then one commencing with half a turf) and beaten. So the work proceeds till all is covered.

It is always wise to lay the turf about 1 inch beyond the ultimate margin desired for the lawn. This extra inch can then be cut away with a sharp edging tool directly the grass has taken hold of the soil, and a much cleaner edge will be obtained than would be possible even with expert laying.

Mowing Established lawns must be mown regularly from about April until October, varying a little according to the season. For the first cutting it is always advisable to set the blades of the mower rather high so that the grass is left at least 2 inches high. Later the blades may be lowered, though there is no point in shaving the grass very close unless the lawn is used for bowls, croquet, or miniature golf. Such treatment only weakens the turf and causes it to die in patches. Another common mistake is the too constant use of the grass box. Short clippings are better left on the turf, where they form a useful mulch; exception to this rule need only be made for sports greens and lawns that are badly infested with daisies.

Maintenance Moss, many creeping weeds, and worm casts can be removed readily by raking the lawn before mowing with a spring-toothed grass rake. Heavy rollers are only required on sports greens, and even then must not be used when the turf is sodden. A light roller employed

Left: Severing a young dahlia shoot from which a cutting can be formed.   *Right:* The base of the dahlia shoot is trimmed just below a joint.

Left: The prepared cuttings are inserted round the edge of a small flower pot.   *Right:* The cutting a few weeks later.   Roots have been formed from the basal joint.

Taking a shrub cutting with a heel of older wood.

Below: The shrub cuttings are lined out in a shallow trench in which a little sand has been scattered. *Bottom:* Soil is returned round the cuttings and made very firm with the foot.

occasionally when the soil is just moist is all that is required to keep ordinary lawns smooth and level. Turf that has become unhealthy through over-rolling or too much wear can be improved by pricking it freely with a fork or using a spiked roller; after this a top-dressing may be given.

Lawn sand is a useful preparation for destroying broad-leaved weeds and at the same time stimulating the grass. It should be applied in spring or early summer. Tap-rooted weeds are best killed by piercing them with a steel skewer dipped in strong sulphuric acid or making use of one of the patent lawn weeders.

CHAPTER TEN

The Herbaceous Border

THE term 'herbaceous perennial' is applied to all those plants that live for more than one year and have soft shoots as distinct from the hard, permanent woody growth that distinguishes trees and shrubs.

The importance to the gardener of the hardy herbaceous perennial has increased immensely during the present century. Formerly tender bedding plants had the monopoly of the summer garden and were raised in immense numbers every year for this purpose. Greenhouse accommodation was, of course, necessary for these great batches of plants for at least six months out of the twelve, involving considerable expense and no little cultural skill. Gradually a reaction set in, headed by such great garden reformers as Mr. William Robinson and Miss Gertrude Jekyll. These ardent enthusiasts demonstrated the latent possibilities of many of the hardy herbaceous perennials which had previously been banished to more or less obscure parts of the garden. The herbaceous border came into being. The demand for more plants of suitable type led to greater attention from nurserymen and plant breeders, with the result that in a very few years new and improved varieties were produced, lists of hardy herbaceous perennials became ever more bulky and exciting, and this class of plant finally established itself as the supreme favourite with the British amateur gardening public.

Suitable Sites The best position for a herbaceous border is one that is open and sunny but sheltered from high winds by a nearby hedge or wall. It is, however, quite possible to select plants for shady sites, and the most dismal north border can be made cheerful and interesting with hardy herbaceous perennials.

Preparation of the Site The preparation of the soil for herbaceous plants must always be thorough and deep. A usual and highly satisfactory plan is to remake the border every fourth or fifth year, lifting all the plants with the possible exception of a few which strongly resent root disturbance, such as peonies, Christmas and Lenten roses, *Romneya Coulteri*, and eremuruses. This means that sufficient nourishment must be incorporated with the soil at the outset to provide at least a mainstay for the plants for several years. It is true that artificial and liquid fertilizers can be applied to established borders, but these should always be regarded more in the nature of stimulants rather than the basis of growth. The latter should always come from the general fertility and good health of the soil—conditions that cannot be greatly improved once the plants are established.

Width of Border It is a common error to make herbaceous borders too narrow. A far better display can be arranged in a border 10 feet in width than in one only 5 feet from back to front, while the 3-foot border so frequently seen in villa gardens is definitely too small for this type of plant. The plants invariably look most satisfactory if grouped in drifts of fair size—preferably long, narrow drifts, so that when one variety passes out of flower others may grow up before and behind it and conceal its barrenness.

Planning Before placing an order with the nurseryman for the perennial plants required it will always be found policy to map out a plan of the

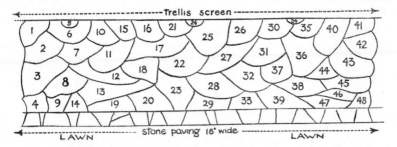

AN 8 FEET WIDE HERBACEOUS BORDER DESIGNED FOR AN
ALL-SUMMER DISPLAY

1. *Achillea eupatorium* 'Gold Plate.' 2. *Cimicifuga simplex.* 3. *Lupin* 'Gaiety Girl.' 4. *Aster* 'King George.' 5. *Climbing Rose* 'Albertine.' 6. *Delphinium* 'Lorna.' 7. *Aster* 'Cardinal.' 8. *Achillea* 'Cerise Queen.' 9. *Heuchera* 'Edge Hall.' 10. *Sidalcea* 'Rose Queen.' 11. *Phlox* 'Elizabeth Campbell.' 12. *Aquilegia hybrids.* 13. *Erigeron* 'Quakeress.' 14. *Armeria pseudo-armeria rubra.* 15. *Aster* 'Blue Eyes.' 16. *Thalictrum glaucum.* 17. *Lupin* 'Blue Jacket.' 18. *Lilium candidum.* 19. *Veronica spicata rosea.* 20. *Dianthus* 'Mrs. Sinkins.' 21. *Aconitum Wilsonii.* 22. *Sidalcea* 'Crimson Beauty.' 23. *Salvia virgata nemorosa.* 24. *Climbing Rose* 'Mary Wallace.' 25. *Delphinium* 'Glorious.' 26. *Aster* 'Gayborder Blue.' 27. *Anthemis* 'Grallagh Gold.' 28. *Centranthus ruber.* 29. *Veronica gentianoides.* 30. *Galega Hartlandii.* 31. *Phlox* 'Mrs. Ethel Prichard.' 32. *Scabiosa caucasica* 'Clive Greaves.' 33. *Aster* 'Gayborder Blue.' 34. *Climbing Rose* 'Emily Gray.' 35. *Helenium* 'Riverton Beauty.' 36. *Delphinium belladonna* 'Wendy.' 37. *Pyrethrum* 'Eileen May Robinson.' 38. *Campanula* 'Telham Beauty.' 39. *Linum perenne.* 40. *Lupin* 'Tom Reeves.' 41. *Aster* 'Beechwood Challenger.' 42. *Phlox* 'Border Gem.' 43. *Campanula lactiflora.* 44. *Papaver* 'Mrs. Perry.' 45. *Oenothera Youngii.* 46. *Aster Frikartii.* 47. *Dianthus Allwoodii.* 48. *Santolina incana.*

border on paper. This, if done roughly to scale, will enable not only the effect that will be produced to be visualized, but the exact number of each kind of plant to be ascertained and the cost calculated to a nicety.

The owner of a small garden will soon find that graduated colour schemes are best left to those with borders of 15 to 20 feet in width and hundreds of feet long. It needs these generous dimensions to get sufficient breadth of planting to make the merging of different tones effective.

This does not mean that there is no alternative to clashing colours in the small one. Groups can be planted near each other to harmonize, and some difficult colours eliminated. In one very successful border scarlet and orange are omitted, partly because the entire garden is enclosed by a hedge of climbing and rambling roses in colours that would clash with scarlet and orange, and partly because these shades have no personal appeal for the owner. This leaves all pinks and crimsons, all blues, mauves, and purples, yellows (particularly lemon), cream, and white. Grey foliage, in the form of santolina, lavender, nepeta, etc., is a great help.

Choice of plants must be left to individual taste. It is best to make a list of plants that are specially favoured and to let these predominate and to keep the number of varieties reasonably small in proportion to the size of the border. This last allows for generous plantings of any one kind, and the ultimate colour effect is very telling.

A useful rule is not to include any plant the height of which is more than the width of the border, otherwise the proportion will be unsatisfying and the border appear top-heavy and foreshortened.

So far as possible individual groups of plants, no matter what their size, should be of irregular shape despite the fact that the plants themselves must be fairly evenly spaced. This will impart an informal air to the whole border, which is what is wanted. Naturally the taller plants will in the main be placed towards the back, with the shorter kinds in front, but the groups should overlap slightly, so that here and there a middle-row plant comes to the front (especially one of good form, such as *Salvia virgata*, veronica, etc.), and some dwarfer ones creep about the feet of the taller occupants. Often a picture of a beautiful flower border is placed on one side with a sigh as unattainable except for those with ample space and professional assistance. But this need not be so, for a border of this type is more easily achieved by the owner-gardener than by one dependent upon paid labour. It only requires enthusiasm and thought in the planning.

The plant destined for the small border should have one more attribute; this is a long flowering season. Gaps in a huge border are not noticed, but the small garden is so much under one's eye, and the quantity of plants so restricted, that blanks become more annoying. For the same reason, plants of different seasons should be intermingled. That there are many such generous givers will be seen from the accompanying plans. In addition, bulbs of narcissus, chionodoxa, muscari,

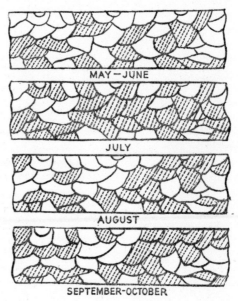

A FLOWERING CHART
This refers to the herbaceous border plan on page 83. The darkened spaces indicate flowers in bloom during the months specified.

crocus, and cottage tulips are planted among the more vigorous growers, thus ensuring bloom during the earlier months of the year, while any gaps that occur through unexpected losses may be temporarily made good with summer-flowering annuals, sown where they are to bloom and thinned out while still quite tiny.

Distance Apart to Plant The actual distance apart at which herbaceous perennials are spaced will depend upon their ultimate size and character of growth. For example, large, rather spreading plants, such as the tall heleniums, rudbeckias, perennial sunflowers, hollyhocks, and tree lupins, will easily occupy 3 feet of ground each way. Delphiniums, kniphofias, and ordinary lupins may be planted from 2 feet to 2 feet 6 inches apart, while at least 18 inches should be left between the clumps of phloxes and other mid-border plants, and from 6 inches to 1 foot between those in the front. The young growths should be thinned to prevent overcrowding, and tall plants should be spread out on three or four canes.

Transplanting Most hardy herbaceous plants can be transplanted quite safely in March or early April. Some gardeners prefer early autumn as a

SOWING AND PLANTING HARDY PERENNIALS

Name	When to Sow	Where to Sow	Position to Plant
Achilleas	May to June	Outdoors	Sun
Aconitums	May to June	Outdoors	Sun or shade
Anchusas	May to June	Outdoors	Sun
Anthemis tinctoria	May to June	Outdoors	Sun
Aquilegias (Columbines)	May to June	Outdoors	Sun or shade
Aster amellus	May to June	Outdoors	Sun
Asters (Michaelmas Daisies)	May to June	Outdoors	Sun or shade
Campanulas	April	Frame	Sun or semi-shade
Chrysanthemum maximum (Moon Daisies)	May to June	Outdoors	Sun
*Coreopsis	May to June	Outdoors	Sun
Delphiniums (giant hybrids)	May to June	Outdoors	Sun
Digitalis (Foxgloves)	May to June	Outdoors	Sun or shade
Erigerons	May to June	Outdoors	Sun
Gaillardia grandiflora	March	Greenhouse or frame	Sun
Galega Hartlandii	May to June	Outdoors	Sun
Geums (in variety)	May to June	Outdoors	Sun
Gypsophila paniculata	May to June	Outdoors	Sun
Helenium	April	Frame	Sun or shade
Helianthus	May to June	Outdoors	Sun
Heucheras (in variety)	May to June	Outdoors	Sun
Hollyhocks	May to June	Outdoors	Sun
Incarvillea Delavayi	April	Frame	Sun
Irises (in variety)	April	Frame	Sun
Kniphofias (in variety)	April	Frame	Sun
Linum perenne	May to June	Outdoors	Sun
Lupins	May to June	Outdoors	Sun
Lychnis chalcedonica	May to June	Outdoors	Sun
*Meconopsis (in variety)	April	Frame	Sun or semi-shade
*Oenotheras	May to June	Outdoors	Sun or shade
Pansies	May to June	Outdoors	Sun or semi-shade
Papaver orientale	May to June	Outdoors	Sun
Phlox decussata	March	Warm greenhouse	Sun or semi-shade
Pinks (Dianthus)	April to May	Frame	Sun
Polyanthuses	March	Warm greenhouse or frame	Shade
Pyrethrums	May to June	Frame	Sun
Scabiosa caucasica	May to June	Outdoors or frame	Sun
Sweet Williams	May to June	Outdoors	Sun
Thalictrums (in variety)	May to June	Frame	Sun
*Verbascums (in variety)	May to June	Outdoors	Sun or semi-shade
Violas (various)	May to June	Outdoors	Sun or shade

* Some of these are biennials.

planting season, on the score that this gives the plants a chance to settle in before the first season of growth. With the majority of varieties this scheme is quite satisfactory, especially if the soil is naturally light, well drained, and warm. There are, however, exceptions to be considered. Varieties of *Aster amellus* and *Chrysanthemum leucanthemum* resent autumn disturbance, while delphiniums, *Scabiosa caucasica*, aconitums, pyrethrums, incarvilleas, and kniphofias are best left over till the spring if the soil is at all inclined to be heavy, sticky, and cold.

Raising Plants from Seed Numerous herbaceous perennials can be raised from seed sown in a sheltered border out of doors or in an unheated frame. There is always likely to be a certain amount of variation in the colour and height of plants produced in this way, as the selected or 'named' varieties produced by plant raisers will not as a rule breed true from seed, but must be increased by careful division at planting time or by cuttings in spring. Nevertheless, seed affords a cheap and interesting method of obtaining a great deal of useful material for the border. Methods of propagation are dealt with fully in Chapter Six, but for convenience a concise table of times and situations for many useful species is given on the opposite page.

CHAPTER ELEVEN

A Garden of Roses

THE notion that it is only the owners of wide areas of rich loam who can grow good roses is all wrong; if it were right, there would be but a few hundred homes of flourishing roses in Great Britain, whereas in reality there are scores of thousands. The beginner may rest assured that, even if he can start with only a dozen plants, and must put them in soil which is far from perfect, he may nevertheless have good roses if he will work for them.

It is quite true that our native dog rose has a preference for good loamy soil, but every observer of countryside hedgerows well knows that the dog rose is not limited to one particular type of soil or district. In fact, it is one of the commonest of our wild flowers, and is also equally common throughout Northern and Middle Europe and Asia. So ubiquitous a plant augurs well for an easy adjustment to garden soil conditions on the part of its horticultural relatives, especially when many of these are using it as a root stock. Incidentally, wild roses do well in chalky districts and marly soils.

Preparing the Ground The best aids to successful rose culture are a strong spade, a good fork, and the will to put them to full use. Work with a wide trench, and get the fork well down to the subsoil, whatever its character. If that subsoil is heavy clay, the greatest need is to incorporate opening material, such as brick rubble, shells, shingle, or ashes. If it is sand or chalk, bury all the rotted garden refuse, lawn mowings, leaves, and humus-forming material available, but mix whatever is buried evenly with the soil.

Poor, hungry ground should have the top spit dressed with bonemeal and hoof and horn meal, 3 oz. per square yard each. There are other things that may be used as substitutes, such as fish meal, and basic slag, hop manure, or Peruvian guano. Old stable or farmyard manure will be beneficial, if there is a possibility of getting either, but do not despair about growing good roses if these manures are beyond reach. It is always possible to feed from the surface when the plants are well established, because there are plenty of good fertilizers for roses on the market.

Planning When planning a rose garden, the first consideration must be the amount of space available and the 'lie of the land.' All roses delight in air and sunshine, so the site chosen should be as open to the sky as possible. Yet some seclusion by means of walls, hedges, or rose-covered screens should be secured where possible, both as a protection from cold winds and so that the rose garden forms a unit of its own planned and planted for completeness of effect. In any case, if space can possibly be spared, it is certainly best that it should be a 'garden of roses,' nothing else.

An exception may be made when forming and planting the walls; apart from this, roses hardly ever seem quite so happy when mixed with other flowers as when growing on their own. A satisfactory compromise can be made in very small gardens by planting groups of roses in the border with plenty of room all round so that they are not jostled and crowded by other plants.

A sunken rose garden is very beautiful; perhaps it would be wiser to say a garden which gives the appearance of being sunk is equally beautiful—and often very much easier to obtain. Creating new levels where there is no natural help in formation means much labour and often loss of the most valuable portion of soil—*i.e.*, the top spit.

If one is determined upon digging out a sunken garden, the top spit of soil should be reserved, and returned after the necessary excavation of subsoil. Drainage will be a serious consideration, and may have to be ensured artificially in order to prevent the ground becoming water-logged or even flooded in wet weather.

A low wall constructed as an enclosure round the rose garden that is to be will give much the same effect. Soil is thrown up from outside almost to the top of the wall, and the slope thus formed is either turfed or covered with low-growing shrubs, with alpines planted on the wall. The soil for forming the slope can be gathered from as wide an area as possible, so as not to rob the rest of the garden too much. At the point of entrance the slope can be well defined, and thus provide means of introducing a couple of steps down to the level, and corresponding steps opposite as an exit. The enclosed space can be marked out with positions for pathways and beds for the roses.

Beds for roses should be oblong, of various lengths, in preference to circular or any fancy shapes, more especially if grass is to be the carpet of the garden. Beds that are straight-edged present much less difficulty to the machine when cutting the grass.

Dwarf (or bush) roses should comprise the foundation of a rose garden; pillars and arches may be used sparingly, and a standard plant introduced here and there, but unless the garden is a large one numerous pillars or arches are not advised, nor even standards in great number; they are too dominating for a comparatively small area. One or two half-standards may be used in the centre of each bed if desired, to break any suspicion of flatness, keeping the pillars and climbers for the sides and corners. Do not be tempted to place an archway in the centre, where it will cut the view of half the garden; one at either end, over the approach and exit, will look very well, especially if varieties that will bloom at the same time are chosen. A plain stone sundial or bird bath as a centrepiece can look charming.

Spacing   Bush roses must always be spaced at least 18 inches apart and a clear foot from the edge of any bed or border. Standards and half-standards require quite twice as much room, while climbers and the less vigorous ramblers should not be closer than 5 feet. Very rampant ramblers of the American Pillar or Dorothy Perkins type will often cover a good 10 foot run of trellis or pergola.

When to Plant   November is the best month of the year in which to plant roses. If the weather is not unusually wet or cold, and the soil has been well prepared some weeks in advance, the plants receive little check and by Christmas will have already commenced to make new roots. However, if November planting is not practicable, the work can be done at any time from then until the middle of March, provided the weather is not frosty.

Planting   The first essential is to prepare the plants. If they are already growing in the garden and are merely to be transplanted to a new site, they should be lifted with as little damage to the roots as possible. Use a strong spade for this, and make four vertical cuts into the soil, to the full depth of the blade and on each side of the bush, about 9 inches from its base. Then lift the rose out with the spade. The hand may be used to steady the top, but on no account must the bush be pulled from the ground. The rose is 'budded' or joined to a stock at about ground level, and, however well the union between these may have healed, there is always a danger of the two coming apart again if subjected to great strain at this point. Standards, which are budded at the top of the main stem and not at ground level, may be handled with a little less caution, but care in lifting is always repaid by better after-results.

In addition to the usual cutting away of damaged portions of roots, recommended in the general chapter on planting, there is one other point that needs particular attention in the case of roses, and that is the 'snag,' or stump, of old stock, which may be still attached to the plant, and, if so, will project as a stump of dead-looking wood just above the point of union between the rose proper and the stock. This must be removed cleanly. As already mentioned, standards are budded at the top of the main stem, and the 'snag', if it has not already been removed, will be found as a lifeless continuation of this an inch or more in length, and above the point from which the branches of the head have their origin. Do not be surprised if there is no 'snag.' Many nurserymen see that it is removed before the roses are despatched. Remember, it is only the roots

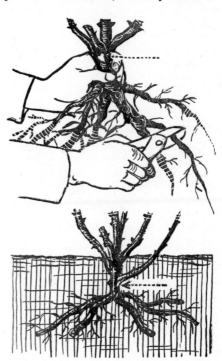

PLANTING A ROSE
Damaged root ends should be removed, also the old snag of stock indicated by the arrow.

Sucker growths from below ground must also be cut away.

and the snag of stock that are to be pruned before planting. Top growth must be left untouched until the end of March.

Planting is carried out in accordance with the general principles fully explained in Chapter Four. Bushes will not require any staking, but standards should receive this attention without delay. Indeed, it is really best to drive a stake into position directly the hole for each plant is made, as this obviates possible damage to the roots caused by driving a stake through them after they have been planted. Inch-by-inch stakes, painted green and tarred at the base, are best. They must be long enough to be driven 18 inches into the ground and yet reach to the bottom of the head of branches. Climbing and rambler roses should also be made secure to some support, such as a pillar, arch, pergola, or wall.

Pruning Bush Roses   In the south of England the annual pruning of all roses except ramblers is done at the end of March, whether the plants are newly put in or thoroughly established. In northern and eastern districts it is wiser to wait until early April. Dwarf or bush roses can conveniently be divided into two classes—those requiring hard pruning and those which need only a moderate cutting back. All newly planted trees, whether put in during autumn or spring, should be cut back hard. With a dwarf rose of average strength, this means to within 3 or 4 inches of the ground, thus leaving two or three good 'eyes,' or dormant buds, to start into growth. This may sound rather drastic, but is essential the

PRUNING A BUSH ROSE
Each strong growth has been cut back to three or four dormant buds, or eyes, while laterals (side shoots) have been shortened to two buds.

first year if a good tree is to be built up. At this first pruning care must also be taken to cut just above a bud pointing away from the centre of the tree. The resultant shoots will not then mingle and cross, but will radiate somewhat, as is so desirable. Slope the cut slightly from the back, starting just above the bud on the far side and finishing about ¼ inch directly above it.

Exhibition roses need fairly hard cutting back always, and not only the first year of growth, though some discretion must be used. Often the very best show varieties are of weakly growth, and it is necessary to cut them down very hard, leaving not more than two buds on a shoot. The more vigorous a tree is, the less pruning it needs, so that a strong exhibition rose, such as Frau Karl Druschki, may have as many as four base buds left on a shoot. Conversely, some of the rather weak bedding roses should be cut annually as if meant for exhibition purposes.

Ordinary bedding roses or roses grown for cut flowers thrive better when pruned moderately once they are properly established (*i.e.*, after the first season's growth). It is well to do the actual operation in two parts. First, cut away all dead, diseased, and weakly wood or shoots; also, unless special considerations ordain otherwise, all those shoots which tend to cross one another, crowd the plant, or make it unshapely. This done, the pruner should have left only well-spaced shoots, mainly of the previous year's growth. These are cut back with a sharp knife or sécateurs, so as to leave from six to eight dormant buds or eyes on each.

There is another section of dwarfs which needs only very light pruning. To it belong the dwarf polyantha roses and certain very vigorous hybrid teas and perpetuals. Rampant growers, such as Hugh Dickson, Frau Karl Druschki, and Avoca, can be dealt with in two ways. If required as bushes, the new shoots should be kept at least a foot in length, and the older branches slightly topped, and their laterals cut to within five or six buds of the main shoot. A better way to treat them, however, is to cut away all the old wood each year, and then bend the young shoots to the ground and peg them down some 4 or more feet away. If well cultivated and allowed plenty of room, they will throw flowers at almost every leaf joint.

The polyantha roses can also be pruned in two ways. All that is really necessary to keep them in health is to cut away the old flower stems and thin the old wood a little each year. In course of time they will make quite large bushes by this method. But when utilized for formal bedding it is better to prune them to within 6 or 8 inches of the ground each year, when they will throw up a large number of shoots of the same height and vigour.

Pruning Standard Roses When dealing with standard roses several fresh details must be noted. Naturally, since the head is so much in evidence,

STAKING AND PRUNING
A STANDARD ROSE

Note the care with which each cut has been made just above the centre of the head of branches. This will help to preserve the shape of the specimen.

shape is of paramount importance. To this end all the branches pruned
should be left very much the same length. More old wood must usually
be retained than with a dwarf rose, which annually throws up new shoots
from the base, whereas new growths from the point of union of a
standard are not usually made after the first two years. Thus the first
year's pruning is again very important. As in a dwarf, all growth should
be pruned to within about three buds of the point of union. In subsequent years pruning will consist, as a rule, of cutting back the shoots
made the previous season nearly to the last year's point of pruning; the
whole head will thus gradually become larger. However, never fear to
cut into old wood if the young growth is weak, or to thin out surplus
branches if the head is crowded, as so often happens in old standards.

When pruning the head, also glance lower, and it will probably be
found that the knife is needed on the stem also. Both brier and rugosa
standards are very prone to throw out suckers from the roots and
growths from the dormant eyes right the way up the stem. Those on the

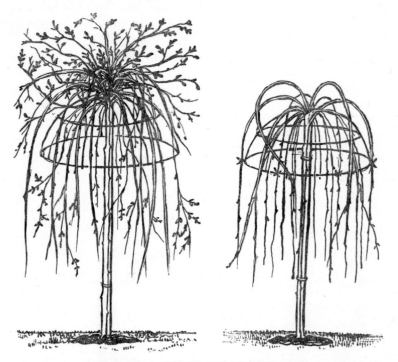

PRUNING A WEEPING RAMBLER ROSE

On the left a weeping rambler ready for pruning. All unnecessary old flowering
wood is removed, as shown on the right.

latter should be neatly pared off with a sharp knife. Suckers on the underground roots should be followed to the point at which they join the main root, and also cut away. Do not attempt to pull them up, as this will very likely damage the roots.

Pruning Ramblers Ramblers of the wichuraiana and multiflora types should be pruned in September, when as much as possible of the old wood should be cut out without sacrificing strong new stems. If there are not enough young canes to fill the space, the healthiest-looking of the old ones may be retained, all the old side growths that have borne flowers being cut back to within half an inch of the main stem.

PEGGING DOWN ROSES
A method sometimes employed with ramblers and very vigorous bushes. Each strong young shoot is tied out horizontally, as shown, and dead wood is removed.

Pruning Climbers The climbing hybrid tea roses are best pruned in spring, early, if grown in a sheltered position. They require very little cutting. It is sufficient to take out any dead growth and thin the old wood to keep the tree open. Try to make a few shoots clothe the base, as this always tends to become bare. The side laterals on main branches need shortening to within four or five buds of the stem, but beyond this no further pruning is necessary.

Feeding Roses After spring pruning and during the summer months roses require a certain amount of routine attention. It is an excellent plan to give the soil round established roses a dressing of Tonk's rose fertilizer in April at the rate of 4 ounces per square yard. This excellent rose food can be purchased ready mixed for applications or can be prepared at home. It consists of 12 parts of superphosphate of lime, 10 parts of nitrate of potash, 2 parts of sulphate of magnesia, 1 part of sulphate of iron, and 8 parts of sulphate of lime (gypsum), all by weight. These are mixed thoroughly, crushed as finely as possible, and stored in an absolutely dry place.

Disbudding When the flower buds appear it will be noted that they are in clusters of varying size, according to the type of rose. In tea, hybrid tea, and hybrid perpetual varieties all the buds on each stem except the central one which terminates it may be rubbed out at an early stage. This process of 'disbudding' results in fewer flowers of greater size, and

A LESSON IN DISBUDDING
A rose bush before and after removal of superfluous buds. Disbudding is of particular importance with roses grown for exhibition.

is always practised by exhibition growers, but is by no means essential if the roses are grown solely for their decorative value. It is never applied to rambler or polyantha roses, with which the bigger the clusters the better.

Summer Treatment The Dutch hoe should be used frequently during the summer, particularly during dry weather. If Tonk's fertilizer has been used, no further feeding will be necessary, except for plants that are to supply exhibition blooms. These should have liberal weekly doses of liquid manure, either prepared by the old-fashioned but highly effective method of steeping a sack of dung in a tub of water or by the handier process of dissolving a little chemical fertilizer in water. Whichever method is used the solution must be very dilute. A reliable compound garden fertilizer is best for this purpose. Seedsmen, nurserymen, and other dealers in horticultural sundries offer many brands, usually

Left: Lifting old worn turf with a turfing iron. *Right:* New turf, delivered in rolls, is laid in position.

Left: A shallow box useful for trimming turves. *Right:* Removing surplus soil from the base of a turf.

Left: Dividing a herbaceous perennial by hand. *Right:* A tougher root which require the leverage of two forks.

Left: Fine soil is worked round the roots of a herbaceous perennial. *Right:* The plan is firmed from both sides at once with the knuckles.

packed in tins of convenient size, thus ensuring that the chemicals are
fresh and in good condition.

As the first crop of hybrid teas and teas passes, the faded blooms
should be cut off, together with a fair length of stem. This will encourage
second growth and further good blossoms later in the summer.

Pests and Diseases Throughout the summer a watchful eye must be
kept for pests and diseases. At first greenfly and caterpillars may be
troublesome. These can be killed by spraying with nicotine or derris,
both of which can be purchased in various proprietary brands, and
should be used strictly in accordance with manufacturer's instructions.
Later on white mildew may attack the leaves. This can be kept in check
with a fungicide prepared by dissolving $\frac{1}{4}$ ounce of liver of sulphur
(potassium sulphide) and 1 ounce of soft soap in each gallon of water.

Black spot causes dark circular patches to appear on the leaves. It can
be controlled by frequent summer spraying with Copper White Oil
Emulsion. A heavy mulch of grass clippings maintained from April to
August will also help.

Red rose rust, a leaf disease, well described by its name, may also be
kept in check by frequent summer spraying with a colloidal copper or
sulphur spray.

CHAPTER TWELVE

Trees and Shrubs

Do not be in too great a hurry about planting such permanent occupants of the garden as trees and shrubs. Careful consideration should first of all be given both to their selection and to the manner in which they are to be placed. One has only to go into an old-fashioned garden in which a so-called shrubbery figures prominently to realize how easy it is to spoil the whole effect through disregard of the above warning. The real trouble with these shrubberies is that they are almost always hopelessly overcrowded with subjects that show too little variation in form or colour. There is not the slightest excuse for this kind of thing, and there is no necessity to go to the other extreme, as some more modern garden planners have tended to do, by leaving shrubs practically entirely out of account when stocking gardens of small or moderate extent. An immense wealth of material is available from which to draw, and shrubs are obtainable ranging from a few inches to 15 to 20 feet in height, and with flower, foliage, or fruit interest extending throughout the year. The same applies to trees. It is a mistake to introduce forest trees such as elms, beeches, ashes, limes, etc., into small gardens, though they are lovely enough when given ample room for full development, but a wide selection can be made from varieties that will keep to quite modest proportions without drastic pruning.

Deciduous or Evergreen? Trees and shrubs are divided into two principal classes—deciduous and evergreen. The former lose their leaves in the autumn, whereas evergreens retain their foliage throughout the year. The distinction is an important one, from both the decorative and the cultural standpoint. Obviously evergreens are most suitable when permanent screens or windbreaks are to be made, while, if judiciously used throughout the garden, some interest can be maintained even during the dullest part of the year. On the other hand, deciduous trees and shrubs have a distinct advantage in town gardens, on account of the fact that they get a new lot of leaves, perfectly clean and clear from grime, each spring. In smoky towns evergreens tend to become heavily coated with grime, which is not only unsightly but definitely detrimental to their health.

When to Plant The best time for planting depends upon whether the tree or shrub is deciduous or evergreen. Practically all deciduous kinds can be transplanted most safely immediately after leaf-fall in the autumn; that is to say, early in November in an average season. If it is impossible to carry out the work just at this period, it can be done with reasonable expectation of success at any time from then until early in March. The one important exception to this rule occurs with deciduous magnolias, which transplant most successfully early in May.

Evergreens do not transplant well during the autumn or winter, and

HEELING IN NEWLY ACQUIRED SHRUBS

If shrubs arrive from the nursery during very wet weather it is often better to heel them in temporarily instead of planting at once.

can be shifted with greater security either in September and early October or alternatively in April and early May. Whenever they are transplanted it is advisable to erect some temporary protection round choice specimens to keep off cold winds or strong sunshine.

Planting In other respects the planting of trees and shrubs is carried out on the same general lines as those already fully explained in Chapter Four. All fairly tall trees should be staked immediately, as there is nothing more harmful to young specimens than to be constantly disturbed and pulled about by wind. This also applies to **certain shrubs,**

and particularly to brooms, which are very susceptible to root disturbance. For this same reason brooms and some other small shrubs are often supplied by nurserymen in pots, so that they can be planted without injury to the roots. If plants grown in this way are obtained they

SHELTER FOR NEWLY PLANTED EVERGREEN

Archangel mats or hessian stretched between posts on the windward side of each specimen will prevent damage during the first few months after planting.

should be placed in a bucket of water to soak for a few minutes, after which the pot may be cracked and removed in fragments without disturbing the roots unnecessarily. Just a few of those coiled tightly round the bottom of the ball of soil should be loosened and spread out in their new quarters.

Pruning The pruning of trees and shrubs is, for the most part, very simple. Indeed, as regards trees one may say that the less that is done the better. The main stem or trunk should, of course, be kept free of growths, but beyond this it is only necessary to thin out the head of branches a little to prevent overcrowding, and to cut back any branches that grow too far. When reducing the size of a tree one should always attempt to cut back each main branch to a point just above that at which a smaller branch joins it. This will prevent the unsightly lopped appearance unfortunately all too common in many of our street trees. Deciduous trees should be pruned between November and February, while evergreen trees are best pruned in April or May.

Most shrubs will also thrive satisfactorily with little or no pruning, but if they grow too much or get overcrowded with shoots they can be thinned and shortened without harm. The best time for carrying out this work will depend partly upon whether they are deciduous or evergreen and partly upon the time at which they flower. Almost all evergreens can be pruned with the greatest safety towards the end of April or in May, but if this happens to be their flowering time it is advisable to delay the operation until the blooms have faded. Deciduous shrubs that flower before June are best pruned immediately after flowering; those that flower later should be pruned between **February and April**. Some, such as *Buddleia Davidii* and its varieties, *Hydrangea paniculata*, and all the deciduous ceanothuses, can, if desired, be cut almost back to ground level each February. They will then make a number of long new shoots, which will flower towards the end of the summer. Very similar treatment can be applied to certain trees grown principally for their foliage, two good examples being *Catalpa bignonioides* and *Ailanthus glandulosa*. Both of these may be allowed to form a standard stem, or trunk, 5 or 6 feet in height, and then the branches that form from this can be cut

PRUNING A FORSYTHIA
Typical of many early-flowering shrubs. Pruning is done immediately after flowering and consists in cutting a few old branches right out (A) and shortening all flowering shoots (B).

back quite close each February. The result will be a much smaller tree with foliage of the largest size. But it should be clearly understood that with both shrubs and trees this hard pruning is not essential to success. It is only carried out where the gardener desires to get certain decorative effects. With brooms it is advisable to trim over the plants lightly after flowering, and particularly to cut out as much as possible of the old flowering wood without sacrificing new growth. The object is to prevent the bushes from getting straggly and bare at the base. Brooms must never be cut back into old wood.

Planning the Shrub Border Shrubs may be planted in several different ways. Mixed grouping in borders is very effective if care is taken to associate colours carefully and to ensure a succession of flowers. The border should be at least 10 feet wide to allow for proper arrangement, with taller shrubs behind and dwarfer varieties in front. The planning as regards colour arrangement and sequence of bloom should be carried out on similar principles to those recommended when making herbaceous borders, and the reader will find these fully set out in Chapter Ten. The great thing is not to have large gaps in the border devoid of all flower, fruit, or foliage interest for long periods.

An alternative is to fill beds entirely with one kind of shrub. This

PRUNING BUDDLEIA VARIABILIS

This shrub is typical of many others that produce flowers fairly late in the summer on the ends of young branches. These may either be cut back really hard each February (A) or else quite lightly pruned (B) and so allowed to form big bushes.

system works well in large gardens, but is not recommended in small ones, as the season of interest is too restricted. Free-flowering shrubs such as forsythias, ribes, *Hydrangea paniculata grandiflora*, philadelphuses, and *Viburnum tomentosum plicatum* are most suitable for this method of planting.

Specimens A third method of arrangement, and one that will appeal to the small garden owner, is to plant shrubs principally as isolated specimens, giving each sufficient space to display its distinctive beauty of form as well as its flowers.

Trees are almost always planted in this manner as specimens, and should be placed to give emphasis to some salient feature of the garden. They are also extremely useful to relieve the flatness and monotony that inevitably creep into a level site if it is entirely planted with herbaceous and bedding plants. For this purpose they should be well distributed over the garden, but not at regular intervals unless the design is of a formal nature or an avenue is to be formed. As a rule ornamental trees should be at least 20 feet apart.

SELECTION OF VARIETIES

It is not within the scope of this book to give detailed selections of trees and shrubs, but the following lists of good, easily grown varieties may be found helpful, especially by beginners:

Deciduous Trees *Acer negundo variegata*, leaves variegated with white; *Ailanthus glandulosa* (Tree of Heaven), handsome pinnate leaves; almond (*Prunus Amygdalus*), charming pink flowers in March; *Amelanchier canadensis*, small pure white flowers in April; *Fraxinus Ornus* (Flowering Ash), white flowers in April; silver birch (*Betula verrucosa*), one of the few forest trees suitable for small gardens; *Catalpa bignonioides*, handsome white and yellow flowers in July; *Cercis siliquastrum* (Judas tree), rosy-purple flowers in July, difficult to transplant; cherries (*Prunus serrulata*, etc.), such varieties as Kanzan, Hisakura, Taihaku, and Apple Blossom are excellent, flowering in April and May; *Cotoneaster frigida*, red berries in autumn, sometimes grown as a bush; *Laburnum Vossii*, the best form, with long yellow panicles of bloom in May; false acacia (*Robinia pseudo-acacia*), ferny foliage and white flowers in summer; mountain ash (*Pyrus aucuparia*), white flowers in spring, followed by red berries; peach (*Prunus Persica*), Clara Meyer is one of the best, flowering in April; *Prunus Blireana*, purple foliage and pink flowers in March; *Pyrus malus Aldenhamensis*, bronze foliage, rosy-crimson flowers in April and May; *Pyrus floribunda*, pink flowers in April; *Pyrus malus* John Downie, blush-white flowers in April, orange-scarlet fruits; thorn (*Crataegus oxyacantha*), Paul's Double Scarlet has scarlet flowers, while *rosea plena* is pink; weeping willow (*Salix babylonica*), beautiful golden pendent branches, ideal for the waterside.

Evergreen Trees Cedars (Cedrus), *C. atlantica glauca* is the best, with blue-grey foliage, requires plenty of space; *Cupressus Lawsoniana* (cypress), good forms are *Stewartii* (golden leaved), *erecta viridis* (bright green), and *Triomphe de Boskoop* (blue-grey); junipers (Juniperus), *J. communis hibernica* is a fine form of columnar habit; pines (Pinus), *P. sylvestris* (the Scotch Pine), *P. austriacus* (the Austrian Pine), and *P. Laricio* (the Corsican Pine) are all good if there is ample space for development; spruce (Picea), the Blue Spruce (*P. pungens Kosteri*) is the best; *Thuja occidentalis* (Arborvitae), often used as a hedge shrub, but will grow into a fine tree; *Thuja Lobbii,* rather similar to the last named; *Sequoia gigantea* (Wellingtonia), an immense tree, very handsome if given plenty of room.

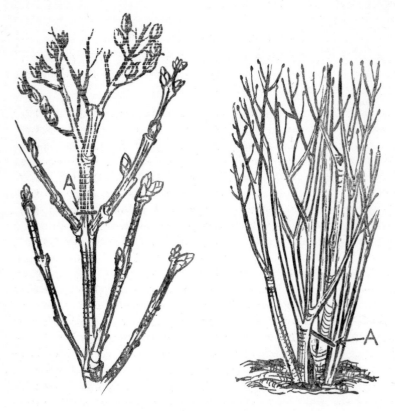

PRUNING A LILAC

Left: the old flower trusses should be removed (A) *as soon as they fade. When shrubs get overcrowded, as on the right, old branches* (A) *may be cut right out in February. Suckers should also be removed.*

Deciduous Shrubs Azaleas, many fine hardy varieties flowering in May (do not confuse with *A. indica,* a greenhouse shrub); Berberis (Barberry), yellow flowers and red berries, the best deciduous kinds are *Prattii, subcaulialata, Thunbergii, rubrostilla,* and *Wilsoniae;* brooms (Cytisus), white, yellow, crimson, or rosy-pink flowers in May, good kinds are Firefly, Dorothy Walpole, *Dallimorei, praecox,* and *albus; Buddleia Davidii* Royal Red, purple flowers in late summer; *Ceanothus azureus,* pink or blue flowers in late summer; *Cornus alba Spaethii*, leaves variegated with yellow; *Cotoneaster horizontalis*, red berries in autumn, flattish growth; *Daphne Mezereum*, fragrant purple flowers in February; *Eucryphia pinnatifolia*, white flowers in July; *Euonymus latifolius*, red fruits in autumn; *Forsythia intermedia spectabilis*, yellow flowers in March; *Hydrangea paniculata grandiflora*, white flowers in late summer; *Hypericum patulum Forrestii*, yellow flowers in summer; lilacs (*Syringa officinalis*), many good varieties such as Mme. Lemoine, white, Souvenir de Louis Spath, dark red, and President Grevy, rosy-lilac; magnolias, flowering in March, April, or May, good kinds are *stellata, Lennei, denudata,* and *Soulangeana*; Philadelphus (Mock Orange), white flowers, usually fragrant, in summer, good kinds are *coronarius, grandiflorus,* and Virginale; *Potentilla fruticosa*, yellow flowers in summer; *Rhus cotinus atropurpurea*, purple foliage and flowers; *Ribes sanguineum atrosanguineum* (Flowering Currant), red flowers in April; *Spiraeas*, many useful species, such as *arguta*, white—*ariaefolia*, cream—*Douglasii*, pink—*japonica* Anthony Waterer, carmine, and *Van Houttei*, white; *Tamarix pentandra*, pink flowers in summer; *Viburnum opulus sterile* (Snowball Tree), white flower clusters in June; *Viburnum tomentosum plicatum,* white flowers in June; and Diervilla (Weigela), Abel Carrière is one of the best, rosy-carmine flowers in summer.

THE UNWANTED SUCKER

Lilacs, sumachs, and some other shrubs produce strong growths from below ground very freely. These should be carefully uncovered and cut out cleanly right to the base.

Evergreen Shrubs *Arbutus Unedo* (Strawberry Tree), white flowers and red fruits in autumn; *Aucuba japonica*, red berries in autumn; Berberis (barberries), good evergreen species, mostly with yellow or orange flowers in winter or spring, are *aquifolium, Darwinii, Gagnepainii, japonica Bealei*, and *stenophylla*; box (*Buxus sempervirens*), fine for topiary specimens; *Ceanothus Burkwoodii*, blue flowers all summer; cherry laurel (*Prunus Laurocerasus*), white flowers in April; *Choisya ternata*, fragrant white flowers in May; cistus Silver Pink, pink flowers in June; *Cotoneaster microphylla*, red berries in autumn; *Cotoneaster Franchetii*, red berries in autumn; *Elaeagnus pungens aureovariegata*, leaves variegated with yellow; *Escallonia langleyensis*, rosy-scarlet flowers in July; *Euonymus japonicus picta-aurea*, leaves variegated with yellow; *Garrya elliptica*, silvery catkins in winter; heathers (Erica and Calluna), many species flowering at various seasons, good kinds are *arborea*, white—*carnea Vivellii*, carmine—*cinerea coccinea*, red—*mediterranea*, rosy-red—*stricta*, rose—*vagans* St. Keverne, rose-pink, and *vulgaris Alportii*, crimson; hollies (Ilex), many forms, some with silver or golden variegated leaves, good kinds being Handsworth Silver, Golden Queen, and *pyramidalis*; *Kalmia latifolia*, rosy-pink flowers in June; laurustinus (*Viburnum Tinus*), pale pink flowers in winter and spring; lavender (Lavandula), Munstead is a good dwarf variety, while Grappenhall is a giant kind; *Olearia Haastii*, white flowers in July; *Osmanthus Delavayi*, fragrant white flowers in April; *Pernettya mucronata*, white, lilac, or crimson berries in autumn; *Pieris japonica*, white flowers in April; Portugal laurel (*Prunus lusitanicus*); rhododendrons, a wonderful selection of hybrids; rosemary (*Rosmarinus officinalis*), fragrant foliage, violet flowers in May; *Santolina incana* (Lavender Cotton), grey foliage and yellow flowers in summer; *Senecio Greyi*, yellow flowers in summer; *Skimmia japonica*, red berries in autumn; and *Veronica Traversii*, white flowers in July.

CHAPTER THIRTEEN

Perennial Climbing Plants

LIKE trees and shrubs, perennial climbing plants are established as a permanent feature of the garden, and so due consideration should be given at the outset both to arrangement and to the preparation of the soil. They can, it is true, be assisted from time to time by feedings and top-dressings, but to ensure continued health the site must be brought into thoroughly good condition in the initial stage. The soil should be dug at least three feet deep, and one square yard should be the minimum space allowed and prepared for each plant. If the soil is already fairly rich and the drainage assured, it will suffice to incorporate a dressing of old manure, and where clematis or ivies are to be grown a little mortar rubble can also be added. On very poor land the wisest course is to excavate about a cubic yard of soil and fill in with a compost of two parts of turfy loam and one part each of leaf-mould and old manure.

The problem with heavy soils is usually drainage. It is useless to dig deep holes in hard, packed soil and fill in the bottom with a layer of clinkers or brickbats, for the result will be that the hole will act as a moisture sump for the surrounding soil. The only really effective measure is to cultivate the entire border to the same depth and provide some drainage facilities in the way of a layer of clinkers or tile drains. This may seem a vast amount of work to undertake, but it must be borne in mind that the benefits accruing from it will be shared by every occupant.

Planting Most nurserymen supply climbing plants in pots. This is a great advantage, as it enables them to be planted with the minimum amount of injury to the roots. Nevertheless, to plant them exactly as they are tapped from the pots, with most of the roots coiled round in a tight mass, would be a great mistake.

As soon as the plants are received give them a good watering and allow them to stand out for an hour or two until the soil and roots are thoroughly soaked. Next, turn them out of their pots, remove the drainage crocks, and gently disentangle the roots with a wooden tally. This is a task demanding the exercise of some patience. Hurried work invariably results in breakages, and it will usually take some considerable time to spread out the entire root system, as the leading roots may easily extend to a couple of feet in length.

As a general rule the soil mark on the stem of the plant indicating the top of the soil ball should be about 2 inches below the surface, though with clematis it is a better plan to plant a little more deeply, as these lovely climbers are usually grafted on to a stock, and deep planting encourages the scion (or good garden clematis) to make roots of its own. The hole taken out for the plants must, of course, be large enough

WATERING A
NEWLY PLANTED
CLIMBER

A drain pipe is sunk vertically into the soil with a little rough rubble beneath. It is filled with water daily, and this soaks down to the roots of the climbing plant.

to accommodate all the roots without twisting or curling them, and in other details planting follows the general principles already fully explained in Chapter Four.

Staking and Tying There is just one more special feature to note, however. Climbers in pots are invariably staked, but they must on no account be put in with the growths still tightly bunched together. The correct procedure is to remove the stake before knocking out the plants, and, immediately planting is completed, train out the stems on to wall, fence, or trellis, so that the space available is covered as evenly as possible. It is a wise precaution to make the ties fairly loose at the outset. Settlement of the soil is inevitable and will put an undue strain on tightly tied shoots.

Among useful climbing plants clematis of all kinds are a host in themselves. In addition to the large-flowered hybrids such as *Jackmanii superba*, *Henryi* and Lord Neville, there are numerous small-flowered, species which are very charming. *C. montana* is white and flowers in

PLANTING A CLEMATIS

The roots should be spread out and not left tightly coiled in the pot ball; moreover it is usually advisable to keep the roots well away from the wall.

May, while *C. flammula* produces its creamy-white fragrant blooms in July or August.

In addition there are the ornamental vines, the vigorous *Polygonum baldschuanicum*—a picture in the autumn, with its masses of dainty blush-white flowers—and the lovely blues of *Wisteria chinensis* and *W. multijuga*. *Cydonia japonica*, often referred to simply as 'japonica,' is a great favourite with its scarlet flowers in early spring. Among the honeysuckles, *Lonicera japonica aureo-reticulata* has fine foliage, while the early- and late-flowering Dutch honeysuckles, if planted together, will provide delightfully fragrant blooms for many weeks. To cover a large space quickly, plant the well-known virginia creeper and the many ornamental varieties of ivy.

Evergreen Climbers Evergreen flowering climbing plants are always particularly useful, and among these some of the best are *Ceanothus Veitchianus*, with thimble-shaped heads of pale blue flowers in May; *Pyracantha Lalandii*, which has white flowers followed by vivid orange berries in the autumn; and *Escallonia langleyensis* with rosy-carmine flowers about midsummer.

Pruning The pruning of climbers is not at all difficult. Indeed, as with trees and shrubs, the mistake which novices usually make is to cut out

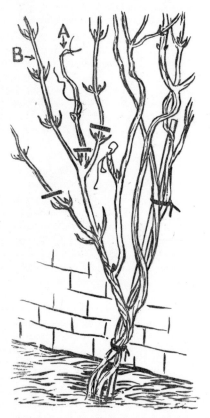

PRUNING A CLEMATIS
Some old or weakly shoots (A) *can be removed to make room for younger and more vigorous growth* (B).

too much growth and so spoil the display of flowers or berries. The best general advice that can be given is, if in doubt, to let well alone and only remove growth that is obviously very overcrowded or weakly. The best time to do this pruning is immediately after flowering with those kinds that bloom before midsummer and are grown for the beauty of their flowers, in February with all late-flowering deciduous climbers, or in April with late-flowering evergreen and berry-bearing varieties. Wisterias that have completely filled the available space are usually pruned in both summer and winter. All laterals are shortened to five or six leaves early in July and are further cut back to within about two dormant growth buds of the main rods in February. *Clematis Jackmanii* and its varieties may be cut back to within a foot of the ground in February, to restrict growth but produce larger blooms. Wall-trained climbers of very shrubby habit may require a small amount of summer pruning, like espalier apple trees.

CHAPTER FOURTEEN

Hedges and Windbreaks

I N most gardens there is usually some necessity for a hedge, either for purposes of division or as a boundary, or else as a windbreak or screen. There is a large variety of shrubs and some trees which may be used for these purposes, the choice depending largely upon the type of hedge and the situation.

The essential features of hedging plants are that they will form a complete mass or screen of twigs and foliage right down to the base and respond to clipping or hard pruning to keep them to a limited size. Those used for boundary hedges are usually also spiny in character to form an efficient deterrent to would-be trespassers, while shrubs for windbreaks are generally very quick growing and exceptionally hardy. Evergreen bushes are usually planted for screens and windbreaks, as the leaves are most valuable in the winter, but both beech and hornbeam can be used, since their leaves, though they become dry and brown in autumn, are retained until the new buds open.

Hedges used merely to divide the garden into sections should be made as ornamental as possible. Any shrub which is compact in growth and which can be kept within the limits of width and height can be used, and such things as *Lonicera nitida*, the barberries, *Olearia Haastii*, rosemary, and many rose species and veronicas are excellent. These will be found to take much less food from the surrounding soil than do the privets and laurel so beloved of the average suburban gardener.

For boundaries impenetrability is usually of more importance than anything else, but many ornamental shrubs can be used. Those in common cultivation include holly, blackthorn or sloe, hawthorn or quick, and the myrobalan plum. In very sandy districts, especially by the sea, gorse and sea buckthorn are invaluable. All the aforementioned have either flowers or berries, which add to the beauty of the hedge, and, though these may not show to full advantage in the hedge proper, it is usually possible to run up a few single stems as standards above the general level. Bushes suitable on account of the stout nature of their growth include the larger cotoneasters, laurels, aucuba and rhododendrons.

Windbreaks These should be higher than most boundary hedges, and

Left: Soaking the roots of a pot-grown climber before planting out. *Right:* The pot is broken to avoid unnecessary injury to the roots.

Left: Planting an evergreen shrub. Note the good ball of soil and roots. *Right:* Firming after planting. This must be thorough and even all round.

Below: The same bush after pruning. This severe treatment is essential the first year.

Above: A newly planted bush rose. Note the correct depth of planting.

Left: A wall-trained climbing rose of the hybrid tea type before pruning. *Right:* The same rose after proper thinning out of old wood.

are therefore normally formed from very quickly growing plants. One of the best evergreens for forming a windscreen in record time is *Thuja Lobbii,* or *T. plicata.* This can be kept at from 10 to 20 feet in height by severe clipping. It will grow on any well-drained land and is perfectly hardy, even in very exposed positions. *Cupressus Lawsoniana* and the taller varieties of this hardy cypress can be used with confidence, but *C. macrocarpa* is slightly tender and should only be planted by the sea or in mild localities where it is known to thrive. For a permanent windbreak the yew is most valuable, but it is so slow growing that it does not form a high hedge for many years, and is therefore usually only planted extensively on large estates likely to remain in one family's care more or less indefinitely. With regular feeding, however, much can be done to hasten its growth, and in its young stages it forms a good dense division or boundary hedge.

A SCREEN ABOVE A FENCE
Formed with lime, elm or hornbeam pruned to form horizontal branches which can, if desired, be plaited together.

Preparation of Site As with other shrubs and similar permanent features, it is most important to prepare the site thoroughly before planting. This is frequently neglected by amateurs, who appear to be under the impression that because hedging shrubs are frequently hungry feeders they should be starved. Ground not previously cultivated needs

H

trenching for good results, and it is wise to incorporate fairly coarse bonemeal in the lower spit to form a source of food for several years. As in planting any shrubs, all perennial weeds must be removed. Very few bushes used for hedging grow well in boggy ground, and therefore where the land is waterlogged and the hedge is not to be planted by the side of a ditch it is necessary to place drainage materials, such as broken bricks, clinkers, and other rubble, at the bottom of the trench and cover this with turves placed grass side downwards. The drainage layer should slope gently throughout the length of the hedge and communicate with an existing ditch or soakaway.

Planting The site of the hedge should be marked out by means of a strained line. It will be found easier to take out a trench in which to

PLANTING A HEDGE

It is important to take out a trench of ample width and to keep roots well away from the foundations of fences and walls.

place all the plants rather than to attempt to put each in a separate hole. This trench must be made large enough to accommodate the roots in a natural manner, and must be in such a position that there will be at least 2 feet of free space on both sides of the hedge to allow of growth. If the bushes are being used as a screen in front of a wall or fence, it is essential that the plants should be not less than 2 feet from this, or they will not remain healthy, very probably suffering from an inadequate water supply as well as from lack of light.

For the actual planting it is a great help if one person can hold the bushes in position while another shovels the soil round the roots. As in all planting, the finest soil should be put in first and the shrub shaken at the same time to ensure that this comes in contact with the roots, which must not be left in air spaces. The stems may be supported by attaching them to wires strained through the row.

Distance apart to Plant This will depend more upon the nature of the plants grown than upon their size at the time of planting. It is possible to establish quick and myrobalan plum as close as 9 inches, but under such conditions it is difficult to keep the hedge growing healthily after the first few years. A foot or 15 inches apart will be found more satisfactory in the long run. Eighteen inches apart is suitable for beech, hornbeam, holly, escallonias, privet, *Lonicera nitida,* and the smaller barberries, but 2 or more feet are needed for the larger cotoneasters and barberries, thujas, cupressus, laurels, aucuba and rhododendrons.

Wherever possible, plants for hedge making should be purchased quite young. If there is no time to be lost in the production of a full-grown hedge, larger size bushes which have been specially pruned for hedging can be obtained, but these are more difficult to establish and, if lost, are often difficult to replace.

TRAINING AND PATCHING A HEDGE

Note the correct stance and different method of holding shears when dealing with sides and top. The hole is being filled by tying some stray side shoots across it.

Pruning and Clipping It is a mistake to let a young hedge grow unchecked for the first few years so that it attains the requisite height in the minimum length of time, for if this is done the base of the hedge invariably becomes bare and trouble is experienced in trying to encourage basal growth, which can frequently only be attained by cutting the plants right back to within a few inches of the soil level. To prevent such a catastrophe the young plants must be hard pruned in the early years. This causes them to branch profusely at the base, and thus ensures a permanent basal screen.

The type of pruning or clipping given in subsequent years will depend upon the shrub used for the hedge and the height to which it can be allowed to grow. Slow-growing ornamental shrubs in division hedges will need little more attention than that given to similar species in a shrub border, but quick-growing plants and hedges which must be kept within a very limited space will need hard pruning or clipping. Some will not stand cutting back into old wood, and must therefore never be allowed to get out of hand, but be kept cut to within a few buds of the base of the new growth. If it is desired to allow the hedge to produce flowers and yet to keep the growth considerably checked, it is best to prune as soon as possible after the blooms have faded.

Small-leaved plants are usually clipped over with shears, but those with large leaves are rendered unsightly by the mutilated portions and must therefore be pruned with sécateurs.

CHAPTER FIFTEEN

Rock Gardens

W HAT amateur gardener has not viewed the splendid rock gardens at the great national flower shows with a feeling of envy mingled with despair? Few have either the space or the means at their disposal to reproduce, detail for detail, such wonderful examples of garden artistry which make the simple stone-covered mound seem a terribly shoddy affair.

Yet, given time, patience, and a sound understanding of the basic principles underlying the setting of stones, there is not the slightest reason why really pretty and satisfying rock gardens should not be constructed on a small scale. An amateur successfully constructed a home for choice alpine plants which occupied only one small section of a garden, 60 by 20 feet. One ton of weather-worn Cheddar stone was utilized, and a charming effect, simulating a natural outcrop, culminating in a jutting spur, was achieved. Even water may be introduced in such tiny alpine gardens, with a variety of miniature aquatics, as described in the next chapter.

Soil The best plan is to set aside a portion of the rock garden for lime-haters and to remove all the natural soil from this, replacing with a mixture of two parts of lime-free loam and one part each of leaf-mould, fibrous peat, sharp sand, and granite or sandstone chippings. For the rest of the garden limestone chippings mixed with good fibrous loam, peat, leaf-mould, sharp sand, and some old mortar rubble will make an excellent mixture. Proportions can be varied endlessly according to the ascertained preferences of various plants, but a good general compost can be prepared with five or six parts of loam to equal parts of the other ingredients. For gentians and many primulas a much spongier mixture is required, consisting principally of leaf-mould and peat with little loam, no lime in any form, and sufficient sand to ensure good drainage at all times.

Position of Stones It is usually advised that the soil be worked into mounds of irregular size before placing the stones in position. This is certainly desirable if the rock garden be of moderate extent, but in very restricted constructions a plain bank, or even an almost flat bed with simple outcrop of stone, may produce a happier result. Such points can only be finally decided on the spot, surroundings and the type of stone to be used being important factors. Only let the beginner beware of attempting the absurdity of reproducing in miniature all the peaks of the Alps in a villa back garden. Aim at simplicity.

Whatever scheme is decided upon, there should be at least 2 feet of good soil in the shallowest part of the rock garden. Most alpines are surprisingly deep rooting, and will soon become sickly if planted in a few inches of soil.

The finest preparation for building a rock garden, large or small, is a holiday in a hilly district. Here note can be taken of the way Nature goes to work. It will be observed that undisturbed stones always have a

BAD ROCK CONSTRUCTION

No attempt has been made to set the stones according to their natural strata.

certain relation one to the other, and that the general formation differs widely with varying types of rock. In parts of Westmorland and Somerset, where beautiful weather- and water-worn limestone holds sway, the hillside outcrops tend to more regular, softer outlines than the rugged spurs of stark granite characteristic of the Welsh mountains. Sandstone, on the other hand, though soft in texture, is usually somewhat angular in outline, straight lines being the rule in a sandstone formation.

Stone The best rock stone is that which is not quarried but merely dug out of the hillside as intact as possible. Such stone may have no less than three distinct sets of markings—one caused by weather, one by water, and one the strata lines which have existed ever since the formation first came into existence in a remote geological period.

Strata lines are regular and parallel, and will be found roughly to follow the same angle of inclination throughout the whole of any given formation. Marks caused by the working of water are much deeper and far more irregular, but a little close observation will reveal the fact that they have some definite relation one to another, for they are caused by water falling through countless ages from stone to stone. Weathering varies immensely in different rock, from a mere surface greying on the mainly smooth Welsh granite to innumerable deep fissures in the Westmorland limestone. Such cracks are closely related to the watermarks, being caused by the tremendous expansive power of frost when the water freezes in winter.

All these marks should be taken into consideration when the stone is being reset. When the rock garden is finished, all the strata lines

A WELL-DESIGNED ROCK GARDEN
All rocks have been sunk into the ground with due regard to their strata markings, the result being an impression of great permanence and natural beauty.

should follow a definite tilt. On no account must one rock be set with the strata lines pointing almost perpendicularly and another with them horizontally.

In the same way water and weather marks should be found principally on the tops and faces of the stones, where water might be expected to trickle down and frost and thaw have their greatest effect. Raw quarried edges should, as far as is possible, be buried beneath the soil, while all the stones must be set more or less deeply into the ground, and not just rested here and there on the surface as though they had fallen from the sky.

In this way an appearance of great permanence and beauty will be given to the whole structure before ever a plant is set in place. With a little ingenuity one large stone may be put alongside or on top of another, with soil packed between, so as to form vertical or horizontal crevices, in which suitable alpines may be planted. It is amazing how many otherwise difficult plants may be grown with perfect success when established in such a position.

All stones should have a slight downward and inward slope, so that rain which falls on them may find its way back into the body of the soil and not be shot off as from the roof of a house. Nor, speaking generally, should one rock overhang another, though departure from this rule is occasionally permissible for the sake of effect. But it must be remembered that the soil beneath the projecting stone will be almost permanently dry, and only plants which are capable of enduring such conditions should be planted in it.

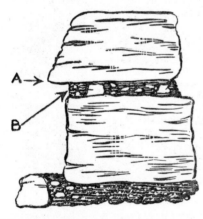

BUILDING UP CLIFFS

Very bold constructions can be achieved in this manner with hard stones or supports between the boulders. Rocks should not overhang, as at (A) otherwise plants will not survive in crevices such as (B).

Planting The planting of alpines in the completed rock garden differs from the planting of other outdoor plants in that, though it is equally necessary to spread out roots as naturally as possible and press soil firmly around them, this cannot always be done by the ordinary methods, because of the limited space available. A great many alpine plants thrive most happily in narrow crevices between large boulders, though it may be mentioned in passing that it is most important that these fissures

GOOD CONSTRUCTION
All the large rocks are slightly tilted inwards and downwards to encourage rainwater to run into the crevices and give the plants in the interstices more light.

A FLAT ROCK GARDEN
Very pleasing results can often be obtained by setting flattish stones on fairly level ground in the manner shown.

should communicate with the main body of soil behind or below, for into this the plants will in time root. It is quite astonishing how extensive a root system a small rock plant is capable of developing.

The first essential in crevice planting is to start with quite small roots. It is a hopeless task to attempt to thrust large plants into such narrow quarters, for the result is certain to be damaged roots and leaves, quickly followed by decay. But with the sturdy young seedling or rooted cutting it is quite a different matter. These have moderate root systems and it is not a difficult matter with a sharpened stick to scrape sufficient soil from the selected fissures to accommodate them comfortably. An old wooden tally, carefully rounded off at the end to avoid bruising, will be found serviceable, both for pushing the roots back into the crevice and for gently ramming compost round them.

When planting alpines in the moraine (which, by the way, is a portion of the rock garden in which the compost contains considerably greater proportions of stones and grit than soil and leaf-mould, and in summer is watered very freely, preferably from underground), it is absolutely essential to shake all the soil carefully from the roots. Cruel though this may seem, it is a very necessary precaution, for experience proves that, if plants are merely tapped from their pots and planted in a hole in the very gritty and comparatively poor compost of the moraine, roots will tend to remain in the old pot ball and will not find their way out into their new surroundings.

TWENTY-FIVE GOOD ALPINE PLANTS

Name	Colour and Flowering Time	Soil and Position
Acaena	Grown for foliage	Any; fine for carpeting
Achillea (dwarf)	Yellow, white; all summer	Gritty; sun
Aethionema	Pink; June	Gritty; sun
Alyssum	Yellow; May	Any; sun
Androsace	Pink, white; summer	Very gritty; sun
Anemone	Various; spring	Leafy; shade
Arenaria	White; early summer	Gritty; sun or shade
Aubrieta	Various; spring	Limy; sun
Campanula (dwarf)	Blue, white; summer	Gritty; sun
Crocus (species)	Various; autumn, spring	Gritty; sun
Cyclamen (species)	Rose, white; various	Leafy; shade
Dianthus (dwarf)	Rose, white; early summer	Peaty; sun
Gentian	Blue; various	Limy; sun
Helianthemum	Various; June	Gritty; sun
Iberis	White; May	Gritty; sun or shade
Linum	Yellow, blue; summer	Gritty; sun
Lithospermum	Blue; summer	Peaty; sun
Phlox (dwarf)	Various; June	Gritty; sun
Primula	Various; various	Leafy; shade
Saxifrage (mossy)	Pink, white; May	Leafy; shade
Saxifrage (cushion and silver)	Yellow, white; various	Gritty; sun
Sedum	Yellow, pink; summer	Gritty; sun
Sempervivum	Grown for foliage	Limy; sun
Thyme	Rose; July	Gritty; sun
Veronica (dwarf)	Blue, pink; summer	Gritty; sun
Viola (species)	Various; summer	Leafy; shade

CHAPTER SIXTEEN

Fish and Lily Pools

A WELL-MADE and properly stocked lily pool can be one of the most charming features in the garden. It is, however, very necessary that the work from start to finish should be done with care and intelligence, for a badly constructed pool can be a great nuisance, continually leaking and causing endless work in patching and refilling. Moreover, if the stocking is not done correctly, the pool will very quickly get into an unhealthy condition, with the result that the water will become offensive and—even more annoying—will breed mosquitoes or gnats in great numbers.

Construction The ornamental pool can be either formal or informal in design. The former is preferable, if the pool is to occupy a prominent site near the house, but an informal design is most suitable when the water forms an annexe to the rock garden, possibly connected to it by a bog or small stream.

The hole for the pool must be excavated 8 inches in each direction larger than the desired size for the finished construction. Two feet is an average depth. It is very necessary that all the soil should be hammered hard, brickbats, small lumps of rock, hard rubble, etc., being pressed in firmly in the process to provide a solid foundation for the concrete lining. The bottom of the pool should be thoroughly soaked before laying on the first coat of concrete.

The first lining should consist of a mixture of three parts of coarse gravel and one each of sand and cement. This is mixed in a dry state, and then water is added little by little, and the whole mass is constantly turned and stirred until it is about the consistency of stiff porridge. The concrete is laid on roughly to a depth of 6 inches, the corners and joins at both the bottom and sides of the pool being buttressed for extra strength. Boards can be used as 'shuttering' to hold up the concrete at the sides if it tends to fall down.

On this first layer of rough concrete a second coating is spread. In this finer ballast takes the place of gravel, the proportions being as before. Before applying it the first foundation must be soaked thoroughly and, after spreading the surface well, should be freely slashed with a trowel to provide a good grip for the finishing layer. This third and last coat consists of two parts of fine washed sand and one part of cement, together with 'Pudlo' powder, according to the amount of cement used. On this point manufacturer's instructions should be followed. This powder waterproofs the pool and holds back free lime, thus obviating the necessity for lengthy soaking before the pool is fit for stocking. The floor and walls of the pool should be kept thoroughly wet when working, and should be covered with sacking to dry as slowly as possible when all the concrete has been applied. This is the secret of a sound pool. If the weather is dry and sunny, spray daily for a week or so with a hose to prevent over-rapid drying.

Planting Water changes need never be thought about if the pool is properly planted. A pool a couple of feet in depth and 50 to 60 square feet in area will hold about thirty plants. For this purpose one or two water lilies should be chosen, or, alternatively, floating aquatics may be used, such as *Limnocharis Humboldtii*, *Villarsia nymphaeoides*, and *Aponogeton distachyon*. In addition, there should be half a dozen submerged aquatics for oxygenating purposes. The best for this purpose are

PLANTING A WATER LILY
The root is placed in a wicker basket and is surrounded with compost. Then turves are wedged round the crown, as shown, to prevent the soil escaping when submerged.

Elodea crispa, *E. callitrichoides*, *Ranunculus aquatilis*, *Callitriche aquatica verna*, and *Hottonia palustris*. These submerged aquatics may be planted in a good layer of loam at the bottom of the pool, a method that can also be applied to the water lilies, though, alternatively, these may be planted in wicker baskets filled with loamy soil.

The remaining plants will be for the margin of the pool, and may be chosen in accordance with taste and pocket from the catalogue of any reliable dealer in aquatic plants. Among the best species and varieties are *Sagittaria japonica, Pontederia cordata, Ranunculus lingua grandiflora, Acorus Calamus, Iris Pseudacorus* and related irises, *Butomus umbellatus, Caltha polypetala, Scirpus zebrinus, Cyperus longus,* and *Juncus glaucus.*

A GARDEN POOL

This sectioned drawing shows how to arrange for the needs of both deep and shallow water plants. The rocky surround helps to give a natural finish.

Animal Life The usual method of calculation is to allow 1 inch of fish per gallon of water. As a rough method of calculation one may reckon 6 gallons to the cubic foot; that is to say, a tiny pond measuring 3 feet by 3 feet by 2 feet deep contains 18 cubic feet of water, equalling 108 gallons, and so should be stocked with about one dozen fish 8 inches in length. The tail is not taken into account when measuring goldfish. From two to four times as many snails as fish will be required, according to the tendency of the pond to produce green, slimy growth. The more of this there is, the more snails should be placed in the pool, and it is advisable to obtain the two species *Limnea stagnalis* and *Planorbis corneus.*

May is the most favourable month for stocking pools.

CHAPTER SEVENTEEN

Bulbs and Their Allies

IT is not essential for a gardener to be able to distinguish between the different kinds of storage organ of plants that are included under the title above; but as there are sure to be some people who are curious enough to want to know why one kind is called a corm and another a bulb or yet again a tuber, a brief explanation is given. These three names are given to different kinds of underground storage organs which enable a plant to live through conditions which are unfavourable to growth above ground. They differ in the part in which the food is stored, and can be distinguished as follows: In all bulbs, such as tulips, narcissi, or lilies, the food supplies are contained in the bases of the leaves of the last season, the tops of which have died away. Corms are swollen underground stems, and none of the leaves surrounding them contains food; they are all dry and papery, as in the crocuses. Tubers may be either swollen roots, as in the dahlia, or swollen stems, as in begonias. They are not surrounded by dry leaves, as in the corm of the gladiolus or montbretia. All these plants are usually lifted, and may be bought when they are dormant—that is, when the leaves have died down.

Bulbs One thing not always realized by beginners is that by no means all of the hardy bulbous or tuberous-rooted plants are spring-flowering. Indeed, with careful selection it is possible to obtain blooms from them all the year round and they may be divided roughly into two groups— early flowering, which are planted during the previous late summer and autumn, and summer flowering, which are spring-planted.

Among the early-flowering bulbs and corms are the snowdrops, many of the crocuses, hyacinths, muscari or grape hyacinths, narcissi (including daffodils), tulips, some of the bulbous irises, and a few species of hardy cyclamen.

The summer- and autumn-flowering groups contain some of the most beautiful of flowers, including, in addition to the lilies, gladioli, montbretias, anemones, and tuberous-rooted ranunculuses, many of which are well known to most people, several delightful smaller plants which are less commonly met with. These include the autumn-flowering crocus species and the meadow saffrons, or colchicums, which are often incorrectly regarded as crocuses, and the hardy little autumn-flowering cyclamen, which will brighten up any north border or group of ferns with their dainty pink blooms.

In warm borders the lovely pink belladonna lily *Amaryllis Belladonna* can be grown, and *Sternbergia lutea*, the lily of the field, in a similarly secluded site in the rock garden.

Almost without exception bulbs, corms, and tubers do best in well-drained soil, and should always be planted on a little sand placed in the bottom of the hole if the drainage of the site is not beyond reproach. If this precaution is not taken the fleshy storage part may start to rot

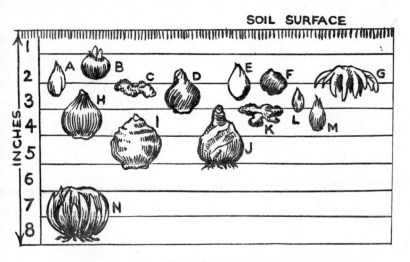

THE BULB PLANTER'S GUIDE TO CORRECT DEPTH

The scale on the left indicates the correct depth beneath the surface in inches. The bulbs shown are: (A) Iris reticulata; (B) Crocus; (C) Dog's Tooth Violet; (D) Early Flowering Tulip; (E) Triteleia; (F) Scilla sibirica; (G) Ranunculus; (H) Darwin Tulip; (I) Hyacinth; (J) Daffodil; (K) Anemone fulgens; (L) Snowdrop; (M) Spanish Iris; (N) Lily.

before the plant has had time to make good growth. Animal manure should always be kept out of direct contact with bulbs and is, indeed, not usually necessary at all, its place being taken by bonemeal at the rate of 4 oz. per square yard when preparing the ground, supplemented by a good compound bulb fertilizer during the season of growth.

Most bulbs and corms planted outdoors in the autumn benefit by as long a growing season as possible, and although quite good flowers may be obtained from November plantings, this is no thanks to the lateness of the planting, and the next year's blooms are almost certain to suffer. An endeavour should be made to plant all daffodils (narcissi),

crocuses, snowdrops, scillas, muscari, and bulbous irises in September
or early October. It will be observed that bulbs left undisturbed from
the previous year will often have made a considerable amount of top
growth by this latter date. Exception to this general rule may be made in
the case of tulips and hyacinths, which, if planted early, are sometimes
liable to start into growth so soon that they get badly damaged during
the winter. From mid-October until mid-November is a good planting
time for these.

When planted out of doors, most bulbs require to be covered by at
least twice their depth of soil, and generally do better if planted a little

PLANTING BULBS IN GRASSLAND

*A special bulb planter is thrust into the soil to make a hole of appropriate size.
The ejected turf is used to plug the preceding hole after a bulb has been put in it.*

on the deep side rather than the reverse. The chart on page 127 will be
found a useful guide in this respect. Bulbs should always be planted in
groups in preference to rows, except for very formal bedding or for
cutting.

If bulbs are required for naturalizing, the groups should be very
informal in character. This is most easily attained by scattering the
bulbs over the surface of the ground in a haphazard manner and planting them where they fall. If large numbers are to be planted in grass it
will be found much simpler to use one of the patent bulb planters now

The first steps in making a small rock garden and pool. Soil from the pool site will be used to mound up the rock garden.

The next step in construction. Hard rubble is being placed under the rock garden to ensure good drainage.

The work nears completion. Rocks are being set to simulate a natural outcrop.

Left: Fumigating soil with dilute formalin, which is being poured into deep dibber holes
Right: The dibber holes have been filled in and the ground is now covered to trap the fumes.

Left: Fumigating a greenhouse with tobacco shreds, which are being ignited.   *Right:* The fumigation started, the house is closed and all cracks are blocked up

on the market rather than a trowel. These cut out a piece of turf to the required depth, which is pressed on top of the next bulb to be planted. Where such a tool is not available it is often wiser to lift the turf from the place to be planted and replace it immediately the bulbs are in place than to cut it up and get the surface littered with soil when using a trowel.

Bulbs for Naturalizing Of the spring-flowering bulbs the various snow-drops and crocus species naturalize well, in addition to the majority of daffodils and narcissi. Tulips, on the whole, do not take kindly to naturalization, for they require much better ripening of the bulbs than is possible in grass in the normal English summer. Contrary to general opinion, hyacinths can be naturalized quite successfully, though naturally they do not produce the enormous flower spikes which are the result of prolonged rich feeding. Similarly the very large varieties of crocus do not make such enormous blooms, and less disappointment is experienced if the smaller-flowered species are selected, for their dainty blooms are almost more at home in short grass than in the rock garden.

In order to obtain a blaze of colour to be viewed mainly from a distance, there is no need to spend large sums of money for high-priced narcissi, whose rightful place is in the greenhouse or borders, but it is always well to get good specimens of the varieties chosen. It pays to put in good-sized bulbs which have sufficient stored food to fight the sur-rounding grasses in the first year, when the grasses have the advantage of being well established, while the bulbs are not. Bulbs should only be naturalized in grass that can be left uncut in the early summer, for it is most important that the leaves should have time to manufacture the necessary food reserves for the next spring's growth and pass it back to the bulb for storage.

Lifting It is generally desirable to move bulbs used in spring bedding as soon as the plants have finished flowering. If this is done with care, so that the roots suffer no damage, they can be ripened successfully in some inconspicuous sunny border. They must not be taken up and dried off at this stage, but only when the leaves have turned quite yellow. All flower heads should be picked off as the blossoms fade. Where the appearance does not matter greatly it is better to leave the juicy stem on the plants, as the storage organ appears to absorb the sap again. An occasional specially fine bloom may be allowed to set seed if desired, but in this case it is better if possible not to move the plant. Narcissi, tulips, irises, crocuses, and numerous other plants of this type grow easily from seed, though it usually takes three or four years for them to attain flowering size, and seedlings usually vary considerably from their parents. Many bulbs will be found, when lifted, to have made one or more daughter bulbs, distinguishable by their smaller size. It is from these that the number of bulbs is increased by simple division and with the certainty of maintaining colour, size, etc., unaltered.

It is by no means essential to lift all early-flowering bulbs at the end of each growing season. If they are grown in clumps in mixed borders it is often much more convenient to lift them only when the border is remade or when they become too crowded. The object of lifting the bulbs at all is to ensure that they are thoroughly ripened. This is much more essential in wet summers than in dry ones. When the foliage has become quite yellow the bulbs should be lifted, thoroughly cleaned, and

STRIPPING GLADIOLUS CORMS

A cool dry shed is the best place to clean and store bulbs and corms. Here dead leaves and soil are being removed before storing.

placed in single layers in a frame, greenhouse or sunny window to ripen off finally. They should then be stored in a cool dry place until the planting season returns. The natural ripening processes of the bulbs should be encouraged as much as possible by giving small doses of a potash or phosphate fertilizer after flowering.

All the information given about the method of planting, depth, etc., applies equally to the summer- and autumn-flowering varieties, with the exception that many of these are more or less tender and so must not be exposed to frost. Familiar examples of this type are tuberous begonias, dahlias, and oxalis species, all of which can be started into growth in a cool but frostproof greenhouse or frame and, after being hardened off, be planted out into their permanent quarters at the end of May or the beginning of June. If frost threatens after they are in the beds they can be protected temporarily by placing an inverted flower-pot over each plant.

Corms The hardy corms, such as the gladioli, of which there are large numbers of delightfully dainty species in addition to the large-flowered and primulinus varieties, and the montbretias and tritonias, can all be planted in March. In England these corms are sold with the scaly leaf bases of the previous year intact. If there is the least suspicion that any of the corms are diseased, it is worth the time expended to remove these skins, for the diseased area is then quite obvious and the infected corms

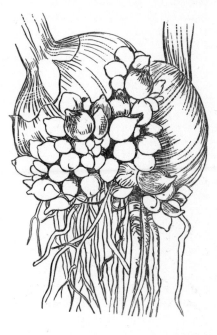

TYPICAL
GLADIOLUS CORMS
The body of the corm is firm and solid, but it is surrounded by dry papery scales. Note the tiny cormels at the side. These will grow on into corms of flowering size.

can be treated or destroyed according to the extent and the nature of the disease. The stripping must be done with great care, or the shoots may be damaged. Any tiny corms, or 'spawn,' found under the different layers should be saved and planted in a nursery bed, where they can be grown on undisturbed.

Lifting Large quantities of spawn are often found attached to the outside of the corms when they are lifted in the autumn. These should be cleaned off at the time and planted at once. It is not absolutely essential to lift gladiolus and montbretia corms every year, but this should always be done if the autumn is a wet one or the soil is cold and clayey, to ensure that the corms become well ripened. Gladioli should be lifted when the foliage has yellowed, cleaned, and laid in shallow trays in a dry, airy, and frostproof place. Montbretias can be treated in the same way, but are really better planted in a frame and not allowed to get absolutely dust dry.

Many more of the summer- and autumn-flowering bulbs and corms need special attention to ripening than do the early ones, which can ripen naturally in the summer. The tiny crocus species all benefit from the protection of a few panes of glass, which may be kept on all the winter, to guard them against excess rain. The tender tuberous plants must be stored in a frostproof place.

Lilies There are two classes of these plants with storage organs which never become quite dormant, and, although it is still quite customary to

A TYPICAL LILY BULB
The fleshy scales distinguish it from a corm or tuber.

purchase them in a dried-up condition, they are all the better for being supplied with water throughout the year. These are the lilies and cyclamen. Lilies in particular suffer badly if allowed to become quite dry for any length of time. The Madonna lily, *L. candidum*, actually moves most successfully immediately after flowering. Other lily bulbs should be planted as soon as possible after they are stocked by the nurseryman, which is usually in October or early November, or, alternatively, they may be purchased in spring—a method specially recommended if the bulbs are obtained from a nurseryman who grows his own stock and so has not got to store dry bulbs for several months.

Prompt planting after delivery is particularly important when bulbs have already had to travel from China and Japan. Dried-up bulbs should always be refused. If it is impossible to plant the bulbs immediately they are obtained, they can be kept fresh for a short period by covering them with damp sand or sawdust, and it is thus that they will be found stored by all reliable stockists. The majority of lilies resent annual disturbance—in fact, any disturbance—and therefore should be placed in their permanent positions at once, and only be moved when they become overcrowded. Except for forcing, it is better to buy small- or medium-sized lily bulbs in preference to the very large ones, for these become established more satisfactorily in the long run, even if they do not make as splendid a display in the first year. All lilies do not require the same conditions, some being the natives of marshes, but they are all alike in requiring soil through which the water drains rapidly, even the bog species, which will not put up with stagnant water. Equally, they all do best if shaded at the root, and thus large numbers flourish best if planted among low-growing shrubs, such as azaleas, where the heads can come out into the sun but the roots are kept cool. A mulch of leaf-mould over the roots is invaluable.

The lily of the valley is in no way related to the true lilies, but has fleshy roots. Strong 'crowns,' as they are termed, should be obtained in September or October and planted just below the surface with the roots spread out horizontally, preferably in a shady place. Solomon's Seal is treated similarly.

CHAPTER EIGHTEEN

Annuals, Hardy and Half Hardy

A N annual is distinguished by the fact that it completes the cycle of its life in one year and then dies. Seed must be germinated afresh each year to spring up rapidly into a sturdy young plant which flowers, bears and ripens a new crop of seed, and then withers away. Annual plants are divided into three sections—tender, half hardy, and hardy. Here we are only concerned with the last two, as tender annuals are exclusively greenhouse plants and are dealt with under that heading.

Half-hardy annuals are those which are liable to injury by frost, but may be grown outdoors with perfect safety during the summer months. Familiar examples are ten-week stocks, annual asters, and annual phlox. Seed of these must be sown in a greenhouse or frame and the seedlings hardened off for planting out in May or early June when danger of serious frost is past. Hardy annuals, however, may be sown outdoors where they are to bloom, as they are not injured by cold.

Popular examples of each type are as follows:

HARDY ANNUALS

Adonis	*Lavatera splendens*
Alyssum	Limnanthes
Bartonia	*Linum grandiflorum*
Calendula	Malope
Calliopsis	Mignonette
Candytuft	Nemophila
Chrysanthemum	Nasturtium
(Tricolor, etc.)	Nigella
Clarkia	Phacelia
Convolvulus	Poppies (Shirley,
Dianthus Heddewigii	Cardinal, etc.)
Dimorphotheca	Night-Scented Stock
Eschscholzia	Sweet Pea
Godetia	Sweet Scabious
Gypsophila elegans	Sweet Sultan
Helichrysum	Ursinia
Kochia	Virginia Stock
Larkspur	Viscaria

HALF-HARDY ANNUALS

*Ageratum	Nemesia
Alonsoa	*Petunia
Anagallis	*Phlox Drummondii*
*Antirrhinum	Salpiglossis
Aster (Callistephus)	Stocks (Ten-Week and
Cosmea	Giant Nice)
*Lobelia	*Tagetes signata pumila*
Marigold (African	*Verbena
and French)	Zinnia

* Strictly speaking, these are half-hardy perennials, but they are almost always treated as half-hardy annuals.

These two classes of plant have both grown immensely in popularity more or less concurrently with increase of interest shown in hardy herbaceous perennials, and for very similar reasons. Both give every gardener the opportunity of enjoying a magnificent display of flowers outdoors without necessity for expensive ranges of glasshouses or great cultural ability. For the poor man there is no type of plant to surpass the hardy annual, which can be purchased for a few pence and be raised with as much ease as ordinary grass seed. Gaps among more permanent subjects may be more easily filled with annuals than with any other class of plant, while for supplying cut flowers for the table and house many varieties are of supreme value.

Half-hardy Annuals The culture of annuals is extremely simple. The half-hardy kinds should be sown under glass fairly early in the year, the precise time being determined by the amount of heat and greenhouse accommodation available. It must always be borne in mind that though the seeds themselves take up very little room, the seedlings will grow very rapidly and must soon be pricked out into boxes or even potted up singly. It will not be safe to place them finally outdoors till May in the south or even early June in the north, so that greenhouse or frame space which seemed adequate at sowing time may be grossly overcrowded long before the planting-out season arrives. A temperature of about 65° will be found necessary for the germination of most half-hardy annuals, and this may fall by five or ten degrees when the seedlings are well through the soil. If the gardener has a heated greenhouse of fair size, together with a good unheated frame in a warm sheltered position, many half-hardy annuals may be sown early in February, but with more limited accommodation it is far better to wait until March. A month will make a considerable difference to the size of the plants and the room they will require by the end of April. Even with only a frame a great deal may be done, especially if the frame can be placed on a hotbed. Full instructions for the preparation of this invaluable aid to early seed raising will be found in Chapter Thirty-one. Seed sowing in cold frames should not be started until about the second or third week in March, according to the weather, and may continue until the middle of April. Apart from this, culture follows the same general lines as in the greenhouse.

Hardy Annuals These may be sown outdoors during April in the beds or borders in which they are to flower. Some gardeners even make sowings in March, but though this may prove satisfactory in mild and sheltered districts, it is more often than not fraught with considerable difficulties, and germination is likely to be much more regular a week or so later when weather is more settled and the days longer. Most hardy annuals can also be sown in September, preferably about the second or

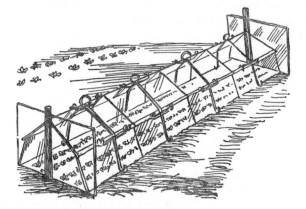

PROTECTING EARLY BATCHES OF SEEDLINGS

Cloches can be placed over young seedlings to protect them in the early part of the year and removed gradually as the weather improves. Note that the ends of the rows must also be protected.

third week in the month. The seeds will then germinate freely before the winter and may be thinned out a little; the final thinning should be left over until the spring. It is not wise to sow earlier than the period indicated, or the plants will get too big before the winter and are more likely to be injured by severe frost. From September sowings one can be certain of wintering all the plants without any protection under ordinary conditions. By sowing in both early autumn and spring a much better succession of blooms will be obtained.

The seeds may either be sown in drills or broadcast, the latter plan giving a far more natural and pleasing effect. In any case they should be scattered very sparingly, for it is surprising how freely they germinate. Rigorous thinning out will be necessary as soon as the seedlings have made two or three leaves and may be readily caught hold of between finger and thumb.

Culture Detailed instructions regarding individual requirements of particular varieties will not be given here, as they are always printed on the seed packets and are also included in most seedsmen's catalogues. The general cultural requirements of both half-hardy and hardy annuals during the summer months are the same. From time to time a small Dutch hoe should be passed between the plants to keep the surface loose and encourage continued growth. All will benefit from occasional liberal soakings with very weak liquid manure, either chemical or animal in origin.

The most important point of all is to remove faded flowers at the earliest opportunity, when most annuals will continue to bloom for many weeks beyond their normal period.

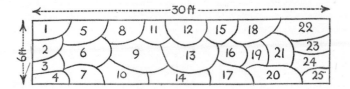

A WELL-ARRANGED BORDER OF ANNUALS

The size of this border can be adjusted to meet requirements. The plants are:
1. *Chrysanthemum 'Northern Star';* **2.** *Anchusa 'Blue Beard';* **3.** *Sweet Alyssum;* **4.** *Candytuft;* **5.** *Clarkia 'Salmon Queen';* **6.** *Sweet Pea 'Olympia';* **7.** *Calendula 'Orange King';* **8.** *Phacelia campanularia;* **9.** *Nigella 'Miss Jekyll';* **10.** *Scabious 'Blue Cockade';* **11.** *Sweet Pea 'Startler';* **12.** *Lavatera rosea splendens;* **13.** *Sweet Pea 'Cynthia Davis';* **14.** *Clarkia 'Firefly';* **15.** *Linum grandiflorum;* **16.** *Stock-flowered Larkspur (red);* **17.** *Godetia 'Sweetheart';* **18.** *Mignonette;* **19.** *Shirley Poppy;* **20.** *Venidium fastuosum;* **21.** *Godetia amoena Schaminii flore pleno;* **22.** *Coreopsis 'Mayfield Giant';* **23.** *Gypsophila elegans;* **24.** *Eschscholzia;* **25.** *Limnanthes Douglasii.*

CHAPTER NINETEEN

Biennials

A BIENNIAL differs from an annual in that, instead of blooming the same year that seed germinates, it must be sown one year in order to flower the next. Like an annual, it dies after flowering, and so a new stock of plants must be raised each year from seed if the display is to be repeated season after season. This is the botanical definition of a biennial, but in garden parlance the term is often used somewhat loosely—for example, to describe such a flower as the wallflower, which is, strictly speaking, a perennial, and can often be seen established on old walls, where it is left for many years in the garden. But from the garden standpoint it proves more economical and satisfactory in the

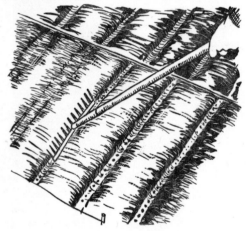

COVERING DRILLS
SOWN WITH BIENNIALS
The back of a rake is used for this task. Note the neatly laid out beds, which make hoeing and weeding simple tasks.

long run to treat wallflowers as though they were biennials, sowing seed one year to produce plants to flower the following spring and destroying them as soon as they have finished blooming. Familiar biennials, including plants that in gardens are usually treated as biennials, are Canterbury bells, sweet Williams, wallflowers, *Coreopsis grandiflora*, forget-me-nots, hollyhocks (but almost as often grown as perennials), many verbascums, double daisies, foxgloves, Brompton stocks, and *Campanula pyramidalis*, all of which are excellent either for bedding or for association with hardy perennials.

Sowing The best time for sowing seed of biennials is in May or early June. All can be sown out of doors, preferably in a sheltered and partially shaded border. There is, however, an advantage in sowing Canterbury bells and also *Campanula pyramidalis* in a frame and covering this with a shaded light until germination takes place. Out of doors the seed of these plants is sometimes a little irregular in germination, and the seedlings make slow progress at the outset.

It is always advisable to sow biennials in shallow drills about 9 inches apart, as this greatly facilitates weeding and hoeing in the early stages. The seedlings should be pricked out into another bed of well-broken soil as soon as they are large enough to be handled conveniently, which is usually when they have formed three or four rough leaves; that is to say, true leaves characteristic of the plant as distinct from the cotyledons or seed leaves. In this 'nursery bed' the plants should be in rows about 1

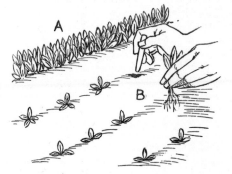

PRICKING OUT BIENNIALS
A task that should be carried out as soon as the seedlings can be handled conveniently. Prick out from the seed rows (A) into other straight lines (B) in a nursery bed of well broken up soil.

foot part with 9 inches from plant to plant, these distances being subject to some little adjustment according to the nature and size of the plants. The point is to allow the seedlings plenty of room to develop into good sturdy clumps ready for planting out either in the early autumn or in the spring in the beds or borders in which they are to flower.

Culture Little attention is required during the summer months except ordinary hoeing to keep down weeds and, of course, thorough watering should the weather turn hot and dry. It is not desirable to feed much during this first summer, because this will tend to make growth too coarse and lush, and it is then much more likely to suffer damage during the winter.

Forget-me-nots In one instance it will often be found advisable to depart a little from the general routine outlined above. This is with forget-me-nots, for experience suggests, at any rate on fairly rich soil, that the best plan is to delay sowing until about the first week in July. Earlier sowing certainly results in much bigger plants, but these do not stand the winter nearly as well as the smaller plants resulting from the delayed sowing.

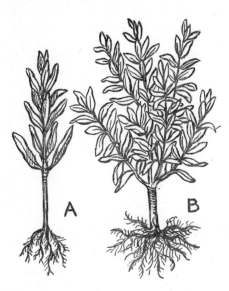

PLANTS FOR PRICKING OUT

Two typical plants from the seed bed. (A) has been grown in over-crowded conditions and (B) has been well grown and is a good sturdy seedling with plenty of root.

Monocarpic Plants Sooner or later the garden novice will probably come across the term 'monocarpic' applied to a plant, and will doubtless be puzzled as to its meaning. Actually a monocarpic plant is very similar to the biennial and dies after flowering in a similar manner, but instead of taking a regular period of two growing seasons to complete its cycle it is usually irregular in behaviour. It simply goes on growing until it attains sufficient size and strength to flower and produce seed, after which it collapses and dies. Typical examples of this type of plant are to be found in numerous species of meconopsis, *Saxifraga longifolia*, *Michauxia campanuloides*, and *Eryngium giganteum*.

CHAPTER TWENTY

Tender Bedding Plants

THOUGH the tremendous vogue enjoyed by bedding plants during the nineteenth century is now a thing of the past, hardy herbaceous perennials and annuals having largely taken their place, it must not be supposed for one moment that they are entirely without value. A visit to any large private or public gardens during the summer months would soon rectify any such false notion as that. For continuity of bloom the bedding or zonal-leaved pelargonium—more familiarly known as geranium—the marguerite, fuchsia, and heliotrope are still unsurpassed and irreplaceable, while there are other plants such as the canna, *Leucophyton Brownii*, and dracaena, which have a unique value in giving height and a pleasing exotic touch to beds that might otherwise suffer from flatness.

Protection The very name of this class of plant gives a clue to its general management. We are dealing with tender bedding plants—that is to say, plants that are very liable to damage by frost and must therefore have the protection of a warm greenhouse from early October until May, but may be placed outdoors to fill beds with summer flowers from May or early June until the autumn. Because of their tenderness it is not possible to handle the majority of these plants without the aid of artificial heat, though it is true that some amateurs work wonders with an unheated greenhouse or even a frame well covered with mats and sacks during the coldest weather. However, such a course is not under any circumstances recommended to the beginner, for considerable experience and judgement are called for in handling such improvised methods satisfactorily. But given a soundly constructed greenhouse fitted with a heating apparatus capable of maintaining a temperature of not less than 45°, and preferably about 10° more during the coldest weather, the care of most tender bedding plants becomes a fairly simple matter. The ideal arrangement is to have hot-water pipes attached to a boiler heated by coke, anthracite, or gas. A very satisfactory and handy alternative is to be found in electric radiators specially constructed for greenhouse heating and preferably fitted with thermostatic control, while yet another method, and one which will appeal with particular force to the man who has only a very small house and little spare cash, is to install one of the fume-consuming oil stoves specially made for the purpose.

Lifting At the end of September, or not later than the first week in October in the south of England, a sufficient number of plants should be lifted from the summer beds to provide stock for the following season. These are placed in pots just big enough to accommodate their roots and brought without delay into the greenhouse. It is important to note that the pots should be well provided with drainage material, for few bedding plants will tolerate stagnation. Only a very little soil will be necessary, and this may consist of ordinary loam with a little sand and peat moss litter added.

Watering During the autumn and the greater part of the winter water will be given very sparingly, though in sufficient quantity at each application to wet the compost in the pots right through. Driblets never do any good. For this purpose it will be necessary to look the plants over about once a week, though actually in the depth of winter water will, in all probability, only be required about once in every three weeks. However, no hard and fast rules can be laid down, as so much depends on the type of soil used, the degree of heat used, and the amount of ventilation given. The only satisfactory method is to examine the soil carefully at each inspection and keep it just moist, but never in a sodden condition.

Temperature Throughout this period a night temperature of round 55° should be maintained. Little harm will be done if the thermometer occasionally falls to 45°, but below this it should not be allowed to go. Ventilation during the day should be given as freely as possible, compatible with this night temperature and reasonable freedom from draughts. In actual practice this usually means that the ventilators can be opened a little during the morning and early afternoon on all very mild days, but should be kept closed when the weather is frosty.

Propagation Towards the end of February the temperature of the house should be increased a little and water given with greater freedom in order to start the plants into growth. A few weeks later firm young shoots can be detached, prepared as cuttings, and rooted either on the greenhouse staging or in a close frame, according to the nature of the subject. Pelargoniums, fuchsias, and marguerites on the whole do better on the staging, but scarlet salvias and heliotropes will make roots more rapidly in the closer and warmer atmosphere of the frame. These cuttings, when rooted, should be grown on steadily in a warm and buoyant atmosphere, being potted on once or twice as the smaller receptacles become filled with roots and finally hardened off very gradually in a frame in readiness for planting out in May or early June.

These general instructions require certain modification in the case of some plants, and particularly those with tuberous roots. Notable among these are tuberous-rooted begonias, bedding dahlias, the blue *Salvia patens*, and cannas. All these go to rest much more completely during the winter than plants with fibrous roots, and so may be stored absolutely dry for several months on end without suffering the slightest harm. With begonias the usual practice is to place the tubers close

RAISING A NEW STOCK OF PENSTEMONS

Cuttings secured in August or September, as shown on the right, will soon make sturdy plants like that on the left.

together in ordinary seed trays filled with dry peat moss litter and store these in any perfectly dry, frostproof, but not too hot place. A cupboard indoors will do very well, or they may be placed under the staging in a warm greenhouse provided they are shielded from drips. Cannas and blue salvias should be potted up, but given no water from November until the end of February.

Dahlias, blue salvias and penstemons can be propagated from cuttings in early spring in a close frame, as already described for the scarlet salvia and heliotrope. Cannas are propagated by very careful division of the old roots in March, a method which may also be applied to begonia tubers if they are sufficiently large to have two or three distinct crowns (or sets of shoots) when growth starts. A knife must be used to cut the begonia tubers into suitable portions, each of which must have at least one crown.

One other popular bedding plant that can be stored practically dry during the winter is the echeveria. A convenient method is to place the rosettes shoulder to shoulder in ordinary seed trays with some light sandy soil between them and stand these in a fairly sunny place in the greenhouse, but practically withhold water from October until early March, after which it should be given in gradually increasing quantity and the plants split up and potted separately as soon as they start freely into growth.

Planting out   When putting out bedding plants in their summer quarters they should be tapped from their pots with as little disturbance as

HARDENING OFF
BEDDING PLANTS

The first stages, from propagating case to greenhouse staging and thence to a shelf near the glass.

FINISHING THE
HARDENING PROCESS

The plants are in a frame out of doors with the lights removed during fine days.

possible and dropped straight into holes of suitable size prepared ready for them. It is most important that the plants should not be put out too early and should be prepared for the change in atmosphere by careful hardening off. Dahlias, heliotropes, and scarlet salvias are specially

Left: Planting daffodil bulbs using a trowel. *Right:* Tulip bulbs, lifted from their flowering quarters, are lined out in a prepared trench.

Soil is pressed firmly round the roots of the bulbs, after which they will be left undisturbed until their foliage dies down.

Left: Planting a group of antirrhinums to make a summer display.   *Right:* Liftin
seedling wallflowers for transplanting.

A section of the well planned annual border at the Royal Horticultural Society's garden
at Wisley.

liable to chills, and it is rarely wise to place them finally outdoors until the first week in June in the south or a week or ten days later in the north. Should an unexpected cold snap occur soon after planting out, the plants can often be preserved by the simple expedient of inverting a large flower-pot over each at night. These must, of course, be removed during the day, or growth will quickly become white and drawn.

Summer Work During the summer months the beds must be hoed occasionally. The plants should be fed periodically with liquid manures, and all faded flowers removed to prevent seed formation and so encourage a prolonged season of bloom. The taller plants will require staking, but trailing plants such as verbenas and ivy-leaved pelargoniums may be pegged down to the surface of the bed.

K

CHAPTER TWENTY-ONE

Sweet Peas

THAT sweet peas will grow and flower in almost any soil and with but the vaguest of cultural attention is well known to every amateur. On the other hand, few flowers will more amply repay the grower for any extra pains that may be taken on their behalf, and their demands are so simple as to be easily supplied by any beginner.

The roots of sweet peas travel a long way in search of food and moisture, and the soil must be deeply dug if the plants are to give of their best. It is not necessary to trench the ground except for exhibition plants, but digging to a depth of two spits is always advisable.

Preparation of the Site   Most soils will be the better for some manure, which should be worked into the bottom spit at the time of digging. The form of the manure will depend upon the nature of the soil, as explained in Chapter Three. It is always a wise plan to supplement the manure with a good sprinkling of bonemeal or crushed bones, placed along the bottom of each trench.

Seed Sowing   Seed can be sown in the open ground at any time during March and April, but if a cold frame is available there is no need to wait until that time before starting. From a sowing in boxes or pots in the cold frame during February first-rate plants can be obtained. These will be ready for transplanting to their flowering quarters in early April.

Boxes should be about 4 inches deep and well drained, and the seeds spaced 2 inches apart each way, or the seeds can be sown singly in small pots. Plenty of crocks and a light compost should be used. Half an inch of soil is ample covering. As explained in Chapter Five, a sheet of glass may be used to encourage rapid germination, but it must be discarded as soon as shoots appear. At all times the plants must be kept as hardy and healthy as possible, and it is only in the event of late frosts that the frame lights need be used.

Planting Out and Subsequent Care   Planting out can proceed at any time after the beginning of April. Breakage and damage to the young root tips must be avoided. Eight inches to a foot apart each way should be allowed between the plants, which must have their roots spread out in sufficiently large holes. The soil should then be made firm round them and watered to settle the particles round the roots.

The main shoot of a sweet pea is very liable to go 'blind,' or stop growing, after reaching a height of about 3 feet, and for this reason most growers pinch out the growing point of each plant after it has

SOWING
SWEET PEAS
IN POTS
The seeds should be spaced out evenly so that the seedlings are given room to develop.

developed three pairs of leaves. This operation greatly accelerates the growth of side shoots, and is always recommended.

Sowing in Open Ground   Soil is in just the right condition for sowing outdoors when it breaks apart after being firmly compressed in the hand. Sowing should then proceed at once in drills about an inch deep. Four to six inches should be allowed between the seeds, as the germination of good seed today makes thin sowing perfectly safe, and any gaps in the row can be made good by transplanting other plants from other parts before they have made too much root.

Pests and Diseases   Several pests are very partial to both seeds and seedlings. Mice will, however, leave the seeds severely alone if they are moistened and shaken in a bag of red lead before sowing. Regular dustings of soot will ward off slugs, and birds can be kept at bay by stretching strong black thread or thin netting over the rows. The two commonest diseases are 'streak,' which causes blotchy yellow discoloration of the leaves and brownish streaks on the stems, and mildew, identified by a white, floury outgrowth on the plants. The former is most commonly met with on exhibition plants, and is usually associated with overfeeding or bad draining. Some gardeners prepare only trenches of soil about 18 inches wide and 2 to 3 feet deep for their peas, instead of digging the whole plot to an even depth. The result, if the weather is wet, is an accumulation of water in the bottom of the trench, with disastrous results. Mildew is most persistent in damp, cold weather and towards the end of the seasons. It can be controlled by dusting with flowers of sulphur.

How to Stake Staking presents a problem to many growers, particularly to city gardeners, who cannot procure the feathery hazel sticks which are ideal for the purpose. All seedsmen offer solutions in the form of wire and string netting, though these are rather expensive. A good, inexpensive method of supporting the plants is to drive a stout stake, 5

FIRST SUPPORT OUTDOORS
Very small branching twigs must be pushed firmly into the ground near each seedling sweet pea as soon as it is planted out.

to 6 feet in height, into each end of the row, and to stretch tarred twine or thin wire between these at 6-inch levels. A few lighter stakes can be driven into the row between the end stakes to help bear the not inconsiderable weight of the plants.

Care during the Growing Period It is of immense importance that young seedlings should be securely supported before they attain sufficient length to bend over and touch the ground, for the bending weakens the plant at a vulnerable point, and any frost occurring will affect the stem at the bend. Also the tissues tend to harden there and check the subsequent flow of sap for all time. Twigs furnished with small side growths are best for this early support.

Regular hoeings and watering during any hot dry spells are necessary until the flower buds begin to form. A light mulch of old, short manure is also helpful in hot seasons, and where the blooms are intended for exhibition a mulch of straw may be extended over the paths. The plants should be given weekly doses of liquid manure after they have started to

flower, to ensure a supply of long-stemmed blooms after the normal
period. Weak solutions of natural manure are best for this purpose and
can be applied in copious draughts. Any of the well-known fertilizers
can also be used, either in solution or sprinkled dry along the rows and
then watered in, but for exhibition blooms should be regarded only as a

**CORRECT STAKING FOR
NATURAL CULTURE**
*Branching pea sticks, pre-
ferably of hazel, are pushed
into the ground with their
upper ends inwards so that
the plants will not straggle
too much and cutting will be
easier.*

special 'pick-me-up' for use ten days before the show, as their regular
use for these plants renders them more susceptible to disease.

All flowers must be cut immediately they begin to fade; if seed pods
are allowed to form, the plants will soon go out of bloom.

Growing for Exhibition When sweet peas are grown for exhibition the
culture differs in that, after the initial pinching when the seedlings are a
few inches in height, the plants are always kept to one stem each, and
that the strongest that forms. All unwanted side growths and tendrils
are pinched out at the earliest possible moment. This is known as the
cordon system of growing. Even flower buds are removed until the
plants have become thoroughly established and the time for showing
approaches. As a rule the plant should be 3 feet in height before any
flower buds are allowed to develop.

To prevent the growth from becoming hard and woody during hot
weather a moist growing atmosphere must be maintained by spraying
the plants overhead and damping down the rows and paths in the early
evening, in addition to mulching.

Lowering the plants on the canes by cutting the ties, laying each
haulm flat along the ground, and restarting its tip on another cane
should be done first when the plants are about 5 feet high. Many
growers never allow their plants to exceed this height, taking them down
and re-layering them as often as necessary.

CHAPTER TWENTY-TWO

Dahlias

THE varieties of heights, forms of flowers, and colours in modern dahlias are so great that there can be but few gardeners who do not find some of these delightful plants essential to their needs, either massed in formal beds, or planted out among the permanent occupants of the mixed border, or even grown specially for cutting.

In height they range from the full 8 feet of well-grown large decorative types, which will often produce flowers a foot across, to the dwarf bedding dahlias, which are all under 2 feet. The unique cactus dahlias make large plants and have curiously curled petals, narrow and spidery. They have been interbred with the decoratives to form the garden cactus race, so valuable for the back of large borders. Then there are tall single-flowered dahlias; collerettes, which are much like singles except for a collar of small florets, usually in a contrasting colour, round the centre; the prim pompons, well described by their name, and the similar but larger show dahlias with ball-like flowers; star dahlias which are small and have two or three rows of rather pointed florets; anemone-flowered dahlias which are like singles with a central boss or pad of tubular florets; and peony-flowered dahlias which have two or more rows of broad, flattened florets. Then there are medium- and small-flowered decoratives, which differ from the large decoratives mainly in the size of their flowers. The smallest of all are the dwarf bedding varieties, which do not as a rule exceed 2 feet in height. Their flowers may be single or double.

These varying types differ in growth, some being very free flowering, as is the case with the small decorative and bedding dahlias. Unlike the old-fashioned varieties, many of the modern varieties of decorative and garden cactus dahlia are characterized by stiff, wiry stems which carry the flowers erectly above the foliage. These firm stems and their long-lasting qualities make the flowers splendid for cutting.

Position Dahlias are ideal amateurs' flowers, for they will grow in almost any situation except deep shade, though they do best in well-drained soil in full sun. To get good results from the larger varieties it is necessary that the soil should be fairly rich, but even this is not necessary for the pompons, and over-feeding of all types produces rank growth at the expense of flowers.

Overwintering The fact that dahlias are tender plants which are damaged by even quite light frosts means that the roots, which are tuberous, cannot be left in the garden during the winter. But this need not deter even those who have no greenhouse or frame from planting them, for the tubers can be stored in a box of dry soil in any frostproof cupboard or spare room.

Starting a Collection The best time to start a collection of dahlias is at the end of May or the beginning of June. At this season young rooted cuttings can be purchased, or the bedding varieties may be sown in a sheltered border out of doors. They may, of course, be germinated from seed much earlier if a heated greenhouse is available.

For the first few days that the dahlias are placed out of doors it may be necessary to protect them at night by placing an inverted flowerpot over each, but this is not sufficient protection against intense cold, and the plants should not be put in the borders until all danger of severe frost is passed. During the summer all tall dahlias need staking carefully,

TRAPPING EARWIGS ON DAHLIAS
Small plant pots filled with dry hay and inverted over the tops of the stakes will attract earwigs. They should be collected daily and destroyed.

using a soft twine or broad raffia to prevent cutting the sappy main stems. It is not necessary to stake the bedding varieties, nor need these be disbudded. Dahlias intended for exhibition should have their growth restricted to three main stems, and all side branches on these must like-wise be removed, only one flower being allowed to form on each. When dahlias are grown for decorative purposes all dead flower heads must be removed at once, or the plants will seed and go out of bloom. Given this attention and constant hoeing of the surrounding soil, all the bedding varieties will flower for a very long period. All dahlias appreciate plenty of water and fairly generous treatment with liquid stimulants.

Enemies of the Dahlia   The blooms are liable to damage by earwigs in the early autumn, and these may be trapped in inverted flower-pots filled with hay, or in lengths of old, hollow broad bean stalks if these are emptied or blown out first thing every morning. Do not leave the traps unvisited, or they will encourage the pest by making excellent breeding-places. Several virus diseases have so far proved incurable, and infected plants should be burnt. The symptoms are stunted growth, blotched, distorted leaves, and streaked stems. Greenfly and other sucking pests (see Chapter Twenty-five) are believed to spread infection.

Propagation   Dahlia foliage is cut by the very first frost and does not

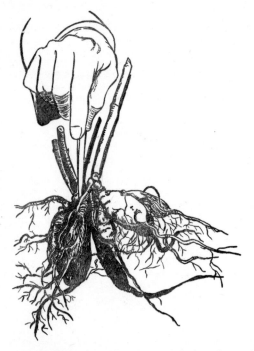

DIVIDING A DAHLIA
A knife must be used to split the crown in the manner shown.

recover from the damage, and therefore the plants should be lifted immediately this occurs. The foliage is then cut off, but the base of the main stem must be left about 4 inches long, for it is from this that the new shoots for the next year will be formed. As previously stated, the tubers should be boxed up in dry soil or peat litter and placed in some dry, frostproof place. They must not be left in this storage place too long

in the following spring, but either started into growth in a frostproof
house during March or April or planted about 9 inches deep in a

PLANTING A
DAHLIA DIVISION
*Fine soil with a little sharp sand
in it is being worked carefully
round the tubers by hand.*

sheltered border in May, so that the growth does not appear above
ground until danger of frost is past.

If it is desired to propagate the dahlias by means of cuttings, the
tubers should be barely covered with soil in pots or boxes and started
into growth in a warm house. A temperature of 55° will give good
results. If watered moderately, a number of strong shoots should soon
appear at the base of the stem, and, if only a few plants of each variety
are required, each of these shoots can be detached from the stem with a
small portion of tuber attached when the shoots are about 3 inches high.
But should a large number of plants be required from each old one, it is
best to remove only the top 2 inches of the shoots, cutting them off in
such a manner that there are a couple of buds on the remaining portion
of new growth. These buds will then give rise to shoots, which in their
turn can be taken as cuttings. The method of taking cuttings is identical
with that described for soft cuttings in Chapter Six.

Large plants with several tubers can be increased by the simple method
of division, provided that each portion consists of a shoot attached to a
tuber or tubers.

CHAPTER TWENTY-THREE

Border Carnations and Border Chrysanthemums

CARNATIONS

For hundreds of years the border carnation has been esteemed in this country as a hardy garden flower. Shakespeare was familiar with it, terming it the 'gilly-flower' and 'sops-in-wine'—the latter name bestowed on account of its ancient use for flavouring wines. It is still as popular as ever, both as an exhibition flower and in the garden and home.

It may be explained here that 'picotee' is merely the name of one of the several classes into which carnations are divided. A picotee carnation is either white or yellow in colour with a narrow pencil line of some stronger hue round the margin of each petal. Similarly a fancy carnation is variously flaked or striped upon a groundwork of one colour, and is subdivided into white ground fancy or yellow ground fancy, according to the ground hue. The self carnation is, as its name implies, entirely of one colour.

Choice of Site The situation chosen for border carnations must be sunny and fully open. It is a great mistake to attempt to coddle the plants in any way. A medium loam that has been well dug and contains a liberal amount of lime is ideal, but almost any garden soil can be made suitable if properly worked. Neither manure nor leaf-mould should be used freely, but sparing applications will improve the texture of both very light and very heavy soils. On the latter grit or sand can also be used freely, while the beds should be raised a little above the surrounding level to prevent waterlogging in winter. As already mentioned, carnations like lime, and this should be added either as air-slaked lime or—a better plan—in the form of old mortar rubble, if it is naturally deficient.

When to Plant Border carnations can be planted either in autumn or spring. Preference should be given to the former period provided the soil is in good condition and not likely to get waterlogged, but in no case should planting be continued after the end of October. September is a better month. Spring planting may be carried out in March or April.

It is customary to grow carnations in beds by themselves, though there is no reason why they should not be grown in groups in the herbaceous border, provided that they are given ample space and larger plants are not allowed to encroach upon them. Whichever method is adopted at least a foot should be allowed between the plants each way; 18 inches is better if the plants are likely to remain undisturbed for two or three years.

Care During the Summer When the young plants start to grow, each should be provided with a short bamboo cane for support. The simplest method is to attach growth to this by means of the small wire rings known as 'Time-Savers.' If blooms of exhibition quality are desired,

FURTHER STAGES
IN LAYERING A
BORDER CARNATION

Making the incision. The slit shoot is pegged down into finely broken soil with a wooden or galvanized wire peg (bottom left). When all available shoots have been layered, a little more fine soil should be heaped over them, after which they are watered freely (bottom right).

each young plant must be restricted to not more than five flowering stems, while even when plants are intended only for garden decoration it is not advisable to allow a young plant to carry more than eight or nine flower stems, the remainder being removed at an early stage. In any case each flower stem must carry only one blossom, preferably the terminal one. Other flower buds will be formed in the axils of the leaves, but should be rubbed out as soon as possible so that strength may be concentrated on the selected blooms. This is known as disbudding. Split calyces can be supported with a ring when the bud is opening.

During spring and summer the soil between the plants should be hoed frequently, and an occasional dressing given of a reliable carnation fertilizer or of soot that has been allowed to remain outdoors for at least three months. Also the plants should be freely watered should the weather happen to be dry.

Growing Plants from Seed Border carnations can be raised from seed, but the plants produced in this way will not all resemble their parents. Indeed, quite a number are likely to be useless, at any rate so far as exhibition is concerned, though it is by careful hybridization, followed, of course, by seed raising, that the expert obtains desirable new varieties.

Layering and Cuttings Once a variety has been selected it must be propagated by layering or by cuttings. The former method is by far the better, as it is more certain and ensures sturdy plants. The general principles of layering carnations have already been dealt with in Chapter Six, and it only remains to be added here that, if the rooted layers cannot be planted in the new beds before the end of October, it is usually best to lift and pot them in September, wintering them in a cold frame, but giving them plenty of ventilation and, indeed, using the lights more as a protection against excessive rain than to ward off cold. In this way really strong plants will be available for spring planting.

CHRYSANTHEMUMS

Border Chrysanthemums These differ from greenhouse varieties in two notable ways. First, they flower in late summer instead of in the autumn, and, secondly, they are considerably hardier—so much so, in

DISBUDDING FOR LARGE BLOOMS

Some varieties respond well to this treatment, and if all side flower buds are removed they will develop the terminal blooms to a surprising extent.

fact, that in many parts of the country they can be left outdoors winter after winter without any protection. It is not in this way, however, that the best results are obtained, for experienced growers prefer to lift the clumps each autumn and place them close together in a cold frame or unheated greenhouse. Then in late winter and early spring these old 'stools,' as they are called, throw up plenty of new shoots from the roots, which are cut off when about 2 inches in length, trimmed as cuttings in the manner already described in Chapter Six, inserted in sandy soil in pots or boxes, and rooted in a greenhouse or frame. Sufficient artificial heat to maintain a minimum temperature of 45° is an advantage for the earliest cuttings, but is by no means essential for those taken towards the end of March and during April. Indeed, during the last-named month it is quite possible to propagate border chrysanthemums outdoors without the aid of any glass, by the simple process of lifting the clumps, detaching any young shoots that have a few healthy white rootlets attached, and planting them quite close together on a sheltered sunny border in rather light and well-broken soil, preferably containing a little peat moss or leaf-mould.

Routine for Early Summer When rooted the indoor cuttings will require careful hardening off so that they may be thoroughly accustomed to the outside atmosphere by the first or second week in May (a little

SUPPORT FOR BORDER CHRYSANTHEMUMS
Square mesh tarred twine netting is strained between bamboo canes while the plants are still small. The shoots grow up between the netting and find the necessary supports.

later in Scotland and the North of England). Meanwhile they should be making good growth and must be potted up separately in 3-inch pots or given more room in a frame to prevent them from becoming overcrowded. For this purpose a compost of four parts of loam, one part of leaf-mould or peat moss, one part of sand and a sprinkling of bone-meal will be found suitable.

The rather complicated processes of stopping and timing which are practised by growers of exhibition chrysanthemums are not in the least necessary with outdoor varieties, which are grown principally for garden decoration or for cutting. With these it is quite sufficient to stop the plants once, about a week after they are planted out. This will induce a good branching habit and encourage plenty of flowers on each plant. Stopping simply consists in pinching out the growing point of each shoot between finger and thumb. If extra-good flowers are required, the final number of stems after the second stopping should be reduced to ten or twelve, and only one flower bud should be allowed to remain on each of these. Surrounding shoots should be rubbed out carefully when still quite small.

Site The outdoor beds for border chrysanthemums must be in an open sunny position. Preparation will consist in deep digging, together with incorporation of a moderate dressing of well-rotted manure and a good

PROTECTION FOR
LATE FLOWERS
A shelter of glass substitute can be erected to protect blooms from rain or soot.

dusting of basic slag or bonemeal as a finish-off. Plants should be given plenty of room. If in rows, these should be fully 2 feet apart, with 18 inches from bud to plant. Each plant will require a good stake, or, better still, three or four stakes, so placed that growth is spread out and light and air admitted. During the summer the soil between the plants must be hoed frequently and growth encouraged by liberal watering, together with the use of liquid manures, for which purpose it is difficult to beat the old-fashioned practice of steeping a bag of dung or soot in a tub of water and using the liquor diluted to a pale straw colour. Reliable artificial fertilizers make a useful variation from this staple diet. A good proprietary brand can be used for this purpose, or a fertilizer prepared at home with two parts of sulphate of ammonia, one part of sulphate of potash, one part of dried blood crystals, and four parts of superphosphate. One ounce of this mixture is dissolved in four gallons of water and applied freely.

Chrysanthemums are very liable to be attacked by aphides and capsid bugs. Weekly syringeing from June to September with a nicotine or HETP insecticide will keep the plants clean.

CHAPTER TWENTY-FOUR

Violas, Pansies, and
Sweet Violets

THE unbotanical reader may wonder why the sweet violet should be included in a chapter with plants as unlike it as the pansy and the viola. The reason is that, though at first sight outwardly dissimilar, all three are very closely related, belonging to the same genus or family, which the botanist comprehensively names 'viola.'

Both pansies and violas are very largely grown for exhibition, especially in the North of England, but they are also first-rate plants for garden decoration, for they are very free flowering and, with proper culture, will continue to bloom for several months. Cultural methods vary considerably according to the purpose for which the flowers are required, while, similarly, varieties that are paramount for show purposes are by no means always the best for bedding.

Pansies The pansy will grow almost anywhere, but if it is to give of its very best it must receive generous and careful treatment. The plants thrive in a cool atmosphere, and so in all gardens they should, if possible, be planted in a situation in which they will be partially shaded during the hottest hours of the day in high summer. A rich, moist, and rather sandy soil is best, and with this should be mixed some well-decayed manure, such as that from a spent mushroom bed or hotbed, some good leaf-mould, and plenty of grit or sharp sand.

Named pansies are now chiefly grown for show, and these are propagated by cuttings. For all ordinary purposes reliable strains from seed, offered by firms of repute, may be grown with all confidence. A catalogue will enlighten the would-be pansy grower as to the amazing range of rich colours exhibited by this grand old garden plant.

Sowing the Seed There are two seasons of the year at which seeds may be sown: in June for transplanting in the autumn, and in August and September for the spring. A June sowing has the advantage that stronger plants are obtained before winter, and there is consequently less fear of loss.

It is convenient to sow the seed in pans or boxes of fine and light soil in a cold frame, but they may also be germinated in the open in a well-

Left: Two good calceolaria cuttings trimmed ready for insertion. *Right:* The cuttings dibbled into an unheated frame in which they will pass the winter.

Left: Removing side shoots and tendrils from sweet peas to be grown on the cordon system. *Right:* Cordon trained sweet peas.

Left: Pinching out the tips of chrysanthemums to encourage branching. *Right:* The result of pinching after a few weeks. Several side growths are forming.

Left: Disbudding a large decorative dahlia. Only one bud per stem will be retained.
Right: Night protection for a newly planted dahlia. The pot must be removed by day.

prepared border, preferably a little shaded, in which the soil has been broken down to a fine crumbling tilth. In either case the seeds should be very thinly covered and kept moist. If the seedlings are overcrowded they are liable to damp off, hence the great importance of always sowing thinly. They should be transplanted into other boxes or into a prepared bed with a fine surface as soon as they can be conveniently handled.

Planting in Permanent Quarters Should the weather be dry, the plants must be watered freely. At no time will pansies thrive in a parched soil. When the plants are well rooted and sufficiently sturdy they may be

BAD AND GOOD PANSY CUTTINGS
The shoot on the left is useless as it is hollow at the base. The one on the right is ideal, the lower leaves need removing as indicated.

transferred to their flowering quarters, in soil prepared as before. The site should be prepared some time previous to planting, in order that the soil may settle and be more easily brought to a fine tilth when required. Rather deep planting is recommended, as it places the roots in a cooler and moister medium than if they were near the surface.

The soil should be stirred repeatedly with a Dutch hoe or a small hand fork, but never deeply, or the roots may be injured.

Pansies for Exhibition If exhibition flowers are desired, only one main shoot should be allowed to remain on each plant, the others being removed as soon as they are formed. When the flowering season begins

L

the plants will benefit from a mulching of old potting soil, leaf-mould, and old manure thoroughly mixed together. This treatment should be repeated later in the season. It will prolong the supply of good flowers and invigorate the plants. All faded blooms must be removed at once. If they are allowed to remain the plants will weaken, with a corresponding paucity of blossoms.

Taking Cuttings As already explained, the best selected and named varieties favoured by the leading exhibition growers must be propagated by means of cuttings. These are obtained towards the end of the

PREPARING FOR CUTTINGS

Pansies or violas required for propagation should be cut back fairly severely towards the end of July.

summer. The first step towards this end must be taken in July or early August. This consists in cutting back a proportion of the old plants and covering the roots with a specially prepared compost of sandy soil. The object is to encourage the production of plenty of new growth from the base.

Do not be afraid to treat the plants fairly drastically. Gather all the top growth in one hand, and shear it off cleanly with a sharp knife about an inch, or even a little less, from the soil. Pass some sandy loam through a ½-inch-mesh sieve, and mix with this half its bulk of sand and the same quantity of sifted leaf-mould. Two or three handfuls of this prepared compost should then be scattered over the crown of the pansy, so as almost to bury the severed stumps. Finally, if the weather is dry, give a good soaking with water, sufficiently to moisten the soil thoroughly to a depth of 6 inches or more.

In a very short time young shoots will start to grow freely from the roots. When these are from 2 to 3 inches in length they should be cut off low down with a sharp knife, trimmed as cuttings in the manner already described in Chapter Six, and dibbled into sandy soil in a cold frame.

INSERTING THE PANSY CUTTING

A correctly prepared cutting which should be inserted in sandy soil to the depth indicated by the line.

They must be watered in very freely and should then be shaded with thin sacking or newspapers until they are rooted. After this shading is dispensed with and ventilation given with increasing freedom until, by the end of September, the lights will be required only at night and during very cold weather. Pansies are really quite hardy and will not tolerate unnecessary coddling.

Bedding Violas The modern bedding viola, as distinct from exhibition varieties, is endowed with all the virtues of the ideal bedding plant. For abundance of growth and continuity of flowering there are few dwarf plants to rival it, and—a most important point—its cultural demands are of the simplest.

The Exhibition Viola This is, practically speaking, a race distinct. For years the raisers of these varieties have been actuated by one ideal only —the size and quality of the flowers. The great majority of the exhibition kinds are coarse, straggly growers, and unless the real intention is to grow flowers for the show bench the amateur will be well advised to steer clear of them.

Though violas may be raised from seed in the same manner as pansies, the usual practice is to grow named varieties from cuttings. These are taken in the late summer in the same way as pansy cuttings, the plants receiving similar preparation. There are, however, nowadays several selected forms which will breed true from seed, a notable example being the fine apricot bedder Chantreyland.

Preparing for Violas The beginner will find no better time than the spring for making a start. Nurserymen then have ready for distribution sturdy young plants raised from cuttings taken in the autumn. They are at just the right stage for successful transplanting. Given good treatment, they will develop into strong clumps by the end of the season, providing an ample stock to work on in future years.

Any soil will grow violas if proper attention is given to its preparation. Contrary to general belief, they are deeply rooting plants, delighting in a cool, moist root run, and unless this is provided there is always a danger of the plants collapsing through lack of moisture during hot, dry weather. For this reason the beds should be dug or trenched and well enriched in the manner already described for pansies. Nine inches apart is a good distance at which to set the plants. For massed effects in beds or edgings they may be a little closer, but do not make the mistake of overcrowding them. A hole large enough to accommodate all the roots without curling or twisting must be made for each plant, and the soil round them must be well firmed down. If the soil is on the dry side it is also as well to water the plants in with a good soaking of clear water.

During the summer months the treatment is the same as for pansies. Similarly, if exhibition blooms are required, each plant must be allowed to form only one strong shoot.

Sweet Violets Few flowers are more welcome from January onwards than the fragrant violet, and it is a simple matter to have an abundance of bloom at that time of the year if a cold frame is available. Indeed, even without the advantage of any artificial protection it is possible to enjoy violets of good quality from quite early in the year.

No mystery surrounds the culture of the violet, the only important points being to obtain sturdy, pest-free clumps during the summer months for lifting and framing in the autumn, and to maintain an abundant supply of air during the winter months. Coddling the violet will not have, and shows its resentment by turning yellow in the leaf and rotting at the crown.

April is a good month during which to make a start, for then young rooted cuttings can be purchased quite cheaply. These are not placed in frames at once, but are grown on during the summer in outdoor beds.

The ideal soil for violets is a rather heavy loam, tending to moistness, though neither stagnant nor cold. The situation should, for preference, be a little shaded—as, for example, a north slope or on the shady side of a fence or wall. But it must not be heavily overhung with trees. If the soil is naturally light or sandy it may be improved by working in well-rotted cow or pig manure and thoroughly decayed vegetable refuse.

Single and semi-double violets are more vigorous than double-flowered Parma violets, and consequently must be given more space in the summer beds. Double varieties may be 9 inches apart in rows 1 foot apart, but single and semi-double kinds should be given at least 3 inches more space each way. A little extra room will be all to the good if plenty of ground is available.

Removal of Runners During the summer the young plants will throw out a number of long trailing shoots or runners. These must be removed

VIOLET DIVISION FOR
PLANTING OUT
*A rooted runner is being
detached for propagation.*

as fast as they appear, for they are useless from the point of view of flower production. Cuttings may be prepared from the best and rooted in a frame in a compost containing plenty of sand and leaf mould.

These will be ready for planting out the following spring. Alternatively propagation can be effected by detaching young rooted pieces from the old clumps in the spring.

Red Spider The only pest that is likely to give serious trouble during the summer is red spider, and this will not prove serious unless the weather turns exceptionally hot or the violets are planted in a dry soil and sunny position. The first noticeable sign of this pest is usually a mottled yellowing of the foliage, and if this condition is noticed it is advisable to spray the plants thoroughly with a solution of soft soap—1 ounce dissolved in a gallon of soft water. Alternatively nicotine may be used, mixing $\frac{3}{4}$ ounce of best 97% purity nicotine with 10 gallons of water. Great care must be taken to wet the under-surface of the leaves thoroughly—not an easy matter with violets, as the plants are so compact and many of the leaves near the ground. However, a much more effective control of red spider is obtained by spraying with a preparation containing chlorparacide according to manufacturer's instructions.

Throughout the growing season the violet appreciates an abundant supply of moisture and plenty of food. Frequent applications of weak liquid manure will aid the production of big, healthy foliage, but it must be understood that it is essential that this feed should be really weak. Continual surface cultivation is also of great service in encouraging healthy growth and keeping down weeds.

Preparation of Frames for Winter Flowers If the plants are to be put in a frame they should be ready for lifting by the end of September. It is a good plan to prepare the soil in the frames some weeks beforehand, so that it may have time to settle. Should there be any wireworms or other grubs in the meadow loam used, these can be destroyed by a good soil fumigant. The frames must have some rough drainage material placed in the bottom, and should be filled with a compost made up of two parts of fibrous meadow loam, one part of sweet old leaf-mould, and one part of sharp sand. This should be made up to within 6 inches of the glass. This is a point of considerable importance, as violets require all the light possible during the dull winter months. If they are a foot or more from the glass, they are almost sure to become diseased and mouldy. Ventilation should be given freely whenever the weather is favourable. Indeed, the lights will only be required at night and during really cold weather. Water should be given sparingly, but in sufficient quantity to keep the soil just moist right through.

Winter Flowers Out of Doors Where it is intended to grow violets out of doors all the year round (and this is quite possible if the right varieties are chosen), it is best to plant them in their permanent positions in May rather than subject them to the further check of a shift in September. A sheltered border or beds between fruit trees should be chosen, so that they may have a measure of protection from winter frosts and be encouraged to bloom early. The flowers should be picked daily, for this encourages further productiveness.

CHAPTER TWENTY-FIVE

Flower Garden Enemies

THE various plants grown in the flower garden are all more or less subject to attack by a variety of foes, and a detailed description of all these would necessitate quite a lengthy treatise. Fortunately, however, such an account is quite unnecessary, for the gardener can very easily learn to counter all attacks effectively if he is able to ascertain to which of three or four principal types the particular foe involved belongs.

Diagnosis The first necessity is to distinguish between a pest and a disease. The former belongs to the animal kingdom and the latter to the vegetable; in consequence the methods of control are fundamentally

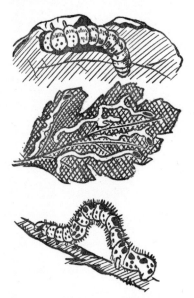

BITING PESTS

Top and bottom are typical caterpillars, while in the centre is a chrysanthemum leaf damaged by the leaf-mining maggot.

different. Typical examples of common pests are caterpillars and greenfly, while familiar diseases are mildew and canker, both of which are caused by fungi. If the foliage of the attacked plant shows clean-edged holes or pale discolorations without any sign of mouldy-looking outgrowths, pests may be suspected, and a closer examination, aided if necessary by a small pocket lens or a night search with an electric torch, will probably reveal the enemy. But should the damage take the form of brownish blotches or streaks, margined by more or less definite zones of a different colour, or, alternatively, if leaves and stems become covered in greyish or whitish mould, it is practically certain that a disease is at work, and probably one of fungal origin. These tests are not infallible, but will serve as a very good general guide.

Let us suppose that the beginner has satisfied himself that his plants have been attacked by a pest. The next step is to discover whether it is what is known as a biting pest or a sucking pest. Caterpillars are an example of the former, for they feed by biting holes in the leaves or

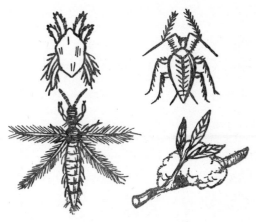

TYPICAL SUCKING INSECTS

Top left; red spider. Top right; greenfly. Bottom left; adult thrips. All much enlarged. Bottom right; cuckoo spit or leaf-hopper.

stems; but the greenfly do not make any holes that are visible, instead they feed on the juices of the plant by inserting a tiny proboscis or sucking apparatus right down into the stem or leaf.

Attacking the Enemy Having got thus far, the gardener is well on the way to deciding the best method of launching a counter-attack, for biting pests can almost invariably be destroyed most readily by poisoning their food, while sucking pests can be got rid of equally quickly by poisoning them with a contact wash such as nicotine or HETP.

If it is a caterpillar, weevil, or some other small creature that is devouring the leaves of the plant, the gardener can spray the foliage thoroughly with a poisonous insecticide. Most effective substances are DDT and gamma-BHC, but derris is also frequently used because it is far less poisonous to human beings and so much safer to handle. These preparations can be purchased through any dealer in horticultural sundries, and the maker's directions as to mixing should be followed closely. The important thing is to cover all the foliage on both surfaces with a thin film of the insecticide, so that the pests cannot take a bite anywhere without getting poisoned. It is always advisable to repeat the application two or three times at intervals of a week or so, in order that new leaves and shoots may also be protected.

Leaf-Mining Maggot There is one important biting pest that lives on the leaves of plants and yet cannot be destroyed by the ordinary methods explained above. This is the larva of the marguerite fly, known as the leaf-mining maggot because it lives within the tissues of the leaf, tunnelling its way along and making very distinctive white, snaky tracks. Ordinary sprays will not reach it, but it can be destroyed by spraying with a special nicotine leaf-miner insecticide that can be purchased from dealers in horticultural sundries.

Slugs and Snails If the attack is from the soil by slugs or snails, it is more practicable to lay a poison bait than to spray the foliage. For this purpose metaldehyde and bran is very effective. The method of preparation is to crush 1 oz. of metaldehyde very finely and mix it thoroughly with 3 lb. of slightly moistened bran. Then little heaps of the mixture are placed here and there where the slugs and woodlice or other pests are likely to come. It is advisable to place a couple of boards or bricks in such a manner as to prevent domestic animals taking the bait.

Mice and Rats These can also be poisoned, one of the most effective substances for this purpose being phosphorus paste. This can be purchased from any chemist, and should be spread thickly on small cubes of bread. Once again it is necessary to take precautions to prevent domestic animals from devouring the poisoned bait.

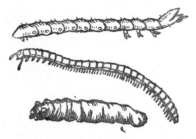

SOIL FOES

Top; wireworm (enlarged about twice). Centre; millepede. Bottom; leather-jacket (slightly reduced).

Soil Pests Biting insects that live deep down in the soil—as, for example, wireworms, leather-jackets, and millepedes—can usually be disposed of most rapidly by fumigating the soil when it is vacant. To do this holes are bored every few inches with a good stout dibber and a little naphthalene is placed in each. Then the holes are immediately blocked up with soil and, if the area is a small one, damp sacks are placed on the surface as an additional precaution against fumes escaping. An average dose is about 4 oz. of naphthalene per square yard, and the ground should not be used for about a month. Many soil pests can also be trapped by placing sliced potatoes or turnips or scooped-out oranges here and there on the surface of the ground and examining them daily. Soil insecticides containing gamma-BHC can also be obtained and are very effective in destroying wireworms. They are forked in according to manufacturer's instructions.

Contact Washes As previously stated, sucking pests such as greenfly, blackfly, red spider, thrips, and cuckoo spit (known also as frog-hopper) cannot be poisoned, as they do not actually eat the leaves or stems. Instead they are sprayed with an insecticide such as nicotine or HETP or with one of the proprietary insecticides advertised for this type of pest. Here the important thing is to get the spray right into contact with the bodies of the insects, which necessitates using an apparatus that is capable of delivering the insecticide in a fairly fine but forceful and penetrating spray. The nicotine, HETP, or proprietary insecticides must be used in accordance with manufacturer's instructions as to strength. For the control of red spider new preparations containing chlor-paracide are being developed and promise to be very effective. These should soon be available commercially.

Fungicides Diseases are, as already explained, frequently of fungal origin and can generally be kept under control by spraying with a fungicide containing either sulphur or some copper salt as its active principle. Probably the safest plan is to purchase a reliable proprietary fungicide and use it exactly as instructed by the chemist who prepared it, but if the beginner prefers to mix his own sprays a useful solution for general purposes can be made by dissolving $\frac{1}{4}$ oz. of potassium sulphide (liver of sulphur) and 1 oz. of soft soap in each gallon of water.

These liquid fungicides should be applied in the same way as the insecticides used against biting insects; that is to say, all leaves and shoots should be covered thoroughly with a fine film of spray so that any spore that happens to alight on them will be killed as soon as it starts into growth. In order that new growth may be protected, spraying should be repeated from time to time. Ordinary flowers of sulphur can also be used dry as a fungicide, either being applied from one of the special blowers sold by nurserymen for this purpose or else placed in a muslin bag and shaken over the plants.

III

THE GREENHOUSE

CHAPTER TWENTY-SIX

Choosing a Greenhouse

WITH the aid of a glass-covered structure a great deal of young stock which would otherwise have to be purchased may be raised from seeds or cuttings for the outside garden. For early vegetables, too, a greenhouse or frame is particularly useful, especially for cauliflowers, onions, tomatoes, and celery. A greenhouse affords shelter all through the winter to plants which could not survive outdoors. Fuchsias, hydrangeas, and heliotrope are good examples. Again, even a small house will usually provide a few plants for the dwelling-house—a primula or cyclamen, a fern or two, or a bunch of late chrysanthemums for Christmas—while, given a larger structure fitted with an adequate heating apparatus, the amateur gardener's interests are immediately widened in the most enticing manner, a whole range of tropical and subtropical plants coming within his scope.

Site for the Greenhouse The type of house to be built will depend very largely on the site at disposal. The main thing to be borne in mind is that, while a greenhouse is best built in the most sheltered spot in the garden, it needs all the light possible. Trees will provide some form of shelter, but it would be quite wrong to have a glass structure immediately below or even close to large trees. Where possible the greenhouse should always be built on the south side of any building, wall, or other high shelter, so that it may not be cut off from any sunlight. If several houses of the span-roof type are to be erected, they should run north and south so that each receives an equal amount of light.

What Type of Greenhouse A very popular type of greenhouse is the 'lean-to' house, built against a wall. Such useful structures have much in their favour, especially the fact that, if built on the sheltered side of the dwelling, they resist the effects of frost far better than a greenhouse built in the open. It is usually possible to carry the roof somewhat higher in

TWO TYPES OF GREENHOUSE

A lean-to house on the left and on the right a modern structure in which the glass is brought down to the ground, allowing more light to the plants.

THE GREENHOUSE SHELF

A shelf near the glass is ideal for hardening off, drying or ripening many plants.

this type, so that the back wall, if covered with a trellis, can be used for growing climbing plants.

The span-roof type of greenhouse, with a path running through the centre and staging on both sides, gives the maximum of light. It need not be very high, though that point governs to some extent the character of the plants that may occupy the house.

Shelves should be placed over the path so that the drip does no damage. They should be far enough away from the glass to allow watering to be done with a short-spouted can, thus avoiding the necessity of taking the plants down each time they require moisture.

Hanging Baskets in the Greenhouse Hanging baskets are best hung from the ironwork of the house rather than from the rafters. Heavy weights suspended from a sash-bar will gradually bend it, and cracked panes of glass will result. The path, especially if a door leads directly into it from the living-rooms, should be made of tile, stone, or cement, but borders of soil may be left with advantage on each side.

Stagings are usually made of battens with 1-inch openings between them. This allows free circulation of air, but there is no reason to suppose this is always essential, because closed staging is preferable for

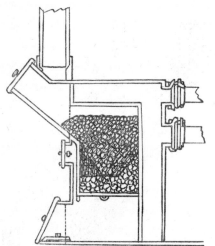

A USEFUL TYPE OF BOILER
This is a good example of the small horseshoe type with automatic draught control, ensuring steady burning for many hours.

some classes of moisture-loving plants; such stages are covered with shingle, shell, gravel, breeze, or similar material. Removable staging is of great advantage in many small houses.

Greenhouse Management Correct ventilation of any greenhouse, large or small, is of the utmost importance, and, when building a span-roofed house, care must be taken to have ventilating lights on both sides of the roof and walls. All plants live partly on air, which must be freely circulated in order that it may be pure and fresh.

Whether the structure is heated or not will govern the type of plant to be grown. It is wellnigh impossible to exclude frost from an absolutely unheated house, and this necessarily limits its occupants during the winter to more or less hardy plants. Given a heating apparatus that will maintain a minimum of 45° on the coldest nights, the range of plants available is vastly increased, while with 10° more there are few subjects, except those from Equatorial regions, that the enterprising amateur may not attempt with at least a sporting chance of success.

Heating The greatest stumbling block for the amateur who really wants a warm house is that of attention to the fire during his absence, but this is being overcome by the type of boiler that needs no attention for twenty hours, by the use of a gas-heated boiler and by electrical

ARRANGEMENT OF
HOT WATER PIPES

(A) *boiler;* (B) *outflow pipe carrying water to far end of house;* (C) *and* (D) *return pipe;* (E) *expansion tank;* (F) *air outlet;* (G) *support for pipes.*

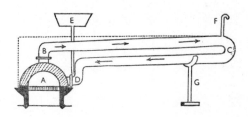

heating. Both gas and electricity may be readily adapted for use with automatic control by means of a thermostat. This will regulate the temperature of the house within a degree or so without any necessity for constant attention. Also there are many heaters of simple design which burn high-grade paraffin, but it is essential to select one that consumes all obnoxious fumes.

Even an unheated frame of the simplest type is an immense asset if properly managed. The sides, if of wood, should be soundly constructed to exclude draughts. Brick or concrete frames are much warmer. Excellent temporary frames may be built with sods of turf stacked grass side downwards. This subject is so important that it is dealt with fully in Chapter Thirty-one.

CHAPTER TWENTY-SEVEN

Greenhouse Management

THE atmosphere in which plants grow is of far greater importance than many people imagine. Out of doors there is little one can do to change its condition, but in a greenhouse the grower has perfect control. It is very little use giving pot plants everything they require in regard to soil and water if the air of the structure in which they are growing is not in the right condition. Frequently amateurs fail, not because they have omitted some detail of routine, but because they have not ventilated their houses in the proper manner.

Humidity Not all plants want the same temperature, and this is well known, but neither do they all require the same atmospheric conditions. Two popular plants, the cucumber and the tomato, provide an excellent example. The former needs an atmosphere heavily charged with moisture, and yet the same amount of humidity would be fatal to the tomato. This means that these two plants cannot be grown in the same house with any degree of success. So it is with many popular greenhouse plants. They need varying degrees of moisture, and it should be the first consideration of the grower to find out just which plants can be grown together under the same conditions. Endless trouble would be saved, for lack of knowledge on this point is the most frequent cause of disappointment with greenhouse plants.

It can be laid down as a definite rule that there are few plants, other than succulents, which really require a perfectly dry atmosphere. For all other subjects there must be some means of creating what is generally termed a 'moist' atmosphere. For many an amateur, who, perforce, must leave his greenhouse from early morning till the evening unattended, this is a very difficult problem; but it can be overcome to a great extent by thoroughly wetting the staging, floor, paths, and side walls of the house (a process technically known as 'damping down') after the daily watering has taken place. In order that this may be effective, all greenhouse floors should retain moisture to some extent, so that this may be supplied to the atmosphere during the day. This cannot happen where the floors are made entirely of cement, but most houses possess only a narrow cement walk, with soil beneath the staging. After

Left: Hessian shading, which can also be used to keep out frost. *Right:* A shelter for the greenhouse boiler to protect it from direct wind.

A neat arrangement for the greenhouse stokehole. Note the coke bin placed conveniently near the fire-box.

Left: Tapping flower-pots to decide whether or not water is required.   *Right:* The correct method of watering established pot plants.

Damping the staging between pot plants to maintain the right degree of moisture in the atmosphere.   Paths and walls may be wetted for the same purpose.

watering a good syringeing should be given between the pots, so as to soak the staging; then, with a can with a coarse rose, all the ground beneath the stagings, the paths, and all walls and brickwork should be watered. These will all give off a good deal of water, and thus an atmosphere in which the plants will grow can be counted on for several hours. If another good damping can be given about midday on very hot, sunny days, so much the better. For some plants, such as gloxinias, gesnerias, *Clerodendrum speciosissimum* (*fallax*), caladiums, and ferns, this midday damping is almost an essential, as they are all lovers of humidity. Plants in bloom always require a drier atmosphere than when they are making foliage.

Night Humidity It may be thought that this moisture in the air is to be encouraged at night to the same extent as in the daytime, but this is not so. That is why experienced gardeners always syringe the greenhouses early in the afternoon. There is then not much danger of the foliage of the plants being wet during the cool hours of the night, nor of the air being overladen with moisture at a time when the plants resent it. Too great humidity at night will only lead to the fruitful multiplication of the most dread of all diseases—mildew.

It is far safer to leave the ventilators open a very little if the afternoon syringeing has to be done rather late, because superfluous moisture will then escape easily.

Ventilation Besides moisture, plants must have fresh air. It is just as necessary for them as it is for human beings. Always try to give sufficient ventilation to ensure that fresh air is constantly available, but never open the ventilators in such a way that a cold draught is created. When wind is blowing, always admit air on the leeward side, leaving the ventilators on the exposed side closed. Even on cold days enough ventilation must be given to ensure that the atmosphere is changed.

For some growing crops the houses must never be tightly closed in summer-time. Tomatoes, especially if grown in small houses, need air continually, and the same advice applies to carnations. This continual fresh air is as important as the soil in which they grow, as they extract food from it.

With certain plants which require a moister and warmer atmosphere, the house must be closed while the sun is still shining, so that some heat is conserved far into the night. The requisite damping down should take place at the same time as the vents are closed. For the majority of what are termed 'greenhouse' plants (begonias, pelargoniums, heliotropes, calceolarias, fuchsias, and verbenas) it will be wise to give a little

M

ventilation all through the night during the summer, and it should be noted that the plants are all the stronger and cleaner—that is, free from pests and diseases—for such treatment.

Shading During the daytime in summer most small greenhouses need some shade from sunshine, otherwise the air will become dry and arid. Shade itself can be equally destructive if used too freely, as it may weaken growth. Careful thought must be given to its density; the

FIXING THE
GREENHOUSE BLIND

A good blind on the sunny side of the house is invaluable in summer. The canvas blind illustrated is moved on a wooden roller (A) *by the cord* (B) *over pulleys* (C).

amateur is always advised to lean towards a light rather than a heavy shading.

The ideal material is a net-like 'scrim,' which, while breaking the direct rays of the sun, allows plenty of light to get into the house. This, if made into roller blinds, can be pulled up and down at will. Alas for many amateurs, the blind must be lowered before they leave for business, and left down until they return. The necessity for thin material is obvious in such cases. Tiffany is a splendid material too, and can be put up temporarily with a few drawing-pins, but permanent shading of this kind is not recommended. The well-known proprietary shadings are best for this type. One point must be stressed, that if put on thickly the plants will suffer. These soluble shadings are all simple to use.

An easily mixed shading is made from starch and whitening. Thin the whitening to the consistency of cream and, after making the starch in the usual way, mix the two together and apply to the glass with a brush or syringe. New lime should never be used for this work. It is injurious to the woodwork and is but a poor substitute for the more suitable whitening.

How and When to Water Correct watering is another matter that the novice must master as rapidly as possible. With this is bound up the equally important question of drainage, a matter that is fully dealt with in the chapter on potting.

THE RIGHT AND WRONG WAY TO WATER	A MOISTURE TEST
Keep the spout of the can close to the rim of the pot as shown on the left, to prevent washing away compost or splashing the plant.	*The pot is tapped with a simply-made wooden hammer or tapper. If a dull note is given the soil is moist, but a hollow ring indicates the need for water.*

How much and how frequently to water are two questions invariably asked by the beginner, and it is quite impossible to answer either of them satisfactorily unless one is on the spot. Moisture must be available to the plants as and when they require it. Too heavy supplies are as detrimental as a shortage, yet it is important to remember that, as the roots of indoor plants are entirely dependent upon the water-can for their supplies, sufficient must be given at each application to soak down to the bottom of the pot, or to the deepest delving roots of plants in the greenhouse border. Once the soil has had time to become consolidated, plants should always be watered from the spout of the can and not through a rose. The spout must be near the soil.

A small wooden-headed hammer or the leg bone of a fowl are invaluable aids when watering pot plants. Each receptacle is tapped before water is given, and according as it rings hollow or dull a supply is given or withheld. The ear will soon become accustomed instantly to detect by this method whether or no a plant is in need of water. It should be noted, however, that cracked pots always give a dull sound, as if the soil within were soaked with water, so this method of testing cannot be satisfactorily applied to them. The soil should be examined carefully instead, and its moisture may also be judged, after a little practice, by lifting the pot momentarily from the stage. Wet compost weighs more than dry.

The supply of water must be varied according to the season of the year and the particular requirements of the plant being cultivated. In a general way less water is required in winter than in summer, but exceptions to this rule occur, particularly with certain plants with tuberous or bulbous roots, such as hippeastrums, nerines, cyclamen, etc.

CHAPTER TWENTY-EIGHT

The Unheated Greenhouse

DURING the summer months artificial warmth is only required in houses devoted to tropical plants, and so at that season the unheated greenhouse is very much on a par with the heated structure for all ordinary purposes. The usual summer-flowering greenhouse plants may be cultivated in it, or, alternatively, it may be cropped with tomatoes. It is, however, necessary to remember that it will be impossible to keep out frost later on, and so it is not advisable to expend much money upon tender perennial plants. Instead, annuals, or at any rate plants treated as such, should be grown so that they may be discarded without loss at the end of the summer and have their place taken by hardier subjects.

Maintaining Interest Through the Winter It is in the autumn that real problems begin to arise, and many a beginner finds himself in a quandary at that season, not knowing with what to fill the house for the winter months. Actually it is quite possible to have something of interest throughout the year, provided the right plants are chosen.

The amateur gardener with limited accommodation under glass will probably find it necessary to make use of the house as a winter store for plants. Summer garden gems that cannot be risked outdoors for the winter may be placed in pots and packed away under and on the staging. Dahlia tubers can be dried off preparatory to being packed away, and all other tuberous plants should have water withheld. Fuchsias will ripen their wood and hydrangeas lose their foliage, all ready for being placed in a safe spot for the winter. Certainly this is all quite good, but there must be something more than this to interest the grower.

First and most important of all, the grower must realize that, as his house is a cold one, he is limited in his choice of plants. Never court disaster and disappointment by attempting to grow things that need a warm atmosphere. It cannot be done. Only such things as will be perfectly safe in a spell of cold weather should be attempted by even the most enthusiastic.

Much can be done to ameliorate conditions, such as making a covering to the roof for use on cold nights. If the house is a small one, this can be done by the simple method of using heavy mats to cover the roof. If it is fairly large, blinds should be fitted that can be let down. A roll of coarse hessian, nailed on to a roller, is a substitute. This covering can be let out each night when frost is expected and will keep out many degrees of frost and in this way extend the possibilities of the house.

Bulbs in the Cold House Up to Christmas many amateurs have their quota of chrysanthemums, and it is from that time onwards that something is most badly needed to give colour. Bulbs will be a great asset in such circumstances. If early hyacinths and tulips are potted up in late summer and buried 3 or 4 inches deep in a bed of ashes outdoors, some of the pots may be brought into the house by the early days of December. The 'prepared' hyacinths, the Duc van Thol tulips, and a few early narcissi, such as Paper White, Golden Spur, Christmas Glory, Cervantes and *N. bulbocodium*, will all come into flower very early and will produce better blooms because they are not hard forced. Pans of crocuses, especially *C. Imperati, C. biflorus*, and *C. Adamii*, will make a show as brilliant as could be desired.

Iris reticulata and its near relatives are far happier in a cold house than in a warm one, and much ought to be made of these plants because they are so lovely and yet so easy to grow. Five bulbs in a 4-inch pot of good fibrous loam, with just a dash of good peat and a little silver sand, will make a lovely potful of rich violet-coloured, delicately fragrant flowers. Early September is a good time for potting, after which the pots should be plunged to the rims for a couple of months in the ash bed out of doors. After that they may be allowed to come along very gently on the shelf near the glass. Do not try to improve the plants by feeding, or they will only make excessive foliage. Rain water is all these little bulbous irises require.

There are chionodoxas, scillas, fritillarias, erythroniums, muscari, tritelias, and a host of other bulbs that are really happy in cool conditions, and which respond easily to pot culture. None of these mentioned requires anything more than the ordinary treatment already outlined for *Iris reticulata*, and none is in any way beyond the beginner. The great thing is to see that they are never over-watered.

Euonymus radicans variegata, cupressus in variety (rock garden kinds), *Eurya latifolia* (with lovely green and white leaves), and small plants of evergreen veronicas all make suitable subjects for growing in pots in the unheated house. They should all be obtainable quite cheaply from any good nursery.

Another excellent method of keeping the house well filled and interesting is to get some forcing plants and pot them up. October is the best month for doing this, because the earlier the plants are potted, the earlier they will bloom. *Dielytra spectabilis, Rhododendron praecox, Prunus triloba, Pyrus malus, Deutzia gracilis, Azalea Hinomayo* and *A. Hinodegeri, Spiraea confusa,* and *S. japonica* are a few that ought to be included in every house. They need only ordinary soil and firm potting, and can be placed outdoors until there is room for them inside.

Primulas Amateurs often ask whether *Primula sinensis* and its *stellata* varieties can be grown in cold houses. They cannot. They may survive, but will never give a really good return for the trouble. A far better type is *Primula malacoides*. It is quite at home in the cold house, and the best varieties are as hardy as the original type. They should never be over-watered, or damping off is likely to result. Though much later flowering, *P. japonica* is a splendid primula and makes a good pot plant. Some of what are termed the alpine primulas are only seen at their best

A PAN OF ALPINES
FOR THE COLD HOUSE
*Included in this collection
are androsace, linum and
erythronium.*

when grown with such protection as the cold house affords. *P. kewensis* is quite safe in a frostproof house and is a good beginner's primula.

Other Flowering Plants There is much to be said for utilizing an unheated house during the winter and spring solely for the accommodation of a collection of early-flowering alpine plants. These may be grown in pots and pans, and a collection can embrace the choicest Kabschia saxifrages, fragrant daphnes, androsaces, and a wide selection of plants that will bloom under glass between January and May. The whole collection may then be transferred either to a frame or to a plunge bed in the open for the summer, when the greenhouse can be put to other uses.

Ample drainage of the pots and pans, a compost freely impregnated with porous stone chippings, and almost unlimited ventilation day and night, except during fogs, are the main principles of successful culture of alpine plants in pans in cold houses.

Another plant worthy of the attention of the amateur is the wallflower. A few plants should be potted up in November and transferred to the house. They do remarkably well if not stifled for want of ventilation. The windows of the house can be wide open for these plants when the weather is mild. The whole of the plant should be kept rather on the dry side, and the soil should never be saturated during a cold spell. Much, if not all, the success wished for will depend on these points.

CHAPTER TWENTY-NINE

Stocking the Warm Greenhouse

I T is astonishing what a difference even a little artificial heat will make to the range of plants that can be grown in the greenhouse. The reason for this is that a great many sub-tropical introductions cannot survive any frost, though they will put up with quite long spells of comparative cold. Some go almost completely to rest in the winter, and this gives them an added power of resistance against low temperatures, and serious damage only occurs when freezing-point is reached.

The reader must not imagine from what has just been written that there is little advantage in being able to maintain higher temperatures. With every rise the gardener's horizon is widened, and, granted the possibility of maintaining a minimum of 70° Fahrenheit, there are few plants that may not be attempted. Usually, however, very high temperatures involve increased cultural difficulties, and so for the beginner the ideal is probably a greenhouse in which an average temperature of 55 to 60° is maintained, falling to 50 or even 45° on very cold nights. The following suggestions are based on the supposition that such conditions are available. Only ornamental plants are dealt with in this chapter. Utility crops, such as tomatoes and cucumbers, will be found in the vegetable section.

A Succession of Flowers The ideal to be aimed at is something of interest throughout the year from January to December. This may tax the ingenuity of the novice, especially if his greenhouse is a small one and he has little alternative accommodation, but it is certainly quite within possibility. A large number of plants can be raised from seed. These will occupy little space while they are still young, and in many cases it is the wisest and most economical policy to throw them away immediately after flowering. Other plants, already referred to briefly, go to rest for some months, usually, but not invariably, in the winter, and while in that state may be stored in cellars, cupboards, spare rooms, and other dry, frostproof places. Then there are autumn-, winter-, and spring-flowering subjects that can be grown outdoors during the summer months, so making way for other plants.

Winter Throughout the winter and spring the beginner could not do better than rely on primulas of the *sinensis*, *obconica*, and *malacoides* types (and particularly the last named, which is very easily grown and does not cause primula rash), cinerarias, greenhouse calceolarias, schizanthus, winter-flowering stocks, cyclamen, and popular bulbs in pots or bowls. The primulas can be raised very readily from seed sown in the greenhouse in June or early July. The young plants are grown in an unheated frame outdoors until the end of September and must be potted on from time to time in sandy loam and leaf-mould. They are usually flowered in pots 4 inches in diameter. In the case of *P. sinensis*

MAKING THE MOST OF THE GREENHOUSE

By judicious use of all available space it is possible to maintain a succession of plants even in a small greenhouse.

it is necessary to be rather careful in watering, as water splashed carelessly over the crown of the plant is apt to cause decay.

Cinerarias and calceolarias can also be raised very readily from seed sown in spring or early summer. It is an excellent plan to make a couple of sowings, one about the beginning of May for early plants and another four or five weeks later to continue the display. The secret of success with both plants lies in cool culture throughout. Like the primulas, they are happiest in a frame during the summer, but must be removed to the greenhouse before there is a danger of frost. Schizanthus can also be sown for spring blooming, but during August and September.

The winter-flowering stocks are always welcome, for in fragrance they rival their summer-flowering cousins. Seed sown in August or September will give sturdy young plants that will commence to flower early the following year. Once again it is necessary to urge that high temperatures are not required. The plants are almost hardy and delight in plenty of ventilation when the weather is favourable.

Cyclamen can also be raised from seed sown during August, but many beginners may prefer to purchase plants just coming into flower in the autumn. Unlike the plants already mentioned, cyclamen are usually grown on from year to year, but their retention need cause no embarrassment during the summer, for from May till September they are best out of the greenhouse. A shady, unheated frame will suit them well during

A METHOD OF GERMINATING
TINY SEEDS

The seeds are sown thinly in a small, well-drained pan which is plunged in peat litter or coconut fibre in a larger pot. Water is only applied to the litter and soaks up gradually into the compost. A pane of glass covers the whole and converts the pot into a miniature close frame.

STARTING AN ARUM LILY

The fleshy roots of this plant should be potted low, with only the crown above the compost. Easily grown in a frost-proof greenhouse, the tuberous roots should be potted in the autumn and given plenty of water.

this period, and for at least a couple of months very little water is necessary, as no growth is made.

Many bulbs can be grown for winter flowering. Hyacinths, daffodils, tulips, *Iris reticulata*, and *I. tingitana* are among the best, as they are showy and easily managed. The important thing is to get them potted or boxed as early in the autumn as possible, so that they may have at least ten weeks plunged outdoors in a bed of ashes or coconut fibre. The bulbs should be covered with at least 4 inches of this, the object being to keep them moist, dark, and at an even temperature, so encouraging vigorous root action before they are transferred to the greenhouse.

The so-called arum lily, so popular for Easter decorations, is neither an arum nor a lily from the botanical standpoint. The correct name for the plant is *Zantedeschia aethiopica*. It can be grown with the greatest of ease in any frost-proof greenhouse. The roots are tuberous, and the plant enjoys a resting season soon after flowering. The usual practice is to pot roots early in the autumn, grow them on in a warm greenhouse with plenty of water until the following June, and then plunge the pots outdoors in a sunny position for the summer months. Little water need

STARTING TUBEROUS ROOTED BEGONIAS

The tubers are arranged close together in trays filled with leaf-mould or peat moss litter, and are watered very moderately.

be given at this season. Care should be taken to prevent water from collecting on the white flower spathes as they are developing.

The spring display can be enhanced with varieties of *Azalea indica* (the well-known Indian azalea), *Deutzia gracilis*, *Genista fragrans*, and other small shrubs in pots. If purchased in the autumn, these may be kept in a frame for a few weeks and transferred to the greenhouse as required. Then when the blooms fade the plants can be returned to the frame until the end of May, when it will be safe to place them outdoors in a sunny, sheltered position for the summer months. During this last period it is an excellent plan to plunge the pots to their rims in a bed of ashes to reduce the necessity for frequent watering.

Perpetual flowering carnations have been purposely omitted, as they are dealt with in Chapter Thirty-three.

Summer For the summer months one may have a great variety of the ordinary annuals so frequently grown in the outdoor garden. Many of these make grand pot plants if sown thinly in 5- or 6-inch pots and thinned to a couple of inches apart when they have made their first rough leaves. Among the best for this purpose are clarkias, *Ursinia anethoides*, rhodanthes, ten-week stocks, salpiglossis, thunbergia, torenia, browallia, alonsoa, scabious, mignonette, verbenas, stock-flowered larkspurs, and *Phacelia campanularia*. Two sowings can be made, one in March and another at the end of April.

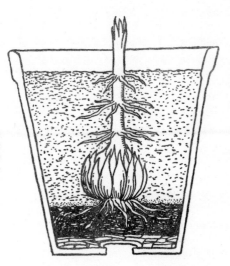

POTTING A
STEM ROOTING LILY
Many lilies make roots from the stems as well as below the bulbs and these varieties should always be potted low and top dressed as they grow.

Tuberous begonias and gloxinias flower freely from June till September and may be raised from seed or purchased as dormant tubers early in the year. The latter method is advised for beginners, as the seed is extremely small and rather difficult to manage. The tubers are started into growth about March in pure leaf-mould and a temperature of 60 to 70°. Later they are potted in an ordinary compost of loam, leaf-mould, and sand, and are watered freely during their period of growth. Shade is necessary during hot sunny weather. In the autumn growth dies down naturally, watering is gradually discontinued, and by the end of October the ripened tubers can be tipped out of their pots and stored in dry coconut fibre in any frostproof place.

Zonal pelargoniums (better known by most beginners as geraniums), heliotropes, and fuchsias are as useful for greenhouse decoration as for bedding outdoors. Moreover, these gay plants are particularly easy to grow, and the only thing that can be said against them is that, as they do not go completely to rest even in the winter, they cannot be removed from their pots at that season and placed in any odd corner. However, there is no objection to cutting the plants back quite hard and arranging them all close together on the most out-of-the-way part of the greenhouse staging.

A number of lilies make admirable pot plants and require little or no artificial heat. The soil used should contain plenty of peat and sand, and generally it is advisable to pot the bulbs singly in pots from 5 to 7 inches in diameter. This work may be done at any time from October till March, after which the pots should be kept in a cool place for a few weeks so that the bulbs may have time to form plenty of roots before commencing to produce flowering stems. Good species for greenhouse culture are *Lilium auratum, regale, longiflorum, Harrisii, speciosum, Henryi*, and *philippinense*. There are also fine varieties of several of these.

Autumn   For the autumn there is, of course, nothing to equal, let alone surpass, the chrysanthemum in all its wonderful variety. But as the culture of this plant is a subject in itself, it is dealt with in a separate chapter. Here it is sufficient to say that, in addition to the Queen of Autumn, the amateur gardener may brighten his greenhouse from September onwards with the ordinary scarlet bedding salvias grown in pots and prevented from flowering in summer by occasional pinching; nerines, which are bulbous plants that are best left undisturbed for several years and given a resting period in a sunny frame each summer; agapanthus, familiar to many as African lilies, and frequently grown in tubs or ornamental vases outdoors; and an early batch of cyclamen.

Foliage Plants   Tender foliage plants are, of course, of interest throughout the year, but assume a special value at times when there are few flowering plants available. One of the easiest to grow is coleus, which has variously coloured leaves and can be raised from cuttings in a close frame in spring (see Chapter Six). Crotons (codiaeum) require a little more heat; the temperature should never fall below 55°. The leaves benefit by an occasional sponging with tepid water containing a few drops of milk, a treatment which also improves the rubber plant, *Ficus elastica*, and the popular aspidistra. Other easily grown greenhouse foliage plants are aralias in variety, *Pandanus Veitchii*, variegated abutilons, and palms (*Cocos Weddeliana* makes a particularly good pot specimen, but likes a rather warm and moist atmosphere).

Potting

O PEN a book on the cultivation of plants in pots, and there will be the familiar formula, 'Loam, seven parts; sphagnum peat, three parts; coarse sand, two parts.' Sometimes more elaborate recipes are given, bringing into use decayed manure, charcoal, bonemeal, and so forth. For succulents burnt earth and pounded earthenware crocks are advocated, but, speaking broadly, it is loam, peat, and leaf-mould for the greater part of potting, seedling-raising, rooting cuttings, and often for preparing beds, borders, or pockets on rock gardens for specially choice plants.

Loam Sometimes, but not as often as it should be, something is mentioned about the widely varying character of loam and of peat, for it is very important to realize that the proportion of leaf-mould, sand, or any other opening material should be regulated in accordance with the density of the other materials. By common consent, turf cut from a meadow or paddock, and stacked until it dies and partially decays, is called loam, but it depends upon the kind of soil in which the grass has grown, and also if the latter was liberally nourished or starved, whether the loam will be strong and substantial or the reverse. If the land is fairly heavy, and sheep, cattle, or horses have regularly grazed upon it, the turf will be strong and full of fibrous roots. Turf cut from a chalky down or a light, sandy waste will not have half the virtue and cannot equal the quality of that cut from good pasture land. Often a stack that has stood little more than six months will be no better than ordinary garden soil when opened out, whereas a good strong pasture, cut 6 inches thick, will still be full of fibre a year or even two years after stacking. That is the kind the plantsman recognizes as first-class potting loam.

Fibre in the Loam The sieve is permitted to ruin an enormous quantity of loam. A heap of freshly sifted soil looks so nice and soft that, to many people, no potting soil is properly prepared if it has not been through the sieve. Actually this treatment invariably robs the loam of a good proportion of its most valuable ingredient—fibre. To discard this is wicked waste, and even for small pots, when the soil must be sifted, it is wise policy to cut much of the fibre into small pieces and remix it with the soil.

When preparing compost for large pots, the proper method is to pull the rough sods of loam apart by hand, tearing them in pieces of convenient size for ramming into the pots to be used. This should always be done for the final potting of chrysanthemums, fuchsias, roses, and other plants in large pots. When using 5-inch or smaller sizes, loam may be prepared by cutting it down from the stack in thin slices, chopping it again when on the ground. Often it is better to sift out the finest particles of earth instead of sacrificing the fibre. Whatever will pass through a ⅜-inch mesh may be mixed with sand and used for seed pans or boxes. The fibre for these is not so essential.

Loam which is deficient in fibre settles down too closely as a result of frequent watering. The fibre helps to maintain a necessary degree of

SIEVING COMPOST

A wooden scraper should always be used when it is necessary to sieve composts, as this enables much valuable fibre to be broken up and pushed through the mesh.

sponginess, which keeps the soil aerated and facilitates percolation of water. There is, in consequence, less need for sand, which has no value as plant food or as an absorbent of liquid manure. It adds porosity only.

Peat The purpose of peat is to help to secure the right degree of sponginess and absorptive power, and to augment the supply of humus when the loam is somewhat deficient in it.

What is known as brown fibrous peat, cut in slabs from either bracken or heather lands, is suitable for hard-wooded plants, which make tough, wiry roots and have an antipathy to lime. Here again hand-pulling is a better method than sifting, for the tough fibre as well as the flaky, spongy substance of the peat is required. For small pots, however, the use of a sieve is sometimes unavoidable, but by using a piece of hard wood, working it to and fro on its edge, it is possible to break and force through the wires the greater portion of the softer parts of the peat, and this does not consolidate, as sifted loam will do. Often in slabs

Left: A lesson in potting. Placing drainage in position. *Right:* Working soil round the roots of the plant to be potted.

Left: The soil is firmed round the edge of the pot with a blunt ended stick. *Right:* The plant correctly potted with the leaves well clear of the soil.

A useful type of frame placed on a hot-bed of decaying stable manure.

A range of frames built against a greenhouse wall. Note the roll of hessian for protection against cold.

PREPARING TO REPOT

The plant is turned out of the old pot by holding it firmly in the pot, inverting it and giving the rim of the pot a sharp rap on the bench. The ball of soil comes away intact and the old crocks can be removed.

of peat one may find pieces of bracken rhizomes, woody bases of heather, etc. All of these should be picked out.

Peat Moss Quite distinct from the peat of moorland or woodland above mentioned there is peat moss or sphagnum peat, which is formed by the accumulation of many years' growth and decay of mosses. It has no stringy fibre, but is light, spongy, capable of opening up close-binding soils, and of holding moisture in loose, porous sands. It is lime-free, and, therefore, cannot do harm to any plant, and, being finely broken, it is convenient for use in quite small pots. Loam deficient in fibre may be mixed with peat moss for potting almost any kind of plant.

John Innes Potting Mixtures What is known as the John Innes potting compost is a standard mixture which may be used for a great variety of plants. It consists of seven parts by loose bulk of medium loam, three parts of sphagnum peat, two parts of coarse sand. It is recommended that the loam be sterilized before use by steaming. The temperature should be raised as rapidly as possible to 200° F. and kept at that for

N

twenty minutes. This should be done before the peat and leaf-mould are added.

A distinctive feature of the John Innes mixtures is that they all contain small quantities of fertilizer. A base mixture is prepared by mixing two parts by weight hoof and horn meal, two parts superphosphate of lime, and one part sulphate of potash. For the standard compost, used for the majority of plants, 4 oz. of this base fertilizer and $\frac{3}{4}$ oz. of ground chalk or limestone are added to each bushel of the mixture of loam, peat, and sand. For very strong rooting plants, such as tomatoes, or for big plants, 8 oz. of base mixture is given, but the chalk or limestone remains as before. For lime-hating plants such as heathers and azaleas the chalk or limestone is omitted.

A similar mixture is recommended for seed sowing. It consists of two parts by loose bulk of medium loam, one part of sphagnum peat, and one part of coarse sand. To each bushel of this mixture is added $1\frac{1}{2}$ oz. of superphosphate of lime and $\frac{3}{4}$ oz. of ground chalk or limestone.

All potting and seed composts should be prepared several days in advance and, if possible, be placed in the greenhouse to warm up before use.

Size of Pot to Use Perhaps the most common of all errors made by beginners in the actual potting of plants is the use of receptacles larger

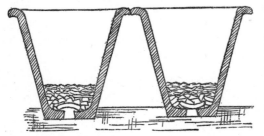

CROCKING

One large crock (piece of broken flower pot) should be placed convex side up over the drainage hole (left) to help to shed the water and not concave side up (right) when it would collect water.

than is necessary. Invariably this overpotting is done under the supposition that the larger the body of soil afforded the roots, the better will be their growth. In fact there is often a danger that, in pot culture, soil that is unoccupied by roots may become sour. In consequence it is seldom wise to use pots many sizes too big. A useful general rule is not to shift a plant into a pot more than two sizes larger than that which it occupied formerly. For first potting use a pot large enough to take the roots comfortably.

There are quite a number of plants which do not flower freely until the roots are quite pot-bound, but with the general run of greenhouse plants it is a mistake to allow the roots to become hopelessly matted round the sides of the pots. Pot-bound roots cannot possibly play their due part in supporting the plant, and there is also a grave risk of their being burnt during hot weather.

In a general way spring is the best time for repotting evergreens and soft-stemmed perennials, whereas greenhouse deciduous shrubs may be potted successfully in the autumn as soon as the leaves fall.

Preparing the Pots There is even a right and a wrong way of crocking

REPOTTING

A large pot is used and the ball of soil and plant are put in the middle, fairly low down.   Compost is added and firmed round the roots.   The finished level should be about an inch below the rim of the pot (right) to allow for watering.

pots. The convex surfaces of the crocks must always be placed uppermost to ensure free outlet for surplus moisture, and to prevent the compost from washing down and clogging up the drainage hole they should be covered with a good layer of very rough material, such as the coarse fibres from loam which has been roughly sifted. One good-sized crock is sufficient for very small pots, but with larger sizes it is advisable to put in a good layer.

One point on which it is sometimes extremely difficult to convince the novice is the folly of using dirty pots. Quite apart from the risk of perpetuating pests and diseases in this manner, dirty pots suffer from another serious drawback—namely, that so tightly will the soil ball cling to them that it will be found almost impossible to knock it out when repotting without breaking the ball and thereby checking root growth. Mossy or slimy growths on the outside of the pots will quickly reduce their porosity, and must also be scrubbed away with a hard brush and water. New pots must always be soaked and allowed to dry naturally for at least twenty-four hours before using. Otherwise the dry earthenware will absorb all moisture from the soil.

Firm potting is an essential in almost every case, but here again some discretion must be exercised, as it is an easy matter to pack the soil so tightly as to render it impossible for the roots to make further progress. The age and strength of the plants must also be taken into consideration, for young seedlings or freshly rooted cuttings can easily be ruined by over-zealous work. As a rule the necessary degree of firmness can be obtained with all plants in pots up to 7 inches in size by rapping the pots on the benches and at the same time pressing the soil down with the thumbs. A blunt-ended potting stick can be used to press the compost between the soil ball and the pot with larger specimens, but again only reasonable pressure must be exerted. The soil should only be filled up to within $\frac{1}{2}$ inch of the rim of the pot to facilitate watering.

Furnishing Hanging Baskets Hanging baskets are first lined with plenty of sphagnum moss, after which the plants are placed in position and surrounded with compost exactly as when potting. They must be well watered.

CHAPTER THIRTY-ONE

The Frame and Plunge Bed

A FRAME is a comparatively shallow wooden, brick, or concrete sided structure covered with a glazed roof or 'light' which is removable at will. It is so useful a structure that, no matter what the size or type of garden, there are few excuses for not possessing one.

Not only can the frame be used as a substitute for a cold greenhouse in gardens where there is no room for the larger building, but, if properly employed with a hot bed, it can form a tiny warm house on its own. Should the gardener already possess a greenhouse, a frame will form a most valuable extension of it, enabling plants to be easily hardened off before being placed in the open. In the tiny concreted yard or roof garden a frame can contain a varied and fascinating collection of alpine plants, while frames are invaluable for raising most bedding plants from seed, for over-wintering them and other half-hardy plants, and for raising early vegetables.

Structure In spite of the perversity of gardeners in referring to frames without hotbeds as 'cold frames,' their object is almost always to keep in as much heat as possible, and for this reason it is essential that they should be well constructed of thick wood, brick, or concrete. It is a waste of money to buy a frame the sides of which are made of thin, unseasoned wood, for the heat will be lost far too readily. The wood should be at least an inch thick and kept in good condition by regular painting every second year.

There is no necessity for a frame to be of any particular size, but the standard size of the lights, which can be purchased separately, is 6 feet long by 4 feet broad, though smaller ones, 4 feet by 3 feet, are readily obtainable. It is a comparatively easy task to make the sides of the frame or row of frames and fit the lights to these, but if this is done the back of the frame must be kept at least 6 inches higher than the front. Where possible the frames should be in a sunny, sheltered position, unless used for propagating cuttings, when the shelter of a north wall is an advantage. Where possible they should be out in the open, so that they can be approached from all sides. This makes for easy working, and the frames can be ventilated by pushing or pulling the lights up or down. Where the frames are built against a wall, as is often the case with structures heated by pipes from the adjoining greenhouse, it is necessary to ventilate in a different manner, each light being propped up on one of its edges and held in position by means of a block of wood suitably notched. In this case the light should be opened on the side away from the prevailing wind.

Drainage The site of the frame must always be well drained, and it is an excellent plan to support the bases of wooden frames on one row of bricks. It is also advisable to remove the soil to a depth of 1 foot from an area slightly larger than that covered by the frame and replace it with

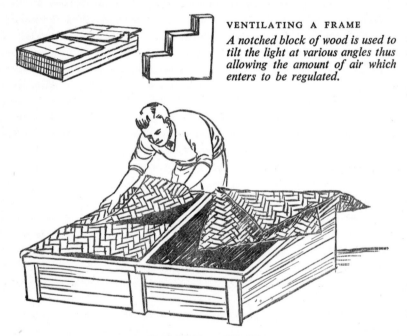

VENTILATING A FRAME

A notched block of wood is used to tilt the light at various angles thus allowing the amount of air which enters to be regulated.

COVERING A FRAME

Stout mats or pieces of good hessian are invaluable for covering frames when frost threatens.   They should be large enough to cover the sides of the frame as well.

at least 9 inches of good drainage material such as broken bricks or ballast. The soil can then be replaced or substituted by a good compost if the plants are to be grown directly in the soil and not in pots or boxes.

Where the frames are to be used solely for housing pots or boxes, the base can be covered with a layer of concrete, which may slope to one corner fitted with a drainage outlet. A layer of washed ashes spread on the concrete will prevent too much moisture from lying in contact with the bases of the plant or seed receptacles.

When cuttings are to be rooted in the frame the sand can be placed directly in the frame, provided it has been supplied with adequate drainage material as just described.

Frames used in the spring for hardening off bedding plants and rooted chrysanthemum cuttings will need to be sufficiently deep to house the rapidly growing shoots. Usually it is possible to raise the sides of an ordinary wooden frame on a row or two of bricks for the last week or two, but alternatively there is no objection to excavating further into the soil. With concrete structures there is nothing for it but to fix boards on the sash bars to take the lights temporarily, but these must be secured very firmly.

A Frame over a Hotbed The hotbed, already referred to, is an ingenious arrangement by which the gardener turns to practical account the heat generated by fermentation. First, a hole is excavated a little larger than the size of the frame available and about 1 foot deep. This is filled with fresh stable manure, preferably rather strawy, trodden firmly down, and more of this material is piled on top to a height of approximately a foot above ground level. This heap, if left for a few days, will soon begin to ferment. A good layer of soil should then be spread over the manure and the frame placed in position on top, but the light should not be put on as yet, nor any plants or seeds introduced, as the temperature will still be too high. After a further day or so, however, the first fierce heat will subside, giving place to a steady, genial warmth which will last for several weeks if the hotbed has been properly constructed. Now is the time to sow seeds, place cuttings in position, or introduce tender plants, such as begonia or dahlia tubers, that are to be started into growth. One warning is necessary—namely, not to start too early with a hotbed, because the heat will not last indefinitely. Hotbeds are most useful if constructed early in March.

Soil Warming by Electricity A modern alternative to the hotbed is soil warming by electric wires or insulated cables buried in the soil. These are most efficient and economical. Both low-voltage and normal domestic voltage apparatus can be purchased. Either should be installed strictly in accordance with manufacturer's instructions.

Frame Management Plants in frames require as much attention as those in the greenhouse. Each will require watering according to its individual needs if in a pot, and the pots should be tapped at least once a day, as explained in Chapter Twenty-seven. Seedlings and cuttings require watering with a very fine-rosed can. Frames containing germinating seeds and newly taken cuttings are usually kept close— that is, given no ventilation—and consequently do not lose as much water as well-ventilated frame plants. These close frames require the extra attention of having the inside of the light wiped regularly early every morning, for during the night drops of water will accumulate freely.

Plunge Beds During the height of the summer, when the frames are used to house tender plants from the greenhouse, it is often a great

A USEFUL PLUNGE BED FOR POT PLANTS

The sides are formed with stout planks, drainage is ensured by a good layer of clinkers, while the pots are plunged in fibre or sand.

saving of labour (and incidentally better for the plants) if the spaces between the pots are filled with washed ashes or small gravel. These materials hold water and keep the pots cool.

From the ashes surrounding pot plants in a frame to a specially made plunge bed is a simple step. A plunge bed is a site used solely for sinking pots in, and is usually made either with the surface flush with the surrounding soil or as illustrated.

In the early autumn the plunge bed will be in great demand for encouraging root growth on freshly potted bulbs. For these pots are not merely sunk to their rims, but covered with 3 or 4 inches of ashes or the more easily handled coconut fibre.

CHAPTER THIRTY-TWO

Greenhouse Chrysanthemums

CHRYSANTHEMUMS are almost hardy plants and so can be grown with ease in a cool greenhouse, but some heat will be needed to keep out frost from the later-flowering varieties. As these are the most valuable flowers for decoration throughout the autumn and early winter months, there are few amateurs who do not try to grow at least a few varieties of the Queen of the Autumn.

There are several different kinds of chrysanthemum. They range from the enormous Large Exhibition (Japanese) blooms through the formal incurved varieties and the late decoratives to the singles, tiny pompons, and cascade forms. It is possible to grow representatives from all the different groups in one collection, as their varying heights allow of their being staged in tiers, and they all require the same atmospheric conditions—namely, as much ventilation as is reasonably possible without creating draughts or lowering the temperature to freezing-point. At no time should the temperature rise above 60°. A night minimum of 45° and a day average of 55° is desirable. While the roots must be kept supplied with sufficient water, the air should not be allowed to become saturated with moisture, and the blooms must be protected from any possible drips from the roof.

One point which will commend the chrysanthemum is the fact that during the summer the plants can be placed out of doors, and in consequence the house is then available for such a summer crop as tomatoes.

Propagation from Seed The young plants can be raised from seed sown early in January in a minimum temperature of 50°, but this method will not yield varieties true to name, and so the more usual method of propagation is by cuttings in winter or early spring. The shoots used for these should be those which grow from the roots rather than from the stem, and they should be firm with short nodes—*i.e.*, spaces between the leaves.

Propagation by Cuttings The method of taking and rooting the cuttings is identical with that described for soft cuttings in Chapter Six. The cuttings may be placed separately in 3-inch pots, or five in a 4-inch pot, or an inch apart in rows in boxes or a bed made up on the staging. As with other cuttings, special care must be taken to prevent loss of water

A 'STOOL'

An old chrysanthemum plant throwing up young shoots suitable for cuttings.

CHRYSANTHEMUM CUTTINGS

The cutting on the left is too small and weak, the one in the centre too spindly and the one on the right is ideal, evenly grown and of medium size.

FIRST POTTING

A healthy young cutting that has made good roots, should be potted up at this stage.

from the soil and leaves before the cuttings have rooted, but it is not advisable to use a high temperature or place the cuttings in a close frame. A light dewing over with tepid water every morning will keep the leaves firm and fresh. As soon as the cuttings start to grow they must be potted on. The plants must never become pot-bound and should be shifted on to larger sizes as they require it. The composts should consist principally of good fibrous loam to which has been added a little fine bonemeal, some well-pounded mortar rubble, and perhaps just a little dried cow or hop manure. As the plants gain in size the composts may with advantage become correspondingly coarser in texture until eventually the sieve is discarded and the loam is simply pulled apart by hand into pieces about the size of a hen's egg.

Stopping When the rooted plant has recovered from the shock of the first potting and reached a height of about 6 inches, it will require to be 'stopped.' This term means that the growing point of the shoot is rubbed

A CHRYSANTHEMUM
CROWN BUD

This bud can be pinched out at the point indicated to encourage further breaking and the shoot to the left of it in the illustration will grow on.

out. The reason for this is that the plant, if left to grow naturally, would form a long stem before it branched, whereas when the growing point is removed the lower buds develop to form branches, making a good bushy plant in much less time. A further reason for stopping the plant is that the side shoots produce much better flowers than the main shoot, and by early stopping these can be had in bloom as much as three weeks in advance of side shoots on a similar but unstopped plant. Stopping is of great importance to those growers who intend to exhibit blooms, for by doing it at just the right times they can have a whole range of plants, the normal flowering periods of which would be some weeks apart, all in flower for a show on a known date.

Results of Stopping After the first stopping several shoots will be formed. The number to be retained will depend upon the type of plant to be grown. If it is to be a specimen plant with countless blooms, as many shoots as possible will be required at each stopping; if a small plant for table decoration on which about six shoots will be needed, three can be retained at this first stopping and two on each of these at the next stopping. The selected shoots should be evenly spaced. Exhibition plants of Japanese chrysanthemums will usually require to be restricted to a single shoot at each stopping, and the strongest should be selected. Exhibition incurved chrysanthemums and exhibition singles are usually restricted to about three or four shoots, and only one flower is allowed to form on each. Only a single shoot is required at the base of one of the trained cascade singles, which are grown at an angle of 45° and bent right down just before flowering.

The first flower bud formed on a plant that has not been stopped is known as the 'break' bud, as its formation causes the buds lower down the stem to start growing, or 'break.' Only under exceptional circumstances is this kept. The flower buds that form on the first side shoots, whether the plant is stopped or allowed to break naturally, are known as first 'crown buds'. A large number of varieties are flowered on these buds; others, however, would be much too early for show purposes if these buds were allowed to bloom, and therefore the shoots are stopped again.

When to Stop The actual date for this operation will vary with the variety, but the shoot or shoots will be at least 6 inches long at the time of stopping. These shoots may produce one of two kinds of buds: either a single bud similar to a first crown bud, in which case it is termed a 'second crown' bud, or one surrounded by smaller flower buds instead of by leafy shoots, when it is known as a 'terminal' bud. If the second crown bud will produce a satisfactory bloom about the time of the main flower shows (usually held early in November), no side shoots must be allowed to grow on the stem. Very occasionally, however, a third stopping is necessary and a side shoot is grown on once again until a terminal bud is obtained, when all the tiny side buds will have to be rubbed out very carefully to leave only the central bloom for exhibition. If the plant is not intended for exhibition, but purely for decoration, there is no need to carry out such elaborate disbudding nor to reduce the number of flowering stems so drastically, though it is always wise to stop at least once to induce a bushy habit. For these plants the first stopping is usually done about the middle of March and a second stopping given in June.

It may appear from the foregoing outline that the novice has a very difficult task before him when he first sets out to grow exhibition chrysanthemums, but as a matter of fact his troubles are considerably smoothed out by the detailed information included in almost all the

CHRYSANTHEMUM TERMINOLOGY

The ultimate object in 'stopping' and the position of the buds is illustrated.

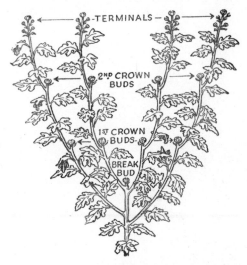

catalogues issued by specialists. These give full instructions as to dates for stopping and buds to be retained. Sometimes the expressions 'natural break,' 'natural first crown' or even 'natural second crown' will be found. These simply mean that no artificial stopping is recommended, but that the plants are to be allowed to grow on naturally, producing one flower bud after another until the desired stage is reached. Of course, the premature buds are removed and not permitted to develop into flowers.

Summer Quarters By the end of May the plants should have been so well hardened off, either in the greenhouse or in a frame, that they can be placed out of doors without damage. There are two methods of dealing with chrysanthemums during the summer, the choice depending mainly upon the water supply available. They can either be set out in their pots on a specially prepared site, or they can be planted out in a border. If the gardener has plenty of time for watering during the summer (and it is almost essential to water pot plants in the middle of the day), the pot method is to be preferred, as the plants then suffer no check due to shifting in the autumn. But if such attention to watering cannot be given regularly, it is far better that the chrysanthemums should be planted out in a well-dug sunny border which has been enriched with rotted manure or bonemeal. In this they are not likely to suffer from lack of water except during severe drought, provided the surface is kept well hoed. The spacing will depend on the number of shoots to be retained. All plants must be adequately staked from the outset. The planting-out method is not suitable for exhibition chrysanthemums.

Plants kept out of doors in their pots should be arranged as far as

CHRYSANTHEMUMS IN SUMMER QUARTERS

The pots have been stood on a plank to keep their drainage holes free of soil and to prevent worms from entering, and the bamboo canes supporting the stems are themselves made secure to a straining wire. Testing the pots before watering is also shown (inset).

possible in rows running north and south, with the tallest varieties at the north end. The plants must be spaced to allow light to reach all the leaves, and the shoots secured by tying them to wires run through the lines. The pots may stand along the edges of the paths of the fruit garden or other similar open place or on a specially prepared concrete site. Where the plants are stood upon soil it is advisable to place a piece of slate under each pot or stand them on planks to keep out worms. The plants should be watered freely as soon as the pots give a hollow sound when tapped with a piece of hardwood or chicken bone. Liquid

stimulants can also be applied in moderation until the flower buds
begin to show the colour of their petals. The more feeding can be varied
the better, it being an excellent plan to keep one tub of water with a
sack of dung steeping in it, another with soot, and to further vary these
natural stimulants with a good proprietary chemical fertilizer or a home-
made mixture of four parts of superphosphate, two parts of sulphate
of ammonia, one part dried blood crystals, and one part sulphate of
potash dissolved in water at the rate of about ½ oz. per gallon, and
applied fairly freely.

The plants should be taken into the house again by the middle of

**LIFTING DECORATIVE
CHRYSANTHEMUMS
FOR HOUSING**
*Cuts are made with a sharp
spade round each plant about
a fortnight before lifting it.
Later they can be taken up
with as little root disturbance
as possible.*

September to prevent damage by early frosts. In order to avoid too
great a shock to the plants taken from the open ground, they should be
treated in the manner shown in the illustration.

Chrysanthemums are sometimes attacked by the leaf-mining maggot
and by chrysanthemum rust.

Fumigating the Greenhouse If it is necessary to fumigate a mixed
greenhouse with tetrachlorethane to eradicate white fly, all chrysanthemums must be removed first, or they will be damaged. The plants
must be looked over very carefully before being taken in again, or the
pest may be reintroduced.

CHAPTER THIRTY-THREE

Perpetual-Flowering Carnations

No greenhouse flower surpasses the tree or perpetual-flowering carnation as a cut bloom, and it is not surprising that most amateur gardeners who possess a greenhouse sooner or later desire to grow a collection of these wonderfully prolific plants. Culture does not present any great difficulties, provided the peculiar needs of the plants are clearly understood and met.

Wherever possible a small greenhouse should be provided for the sole purpose of accommodating carnations. For preference it should be of the span-roof type, fitted with ventilating windows each side of the ridge, also in each gable end of the roof, but a lean-to house may be used. For winter flowering the house must be heated with an apparatus capable of maintaining an even temperature of 50° throughout the winter nights. The house must be situated where it can receive full sunlight.

Building up a Stock A start is usually made by obtaining small plants to grow on. Choice of colours and varieties is a matter for the grower to decide. Most of the leading specialists in carnations offer collections of good kinds for the convenience of the beginner. Naturally, after the first stock is obtained growers will wish to raise their own plants. This is done by means of cuttings, which are made from growths put out from the leaf joints on the flower stems, sometimes before the bud opens, sometimes after the flower has been removed. If suitable growths are slow in appearing when required, it is a good practice to take off the bud. This causes them to grow more quickly. The growths most suitable for the purpose are usually about half-way up the stem. They should be stiff, about 3 inches long, with very little space between leaves. Sever the shoots from the plant by gently pulling them away. A small fragment of bark should come away from the older stem with each shoot. This, when trimmed neatly, as described in Chapter Six, makes the 'heel.'

Striking Cuttings The time for rooting cuttings is from November into March, though some very successful growers, especially in the colder northern counties, take their main batch in late summer and early autumn. For easy rooting, plain silver sand or a very sandy mixture is

Left: Summer pruning raspberries by removing the old fruiting canes. *Right:* Summer pruning side growths of a gooseberry bush to encourage production of spurs.

Left: First thinning out of pear fruitlets after a heavy set. *Right:* Testing a pear to find out if it is ready to be picked. It should part easily from the tree.

Summer pruning the laterals on a cordon trained apple tree to five leaves.

Left: Reducing an old and overgrown spur on an apple tree. *Right:* A young bus apple after correct pruning to encourage branch development.

used. This should be well firmed into 5- or 6-inch pots or pans. After a thorough soaking with water, the cuttings are inserted round the edge of the pot, and about 2½ inches apart, if pans are employed. Care must be taken that cuttings are not put in deeply; ½ inch is quite sufficient, and the base must rest on the medium, and not be suspended in air in a deep cavity made by the dibber.

To facilitate successful rooting, a little bottom heat is required. This is obtained by the use of a propagating frame, in which the receptacles

PERPETUAL FLOWERING
CARNATIONS

A good cutting with 'heel' is shown (F) and a typical plant with side shoots on the left. Of these (B). (C) and (D) will be found most suitable for removal as cuttings, (A) being too near the top and (E) too close to the bottom.

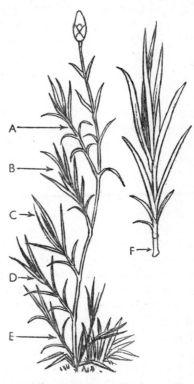

are plunged to the rims in a moisture-holding substance, such as coconut fibre. An illustration is to be found in Chapter Six.

Prepare for Potting For the first three days cuttings require little air, the glass covering only being removed to wipe free of moisture. After this time the glass must be so arranged that just a little air has entrance. This space is increased daily until, by the time the cuttings are rooted, the glass has been dispensed with altogether. The time taken under these conditions is usually just over a month. As soon as rooted, the plants need potting into 2-inch pots. A compost should be made up and warmed

O

in the greenhouse to be ready when required. It should consist of two-thirds loam, one-sixth sand, and one-sixth equal parts wood ash and crushed limestone. Watering should not be overdone, but the plants must never feel the want of it.

Soon the plants will require a further move into 3-inch pots, the potting material being the same as before. Syringeing the plants with clear water now becomes a routine matter; it will be performed daily, except on dull days, and does much to get the wood into a nice state to make free 'breaks' after 'stopping.' This is done by taking the growing point off when the rooted cutting is a matter of 4 inches, or a little more, in height. Six or seven pairs of leaves will have been made; after stopping, five or six pairs will remain to produce side shoots. Plants obtained from carnation specialists, described as 'stopped' and 'broken,' are in this state of making side growths.

Summer Care In April, when weather permits, young plants may be removed to a cold frame, the bottom of which should be covered with coal ashes, to keep the roots cool and moist. One may guard against frost by covering the lights at night with mats or other protection until that danger is past.

Routine work now consists in watering when necessary, and spraying in dry weather until the plants again require a change of pots. Many growers pot direct into a 6-inch pot in which the plants are to bloom, but an intermediate potting into the 5-inch size is well worth the extra trouble, afterwards the plants being moved into a final 6-, 7-, or 8-inch pot, as is judged to be necessary by their individual size and vigour.

The compost used this time, and for all subsequent potting, will consist of two-thirds loam, one-sixth cow manure (half-rotted), one-sixth wood ash and mortar rubble, with enough sand to give free porosity. Potting must now be done very firmly; perpetual carnations, being fine-rooted, like a compact root run. Staking is now necessary.

After the plants are established in their final larger pots, with the side growths of sufficient length, they should be 'stopped' again, leaving three or four pairs of leaves, after taking off the top of the shoot, as was done at the time of first stopping. As a rule, all growths will not be ready at the same time, and it is sufficient if the longest are done first, leaving the others until they, in their turn, are large enough.

Autumn and Winter Flowers To get autumn and winter flowers, no stopping should be done after the first week in July, any shoots that remain unstopped then being left. All potting, too, should be finished by the end of July.

Perpetual carnations should be taken into the greenhouse at the end of September. The house at first must have full ventilation day and night, in order that the plants may become accustomed to their new conditions before winter.

The grower's whole attention in autumn and winter will be devoted to keeping the atmosphere in the house buoyant and airy by using the

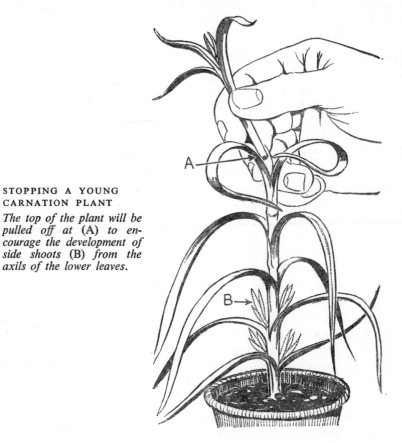

STOPPING A YOUNG CARNATION PLANT

The top of the plant will be pulled off at (A) to encourage the development of side shoots (B) from the axils of the lower leaves.

ventilators with sufficient fire heat to keep the temperature right. When the days are fairly warm and sunny a morning spray may be given over the plants, but it must not be done on damp days, and, as winter comes on, should be discontinued altogether, dry remedies then being used against insects and diseases.

For winter bloom the night temperature in the house should register 50°, and be kept as even as possible, with a daytime rise of 5 to 10°.

Care of Buds and Calyx   Carnations must always be kept well staked to keep the growing stems upright, not only for the sake of tidiness, but for strength also. When buds form, if they grow in clusters and come out on the flower stem, they should be thinned, leaving only the one at the top of each stem to flower. Care must be taken to prevent harm to the flowering bud and stem while this is being done. Many of the newer varieties are not so troublesome in this respect, in many cases just making the single bud, especially at the commencement of the season.

DISBUDDING

A carnation shoot before and after disbudding to encourage fine blooms.

If the calyx of any bud splits, as it is sometimes prone to do if the plant is checked by fluctuations in temperature, improper feeding, or other cause, a calyx band should be put on; the thin wire rings are best for the purpose, though rubber rings or raffia grass may be used. They should be put on just as the bud is opening into flower, to prevent the petals falling outwards.

CHAPTER THIRTY-FOUR

Greenhouse Hygiene

O NE of the advantages—and sometimes disadvantages—of a greenhouse is that it is practically a little kingdom on its own, separated from the outer world by its glass walls. This means that many pests or diseases may be rampant in the garden and yet not find their way into the greenhouse, especially if proper cultural methods and good hygiene are the rule within that structure. On the other hand, an obvious disadvantage of the self-contained kingdom idea is that, once a foe does find its way within the walls, its efforts are concentrated in a very unwelcome manner. For this reason every effort should be made to keep greenhouse plants in perfect health and nip an attack at the earliest possible moment.

Fumigating Outdoors it is necessary to attack the pests by means of sprays or dust spread upon the foliage and stems of the plants. In the greenhouse a far more efficacious and rapid method is possible. Pests can be gassed or, to use the gardening expression, fumigated. If the greenhouse is properly constructed it will not be a difficult matter to make it reasonably airtight by closing the ventilators and sealing the door, and within the house a sufficient concentration of some powerful airborne insecticide can then be obtained to kill every live foe, no matter where it may be hiding.

Nicotine For this purpose various chemicals are available. One of the most generally useful is nicotine. This can be purchased from a dealer in horticultural sundries either in the form of shreds or cones, which have merely to be placed in the house as directed by the manufacturers, lit, and then left to burn themselves out and distribute the fatal fumes, or else in liquid form to be vaporized on special fumigating lamps.

Nicotine fumigation will quickly rid a house of greenfly or any other aphides, but should not be used in greenhouses that are carrying crops of tomatoes, cucumbers, grapes, etc., which are approaching ripeness. The reason for this is that the fumes possess a certain penetrating power, and, as nicotine is poisonous to human beings, it is undesirable that even a minute quantity should be carried to the table.

White Fly needs Special Treatment Unfortunately, one of the commonest of greenhouse pests—namely, white fly—is not affected by nicotine. This foe is very minute, but often present in such immense numbers that if a plant is shaken it appears to be immediately enveloped in a white cloud of tiny flies. To counter this enemy a chemical known as tetrachlorethane is frequently used. It can be purchased under various

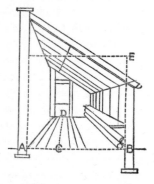

CALCULATING
GREENHOUSE VOLUME
FOR FUMIGATION
In a lean-to house the breadth (AB) *is multiplied by the length* (CD) *and the height* (BE) *halfway up the slope of the roof. If all these measurements are taken in feet or fractions of feet the result will give the volume of the house in cubic feet.*

proprietary names, such as White Fly Vapour, White Fly Death, etc., and is simply sprinkled on the pathway of the greenhouse in the quantity indicated on the container.

Calcium Cyanide   The most powerful of all greenhouse fumigants, and one that is effective against white fly as well as other pests, is calcium cyanide, usually sold under the trade name Cyanogas. This is a dry white powder which gives off deadly fumes as soon as it comes in contact with any moisture. It is only necessary to sprinkle the correct amount on the path in the greenhouse, and atmospheric moisture will do the rest. However, Cyanogas is not a fumigant which can really be recommended to the gardening novice, as it is exceedingly poisonous to human beings, and therefore must be used with the utmost care. On no account must the fumes be inhaled.

Azobenzene   Red spider, another common greenhouse pest relatively unaffected by nicotine, can be killed with azobenzene either applied as a smoke from a specially prepared canister, or as a very fine spray known as an aerosol, from a special apparatus which can be purchased for the purpose.

Newer Insecticides   Preparations are now available which contain newer insecticides, BHC, HETP and TEPP. These are easy to use and effective against a wide range of pests. Thus BHC (benzene hexachloride) available in dusts, smokes and sprays is effective against thrips and soil pests such as wireworms and springtails. HETP (hexaethyl tetraphosphate) and TEPP (tetraethyl pyrophosphate) both organic phosphorus compounds, available as sprays and smokes, are extremely effective substitutes for nicotine against white fly, thrips, aphides and red spider. Both are very poisonous to warm-blooded animals in concentrated solutions but this effect wears off after 48 hours. When using all these preparations the manufacturer's instructions must be followed carefully.

A new and most effective control for red spider is being developed and is now available commercially. This is known as chlorparacide.

How and When to Fumigate The best time for fumigation or for using smoke canisters is in the evening. After lighting the shreds or canister or placing the fluid or powder on the path, the greenhouse should be

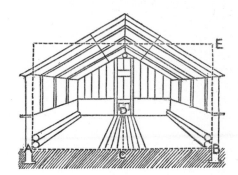

VOLUME OF A
SPAN-ROOFED HOUSE
Here again the breadth (AB), length (CD), and height (BE), to halfway up the roof slope are multiplied together.

instantly left, the door closed and sealed with paper and gum or damp sacks. If the ventilators do not fit closely, these should also be sealed in some similar manner. It is advisable to lock the house securely and remove the key so that no unauthorized person may enter. Not until twelve hours later should the house be visited, and then only momentarily in order to open the ventilators and allow any fumes that remain to escape. It is usually a good plan to repeat the fumigation after two or three nights to destroy any pests that may have hatched out since the earlier application was given.

Treatment of Diseases It must be understood that this fumigation is only effective against pests and not against diseases. The latter can to a great extent be kept at bay by proper ventilation and watering combined with thorough annual cleansing of all woodwork and glass with a scrubbing brush and soapy water. Mildews, in particular, are usually an indication that the atmosphere is too moist and heavy and that more ventilation is required, with less moisture in the air and possibly more at the roots.

Sterilizing the Soil Another most effective method of keeping diseases out of the greenhouse is to sterilize the soil that is to be used for seed trays, tomato borders, etc. Soil sterilization provides a reliable method of controlling eelworms, stem or collar rot diseases, damping off disease, aster wilt diseases, and other harmful fungi which may be carried in the soil. Such sterilization may, of course, be employed outdoors, but is even more useful with greenhouse plants, as the comparatively small volume of soil can be handled easily. Formaldehyde of commercial (40 %) strength and cresylic acid (97-99 %) are two chemicals commonly used. The former must be mixed with fifty and the latter with forty times its own bulk of water before use. In both cases the soil is soaked as thoroughly as possible and then covered with sacks or tarpaulins for a few days to keep in the fumes. The soil must not be used for the plants until it has completely lost the smell of the chemical.

Soil can also be sterilized by heat. A simple method with small quantities is to place it in a small sack and suspend this over a few inches of boiling water. Continue to boil rapidly for an hour with a lid or sack over the top to trap the steam.

Preparing Cheshunt Compound Cheshunt compound is a sterilizing preparation which may be used on the soil while plants are actually growing in it. Even seedlings may be treated, and the compound is particularly useful for checking the spread of damping off. It can be purchased ready for dissolving in water according to manufacturer's directions. Alternatively Cheshunt compound can be prepared at home as follows: Mix eleven parts by weight of carbonate of ammonia with two parts of sulphate of copper. Store in a stoppered vessel for twenty-four hours. Prepare for use by dissolving $\frac{1}{2}$ oz. of the mixture in 1 gal. of water. Do not use or mix in iron, tin, or zinc vessels.

Sulphur Flowers of sulphur can also be dusted freely over leaves and stems to ward off attack by fungi, and is particularly useful against mildews.

If in spite of all precautions diseases still make their appearance, it will be necessary to use one of the fungicides described in Chapter Twenty-five. The method of application is the same as for outside plants. Flowers of sulphur scattered dry on the foliage are particularly serviceable, as no extra moisture is then added to the air.

IV

THE FRUIT GARDEN

CHAPTER THIRTY-FIVE

Laying Out and Stocking a Small Fruit Garden

THE planning and stocking of a small fruit garden require even more skill and forethought than the laying out of a large plantation. It is no easy matter to ensure a good variety and succession of fruits from the limited space available in the average garden; yet it is quite possible to grow a large amount of fruit in a comparatively limited area, and by careful selection of suitable varieties to make certain that at all times when outdoor fruit is in season the gardener still has something to offer.

Suitable Root Stocks The secret lies in the free use of dwarfing stocks for apples and pears, and intensive methods of culture for all fruits. First as regards the stocks. The novice must understand that although it is possible to grow such fruits as currants, gooseberries, raspberries, and blackberries on their own roots, the larger fruits, such as apples, pears, plums, cherries, peaches, nectarines, and apricots, must almost invariably be grafted on to a suitable root system. Though it is sometimes possible to raise these fruits from cuttings, they are hardly ever satisfactory when grown in this manner. Much valuable research work has been carried out with a view to testing the influence of stocks upon the trees grafted on them, with the result that it has been conclusively proved that whereas some root systems encourage vigorous growth and delay fruiting, others induce a dwarfing habit and encourage early bearing. In the case of apples, a number of stocks have been carefully classified at the East Malling Fruit Research Station. They are known by numbers, such as Malling I, Malling II, etc. Of these, Malling IX, a paradise apple, formerly known as Jaune de Metz, is extremely dwarfing. Even such apples as Bramley's Seedling and Blenheim Orange Pippin, which normally make very large trees, assume quite small proportions when grafted on Malling IX stock, and, moreover, instead of having to wait fifteen or twenty years before the trees come into bearing, the fruit gardener is able to commence harvesting after three or four seasons. For pears the selected quince stock known as Malling A has proved to have a dwarfing effect, and so is suitable for the owner of a small garden.

With apples and pears worked on these selected stocks it is possible to have bushes of very small proportions, or, better still, to grow them

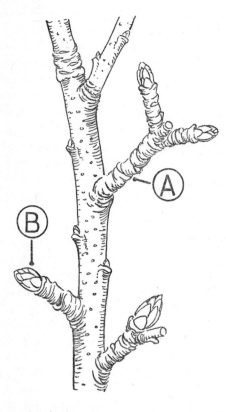

FRUIT AND GROWTH BUDS
A typical apple shoot showing the difference between (A) a growth bud and (B) a fruit bud.

on the single-stemmed cordon system, fuller particulars of which will be found in the next chapter. In this way a great number of varieties can be included in quite a small garden. Unfortunately very dwarfing stocks have not yet been discovered for the stone fruits, such as plums, cherries, and peaches; but all can with a little care be trained against walls or fences on the fan system, and in this form may be introduced into the small fruit garden. Even red and white currants and gooseberries can be grown on the cordon system.

Self-Sterility In a small fruit garden the question of self-sterility must be considered carefully, while the very best varieties for providing a succession of high-class produce and their suitability for cultivation under a severe system of pruning must also be taken into account. Self-sterility is the name given to a characteristic of certain varieties of fruit, the blossoms of which will not set fruit unless fertilized with pollen (the yellow dust found in flowers) of another variety of the same type of flower. Self-sterility is quite common among cherries and plums, and also occurs in a modified form in apples and pears. Thus the popular cherry Napoleon Bigarreau refuses to bear if it is the only variety in the garden, no matter how many trees there may be of it, but if the variety

PROTECTION FOR A WALL-TRAINED FRUIT TREE

Rather tender trees such as peaches, nectarines, and apricots should be planted against sunny walls, preferably with a small glass coping to give additional shelter. Canvas can be suspended in front of the trees during the blossoming period or used when frost is expected.

Bedford Prolific is planted sufficiently near to ensure that pollen is distributed by wind and insects from one variety to the other, good crops will be produced. If there are few insects about, as under glass, it is necessary to ensure the distribution of pollen even among varieties that are normally self-fertile. This can be done with the aid of a rabbit's tail or camel-hair paint brush, or by jarring the supporting wires. Self-sterility has accounted for the barrenness of many a lone tree.

Planning the Garden The precise way in which a fruit garden should be arranged must depend upon the shape, size and surroundings of the plot available. But, speaking generally, given a rectangular plot in a fairly open situation, apples, pears, and some cherries are best trained to wires running as near as possible north and south, and in rows at least 14 feet apart. This will allow space between for the lower-growing soft fruits. Bush gooseberries and red, white, and black currants should be allowed at least 4 feet each way, but the first three named, if grown as single-stemmed cordons, can be planted much more closely. It will be sufficient if the rows are 2½ feet apart, and the plants 1 foot one from the other. Cordon apples and pears may be as close as 2 feet in the rows. Comparison with the general distances for planting given in the next chapter will show at once what an immensely increased number may be grown in the same area when these restricted forms are used instead of bush or standard trees. In addition, the crop is continually under the gardener's control, and the highest quality fruit can be obtained. Cordon trees should be planted at an angle of 45°. By this means a longer stem is obtained with the same height of wall or wire, while the slight check given to the rising sap is an advantage, as it curtails pruning.

Unfortunately plums and cherries do not readily submit to such restrictions upon their growth, and, although experts do manage these as cordons, the average amateur will be well advised to plant fan-trained trees. If a wall or fence is available it should be utilized for these. But, with regard to cherries, another suggestion may be made—namely, that in the small garden such handsome early varieties as Kentish Red and Flemish Red should be planted in bush or standard form in the shrubbery or other position where they will be of decorative as well as utilitarian value.

The plan on page 221 shows a small fruit garden, 25 feet wide and 30 feet long, suitable for the amateur. Cordon trained red currants and gooseberries border one side, raspberries another, and fan-trained loganberries and blackberries make a border for a third side of the plot. The apples and pears are cordon trained on either side of the path to save space, and standard plum trees and black-currant bushes take up the space between the path and one side.

Apple Varieties to Span the Season Dealing with apples first, the gardener will require dessert and cooking varieties which may be used direct from the tree during the summer months. For eating he can scarcely do better than select Gladstone for July, with Beauty of Bath for August, while Early Victoria will fill the bill for culinary purposes. The last named is well adapted to the cordon system, is a very prolific variety, and is also an excellent pollinator which may be counted upon to set the fruits of several other first-class apples that should find a place in this model fruit garden.

As September apples, James Grieve and Fortune are recommended for dessert, with Golden Spire and Grenadier for the kitchen; while for the three succeeding months Ellison's Orange Pippin, Rev. W. Wilks, Cox's Orange Pippin, and Lane's Prince Albert is a selection which could

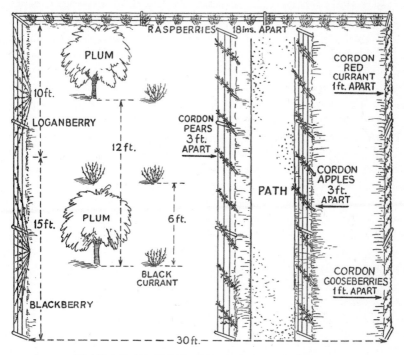

PLAN OF AN IDEAL SMALL FRUIT GARDEN

The path is lined by cordons, apples to the right and pears to the left, and the fences are well utilized for soft fruit. Two standard plum trees are interplanted with blackcurrants in such a way that the bushes do not get too much shade from the trees.

hardly be improved upon, unless the gardener is unfortunate enough to live in a district in which Cox will not succeed. In that case he would be well advised to try Charles Ross or Rival.

If it is desired to store apples until the early summer, room should be found for Sturmer Pippin and Crawley Beauty grown as bushes or standards, but where space is very limited the amateur will be well advised to concentrate on the earlier varieties.

Pears Pears are particularly adapted to the cordon system, as they are naturally spur-fruiting, and do not object to hard pruning. If room can be found for a dozen trees, six varieties for succession may be chosen and two of each sort planted. In this way it will be possible to have a few choice pears for dessert for six or seven months of the year.

Laxton's Superb is a very early variety that may be selected with confidence. William's Bon Chrétien is still the best variety for September use. Fertility lives up to its name, but is of inferior quality, though useful for cooking. For October use, Louis Bonne of Jersey and Conference

CORDON FRUIT
The cordon system is an excellent way of training apples or pears, and makes picking an easy matter.

have every qualification. Pitmaston Duchess always commands high praise by reason of its great size and handsome appearance, and given good cultivation is of fair quality, though it can never compare in flavour with Doyenné du Comice, which stands in a class by itself. Unfortunately the latter does not succeed everywhere. It should, however, be planted unless it is known that it will not fruit well in the district. Should it not make satisfactory progress, it may be replaced by Beurré Superfin. Pears are not so easy to keep as apples, and the suggestion is repeated that, if the area is restricted, the gardener should confine himself to such varieties as may be consumed before the New Year. But if a late keeping variety is required, plant Joséphine de Malines, which is one of the best.

Choosing Plums and Cherries Plums and cherries require very careful selection, as the self-sterile peculiarity is particularly noticeable among them. The following varieties have been chosen with special regard to this point, and they are all varieties that may be expected to succeed under ordinarily good cultural conditions. The dessert plums are: Rivers' Early Prolific, which is really a good cooker, but is quite good for eating in July and early August; Denniston's Superb Gage or Early Transparent; Jefferson's Gage; Coe's Golden Drop and Kirke's Blue. For cooking: Rivers' Early Prolific, Czar, Victoria, and Monarch. Merryweather is one of the best damsons.

Dessert cherries will not appeal to every amateur, but where room can be found a few should certainly be grown. Several will succeed very well against a north-west or east wall, which may be of very little service for any other purpose. Early Rivers is a good black variety, ready for the table by the end of June; Kentish Bigarreau and Black Heart follow in July, while Napoleon Bigarreau extends the season into August. Among cookers Morello is easily the best for small gardens and is too well known to need further praise. It is perfectly self-fertile and so may be planted alone. It will grow on a north wall.

Soft Fruit Varieties Red, white, green and yellow gooseberries should be represented if possible. A selection, including first-rate representatives of each class, and at the same time ensuring a succession of berries throughout the season, would be Keepsake, Leveller, Careless, Whinham's Industry, and Cousin's Seedling.

Three varieties of red currants and one of white will be ample for most amateurs, and one may hardly do better than plant Earliest of Fourlands, Laxton's No. 1, Rivers' Late Red, and White Versailles. All these and the gooseberries are suitable for cultivation on the cordon or fan-trained system.

Among black currants Baldwin is one of the heaviest croppers, though Boskoop Giant has larger fruits and trusses. Daniel's September is recommended for late use.

Royal Sovereign is still a good strawberry if a disease-free strain can be obtained. That known as Malling 40 is reliable, and it should certainly find a place in the model fruit garden. Indeed, if it is decided to grow one variety only, this is the one to choose. Huxley Giant is a very heavy cropper which is not, however, first class in quality. Auchincruive

Climax is vigorous and free, and **Tardive de Leopold** will extend the season for several weeks.

In making a selection of raspberries, allowance must be made for the soil and also the district in which planting is to take place. Lloyd-George is a favourite kind, and has much in its favour, for the flavour is good, the fruits are large and, moreover, it fruits on young as well as old canes. Unfortunately it suffers badly from a disease known as mosaic, for which no cure is as yet known. Malling Promise and Malling Landmark are newer varieties with greater resistance to disease, and Norfolk Giant is favoured by some on account of its great vigour.

Blackberries and loganberries may well be planted on a fence. There is only one variety of loganberry, but there are many blackberries, and selection may be made from John Innes, a heavy cropping late variety; Bedford Giant, one of the earliest of all; and the Himalayaberry, which is a good cropper but too vigorous for small gardens.

Tree Fruits for Milder Localities   No mention has yet been made of peaches, nectarines, and apricots, as these are not sufficiently hard to be grown outdoors with satisfaction in all parts of the country. However, if a sheltered wall is available, it is quite possible to produce satisfactory crops, especially if the trees are protected by fish netting at blossom time and are carefully pollinated by hand. Good varieties are: apricot, Moorpark; nectarine, Elruge; and peach, Hale's Early.

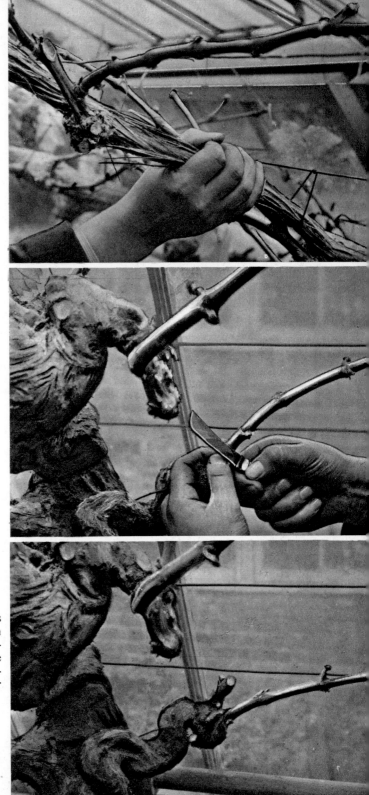

Removing old loose bark from a vine rod by rubbing with the palm of the hand.

Winter pruning a vine side growth which has borne fruit during the preceding summer. The cut is made just above a bud.

The side growths after pruning, with only two buds remaining. Other side growths will be treated in a similar manner.

Left: Winter spraying a bush apple with tar oil wash to kill insect eggs, lichen, etc
Right: The correct method of placing a grease band on a standard fruit tree.

Dusting strawberries with flowers of sulphur to prevent mildew or other fungal diseases

CHAPTER THIRTY-SIX

Selecting and Planting Fruit Trees

THE selection of varieties of fruit trees for the small or medium-sized garden has already been dealt with in the previous chapter. There is, however, another important element of selection which has not yet been fully entered into. This is the decision as to the type of tree which shall be planted, together with such important matters as the kind of root system to be employed and the age of the tree.

Training Nurserymen prepare fruit trees in a large number of different forms, which will be found fully described in their catalogues. The most important from the amateur gardener's standpoint are the standard, bush, fan-trained, espalier-trained, and single-stemmed cordon. The standard is only used for the larger fruits, such as apples, pears, plums, and cherries. It is particularly suitable for the last two, as both succeed well when allowed to grow freely, unrestricted by severe pruning. When forming a standard the tree is allowed to make a main stem or trunk 6 feet in height, which is kept free from all side shoots and is then encouraged to form a large spreading head of strong branches arranged in the form of an open goblet. The half-standard is similar in every respect, except that the main trunk is only about 4 feet in height. Standards and half-standards of apples, pears, plums, and cherries require a considerable amount of room and should be planted from 25 to 30 feet apart. They are more suitable for orchard planting than for the average garden, though isolated standards can sometimes be used most effectively for the dual purpose of ornament and utility.

Bushes are similar to standards in that they possess a number of main branches arranged in goblet fashion, but they have only a very short main trunk. Usually this is no more than 18 inches in height. They do not occupy so much room as standards, and bushes of apples, pears, plums, and cherries can be planted from 15 to 20 feet apart if worked on ordinary stocks. Bush apples grafted on dwarfing stocks can often be planted as close as 10 feet without overcrowding. Gooseberries and currants are usually grown as bushes, in which case they should be planted at least 4 feet apart each way. It is an advantage if rather more space can be given for black currants, as these soon make large plants.

The fan-shaped system of training is particularly valuable for all stone fruits grown against walls or fences. Plums, cherries, peaches, nectarines, and apricots do not submit to very restricted forms of training and pruning, but succeed well when allowed to form a number of main branches which spread out laterally in the form of a fan. It is important to note that no central stem should be retained, or it will monopolize the flow of sap and grow very vigorously at the expense of the side branches. Fan-trained plums, cherries, peaches, nectarines, and apricots should be spaced from 12 to 15 feet apart.

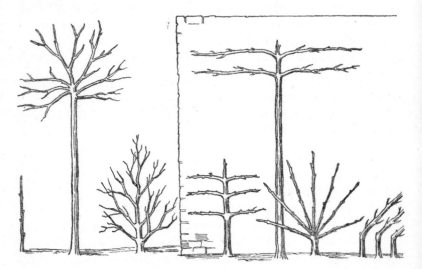

FRUIT TREE FORMS

Left to right: maiden (this can be trained to any form later); standard; bush; espalier; standard espalier; fan-trained; sloping cordon.

Under the espalier system, which, by the way, is used for apples and pears and is hardly ever applied to stone fruits, a central vertical stem forms the basis for horizontal arms parallel to one another and spaced a foot or 15 inches apart. Each arm is pruned in exactly the same manner as a single-stemmed cordon. Espalier-trained trees should be allowed a good 15 feet each, unless grafted on a very dwarfing stock.

The typical cordon tree, which has already been referred to in the previous chapter as one of the most suitable forms for apples and pears in small gardens, is restricted to one stem only. This can either be trained vertically or at an angle of 45°, and may be against a wall or fence or out in the open with wires to provide the necessary support. All side shoots are pruned comparatively severely and so encouraged to form fruiting spurs. Cordon apples and pears may be planted 2 feet apart in rows 6 feet asunder, but a better plan is to allow 14 feet between the rows and intercrop with currants and gooseberries. Both these fruits are also sometimes grown as cordon trees, either with one stem or occasionally with two or even three parallel stems about 6 inches apart. These should be planted in rows 2½ feet apart with 1 foot from tree to tree in the rows, if single-stemmed cordons are planted, or 18 inches for double-stemmed cordons.

Selecting the Stock Fruit trees can be obtained grafted on various stocks. In a general way the nurseryman's advice should be taken as regards the stock considered most suitable for any particular variety, the most essential thing being that each tree should have a good supply of healthy roots and sufficient sturdy branches. However, in the case of apples and pears it is definitely worth specifying a dwarfing stock such as quince for pears and Malling IX for apples, if the intention is to grow cordon trees in a restricted area. Malling II is more vigorous than IX, and so is suitable for poor soils and naturally weak varieties, especially where the apples are to be grown as bushes rather than as trained trees.

When to Purchase The most suitable age at which to purchase almost all the larger fruit trees is at two to three years. Older than this they are more difficult to move satisfactorily, while younger trees require the attention of an expert to ensure the proper foundation of growth. The only exception to this general rule must be made with standards, which are always a few years older on account of the time taken to form the main stems. Small fruits such as gooseberries should be purchased as one- or two-year-old bushes, while raspberries, loganberries, and blackberries are purchased as young, well-rooted canes. The first-named are usually planted 3 feet apart in rows 6 feet apart, the two latter at least 8 feet apart against walls, fences, or trellis screens.

Preparation of the Ground Ground for fruit trees should always be prepared some time in advance so that the soil may have time to settle and at the same time become well weathered. It must be borne in mind that, once planted, most fruit trees will occupy the ground for many years and render further deep cultivation impossible. For this reason the soil should be well trenched at the outset and receive a thorough dressing of farmyard or stable manure, together with either bonemeal or basic slag. The bulky animal manure is worked into all except the surface soil and the fertilizer given as a top dressing to be forked in later on. It is most important that the ground for fruit trees, and particularly for apples and pears, should be well supplied with potash. Shortage of this encourages the disease known as leaf-scorch and greatly reduces fruitfulness. Kainit is a useful and cheap form of potash which may be given as a top dressing in autumn or winter when the ground is prepared. It should be used at the rate of 3 oz. per square yard.

Feeding In subsequent years it is advisable to carry out routine feeding by means of surface dressings. Kainit at 3 oz. or sulphate of potash at

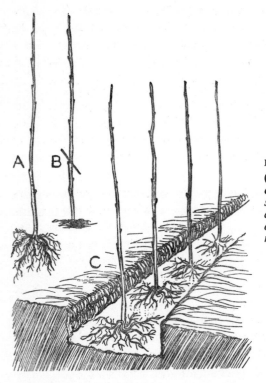

PLANTING RASPBERRIES
(A) *a well-rooted raspberry cane ready for planting should be cut back as shown at* (B). (C) *a trench of ample width in which the roots can be spread out.*

1 oz. per square yard may be given each autumn, followed by a mulch of well-rotted dung in the spring. If this last is not available, give a spring dressing of Nitro-chalk at 1 oz. per square yard. Basic slag should be given in autumn every second year at 4 oz. per square yard, except with strawberries, for which it is better to apply superphosphate of lime at 1½ oz. per square yard every spring.

Planting Fruit trees can be planted any time during the dormant period—that is to say, from the date when they lose their leaves in autumn until the buds commence to grow in the spring—but the best time is undoubtedly as soon after leaf fall as possible, which in normal seasons means the first week in November. On no account should planting be attempted if the ground is frozen or sodden.

The general principles of planting have already been detailed in Chapter Four. Holes must be large enough and in depth sufficient to allow the uppermost roots to be covered with at least 3 inches of soil. It is, however, necessary to guard against planting too deeply. Unlike roses and clematis, fruit trees are not to be encouraged to make roots from the scion, as this may completely upset the particular action of the root stock used. The union between stock and scion must be well above ground level.

General Care All standard trees must be staked and tied securely. A simple and effective tie is made by wrapping a piece of old motor tyre round the main trunk and then placing a tie of soft tarred twine round this. Trained trees should have their branches spread out on the wall, trellis, or wires at once and made secure with ties of soft tarred twine.

In the spring following planting it is an excellent plan to spread a good mulch of very strawy manure or grass clippings on the ground for a yard or so round each tree. This will keep the soil cool and moist and encourage roots to establish themselves rapidly.

CHAPTER THIRTY-SEVEN

Pruning, Thinning, and Training

As fruitfulness of the trees will depend to a large extent upon correct pruning, it is most important that the amateur fruit grower should at the outset master the principles involved.

Reasons for Pruning When pruning, the gardener has two quite distinct ends in view. Firstly, he is concerned that the trees should make a sufficient quantity of healthy wood well spaced so that both fruits and leaves get plenty of light and air. The second objective is to encourage regular and reasonably heavy fruiting. It is most important to realize that these two aims are not only distinct but, sometimes, actually opposed to one another.

In the early stages of a fruit tree's career it is the first of these objects that the pruner should have in mind. Fruiting has not to be considered except with currants, gooseberries, and raspberries, but it is a matter of great importance that the trees should be provided with an adequate framework of strong growth that will later be capable of producing healthy fruit buds and fruit. The golden rule to remember when using sécateurs or pruning knife is that the more severely branches are cut back, the more vigorously will they restart into growth. Light pruning means little wood and more fruit; hard pruning induces sturdy growth at the expense of the crop.

Winter and Summer Pruning For the first few years all the larger fruit trees must be pruned fairly severely. The work is divided between two periods, summer and winter. During the former season all lateral shoots, by which is meant the side shoots from main branches, have their growing points shortened to prevent needless extension. This work should be done when the shoots start to get woody, usually in late July and early August. Each sturdy growth is shortened to five well-developed leaves. The leading growths—that is to say, the young shoots growing at the ends of the main branches and so extending the area of each tree—are not pruned at all in summer. Winter pruning is done at any time from November until the end of February, according to convenience. It is, of course, best to choose a time when the soil is fairly dry on the surface. At this winter pruning the laterals of trained trees are further shortened to within 1 inch or so of the main stems, the object being to prevent the trees from becoming crowded with long shoots. Less formal specimens such as bushes and standards may be left unpruned or be shortened to fruit buds on the two-year-old wood, where this will prevent overcrowding. As a result of this treatment, spurs—that is to say, complex clusters of fruit buds—will be formed in time. The leaders are also cut back, the strongest by about one-third, while more weakly shoots may be cut back a half or even two-thirds. Every cut on leaders should be made just above a growth bud, and if possible buds should be chosen that point in the direction it is desired that the new shoots should take.

Lighter Pruning for Some Fruits These general rules apply to the early pruning of almost all the larger fruits. The only important exceptions to this principle of hard pruning for the first few years are made for

SUMMER PRUNING A TYPICAL APPLE BRANCH
The soft ends of all side shoots are pruned to encourage spur formation. This method is also applicable to pears, plums and sweet cherries.

peaches, nectarines, and Morello cherries, all of which can with advantage be pruned somewhat more lightly. The leaders are shortened, the weakest side growths removed, and stronger laterals allowed to remain at their full strength, provided there is sufficient room for them to grow freely.

Espalier A little extra care is called for in forming good espalier-trained trees. With these the object is to get a new pair of horizontal arms every foot or 15 inches. To do this the central upright stem should be cut back to a point about 15 inches above the topmost pair of lateral branches. When possible the cut should be made immediately above the uppermost of three strong growth buds situated close together. Then in spring, when these three buds produce shoots, the topmost is trained vertically to continue the central stem, while the two lower shoots are trained horizontally to form the basis of a new pair of lateral arms.

Pruning for Fruit Buds Season by season the pruning of bush and standard fruit trees should become lighter, for, as the trees become firmly established and form a good framework of wood, it is advisable that they should be encouraged to fruit. Now, as already explained, hard pruning produces plenty of growth, but the tree that has used up all its energy in making much wood cannot also bear heavy crops of fruit. So wood production is gradually slowed down in order that fruiting may be encouraged. In time it will only be necessary to tip the leading growths and cut out an occasional old or crossing branch to prevent overcrowding. With standard trees even the laterals may be allowed to go more or less unpruned unless they are overcrowded or diseased. With more restricted forms of training, such as bush, cordon, espalier, and fan-trained trees, it is not possible to be so lenient, as the distinctive shape of the specimen would soon be lost and—a more

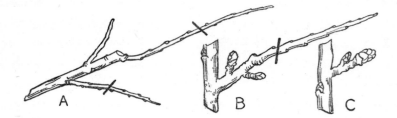

A FURTHER STEP IN SPUR PRUNING

(A) *The good leader and laterals are shortened in winter, and sturdy laterals* (B) *are shortened to encourage spur buds.* (C) *shows very short growths known to the fruit grower as 'darts,' these require no pruning as they readily form fruiting spurs.*

serious point—growth would become grossly overcrowded. This difficulty is partly overcome by regular summer pruning, which reduces leafage and so checks superfluous vigour, and also by judicious root pruning or ringing or by growing the trees on selected dwarfing stocks, as explained in Chapters Thirty-five and Thirty-six.

It now becomes necessary to explain more fully certain important differences in methods of fruiting. Broadly speaking, fruit trees can be grouped into two classes: those that fruit largely on the mature wood, even though it may be many years old, and those which bear most satisfactorily on one-year-old shoots. Apples, pears, plums, and sweet cherries belong to the former class, while peaches, nectarines, and Morello cherries come into the second group.

The method of pruning just described is ideal for the former class, as it will encourage the branches to become covered with short, spur-like growths which, though they take up little room, are crowded with fruit buds; but it is not a suitable system for established trees of the second group. The object in view in their case is to keep up an adequate but not over-abundant supply of one-year-old laterals. Let us suppose that the amateur fruit grower is faced with a fan-trained tree that has been well pruned in its early stages and has a good framework of main branches evenly spaced and each carrying a good number of laterals. The first task is to reduce the latter so that each can be tied to the wall or trellis with plenty of space for the foliage and fruit. Of course, the weakest must go first. During the following summer each lateral will, in addition to producing leaves and fruit, also throw out a number of new shoots. These should be gradually pinched out while they are still quite small, until only two are left—one as near as possible to the base of the

PEACH PRUNING

(A) *Main branch.* (B) *Fruiting lateral with all young shoots removed except the terminal shoot* (C) *and basal growth* (D).

old lateral, and the other at its tip, to draw the sap through it and make the fruits swell. Then in winter the old lateral is cut out and the new shoot that was retained near its base is trained to the wall or trellis in its place.

As already mentioned, sweet cherries, plums, and apricots bear their fruit on spurs, like apples and pears, and may be pruned in precisely the same manner. But where there is room for free development it is an advantage not to practise hard pruning, because a disease peculiar to these trees, and known as gumming, appears to be encouraged by continued and severe cutting back. It is for this reason that sweet cherries and vigorous plums should, if possible, be planted as standards and allowed to grow with little or no restriction once the heads are well formed. Choice varieties, however, and also all apricots, benefit from the protection of a wall, against which they should be trained in fan form, and a mixture of spur pruning and tying in of young growths, as recommended for peaches, applied.

Soft Fruit Gooseberries and red and white currants fruit freely on old and young wood after the manner of apples, and may be pruned in exactly the same way. However, it is often a good plan to leave some strong laterals and even leaders at almost full length if there is plenty of room, as they will fruit right along the length of these if well ripened.

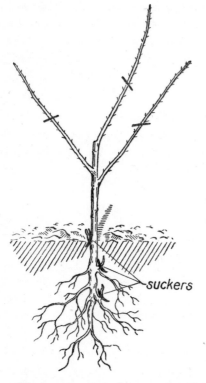

A YOUNG GOOSEBERRY BUSH

The shoots should be cut back after planting at the point indicated, and the heavy black lines show where suckers should be removed.

Black currants fruit most plentifully on one-year-old wood, and the object in pruning is to maintain a plentiful supply of this. When the bushes are planted they should be cut back to within 6 inches of the ground. There will be no fruit the first summer, but plenty of strong young growth which will bear a crop the second season. No pruning is necessary at the end of the first season's growth, but the autumn following fruiting sufficient of the older wood that has borne a crop should be cut out to make room for strong young growth that has not yet fruited. Subsequently this process is repeated each autumn.

When to Prune Raspberries Raspberries fall into two classes—summer and autumn fruiting. The former bear on year-old canes, and are pruned in exactly the same manner as black currants, with the one exception that *all* old canes that have fruited *must* be cut out, and not merely sufficient to make room for the young canes. The work should be done as soon after fruiting as possible. Autumn fruiting raspberries are cut back to within a few inches of the ground each February. A mixture of the two systems may be applied to the variety Lloyd George, which is summer and autumn fruiting; the autumn fruiting canes are either shortened or cut back almost to the ground in February, while the summer fruiting canes are removed in the early autumn.

Blackberries, loganberries, wineberries, and other bramble fruits all bear on year-old canes, and all old wood is cut out after fruiting in the same manner as advised for summer fruiting raspberries.

Pruning after Planting A point round which controversy often rages is whether fruit trees should be pruned immediately after they are planted. In my opinion unless fruit trees are moved very late in the season, when the sap is already on the move, it is best to carry out the ordinary pruning just as if transplanting had not taken place.

Root Pruning Root pruning is often used to check excessive vigour in fruit trees that are growing too freely and persisting in making great quantities of wood at the expense of fruit. It should be done during the dormant period in autumn or winter. A 2-foot-deep trench is opened half-way round the tree and a couple of yards from its base. Then the soil towards the base of the tree is gradually loosened into the trench with a fork, so exposing the roots. Any very thick roots should be severed, but the finer fibrous roots must be carefully protected from injury, then the soil is replaced very firmly.

Ringing An alternative to root pruning is ringing. This can be applied to apples and pears, but should not be used on stone fruits such as plums and cherries. It is done in May and consists in the removal of a ring of bark ¼ inch deep right round the main trunk. Only the bark should be taken away, and the cut must not be made down into the hard wood beneath. By the end of the summer the narrow scar will have completely healed over, but the check given will prove sufficient to retard growth and so encourage fruiting.

Thinning There is another aspect of pruning that must not be over-looked—namely, the thinning of fruits. Apples, pears, peaches, nec-tarines, and apricots nearly always have far more fruit than they can carry to full maturity. The number should be reduced little by little while the fruits are still very tiny, but the thinning of all stone fruits should be delayed until the stones are formed for certain, as quite a number of fruits fall during the process of stoning. A simple test is to remove one fruit and cut it with a knife to ascertain whether the stone is formed or not. With apples and pears two fruits per spur will be ample for ordinary

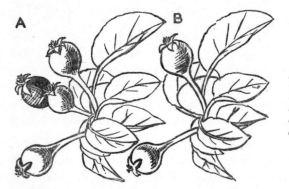

THINNING PEARS
Each cluster as (A) *requires thinning to one or two fruitlets as* (B).

purposes, and only one should be allowed for exhibition. Peaches may be allowed to bear one fruit per lateral, or two if the laterals are trained, while nectarines and apricots may be permitted to fruit a trifle more heavily. Gooseberries may be thinned as soon as those on the more forward shoots are large enough for cooking. The remainder are left to attain a fair size.

CHAPTER THIRTY-EIGHT

Harvesting and Storing

I is a thousand pities that many months of painstaking labour should
be rendered of little value by last-moment carelessness, yet it is
impossible to avoid the conclusion that a vast amount of fruit is ruined
every year by bad methods of picking, resulting in early decay in the
store room. Tender fruits need careful handling, so that the skin is in no
way bruised or damaged. Too often, however, the somewhat thick
skin of apples and pears leads the picker to suppose that these fruits
will stand a certain amount of rough handling without serious harm
resulting. Every effort should be made to preserve the fruits from injury.
Two or three thicknesses of paper lining the baskets will afford much
protection. Fruits that have fallen should on no account be mixed with
the rest, even though there be no apparent injury. They must be kept
separate and decay watched for; there will then be no risk of their
decaying and damaging sound specimens.

When to Pick As to the best time for gathering, it is not good policy to
start picking from a tree and continue until the whole is cleared. Fruits
mature unevenly, and, quite apart from the better eating qualities of a
fully ripened crop, if apples and pears are required for storing, those
that are forcibly removed will shrivel before the time arrives for them
to be in prime condition.

With currants, cherries, plums, and other soft fruits, it is a simple
matter to estimate the degree of ripeness by appearance and feel.
Gooseberries are usually picked over at least twice, first when the fruits
are just large enough for cooking and again when they are fully ripened.
The first gathering serves instead of thinning and makes it possible for
the bushes to bring the remaining fruits to a high degree of perfection.

It is not quite so easy to tell when apples are ready for gathering.
Usually two pickings are necessary. When fit for picking an apple comes
away from the tree easily if raised in the hand or given a twist sideways.
Further, the pips are brown, whereas those of an immature apple are
green or white. No apples should be allowed to hang on the trees much
after mid-October. It is not very important to have culinary apples
matured, for with them size is the chief consideration; but dessert
apples must be gathered in the best condition. It is desirable to store late

237

varieties of apples only. Early kinds require to be eaten as gathered, some of the very earliest going mealy in a few hours.

Early culinary apples of the codlin type may advantageously be picked over as soon as the biggest specimens are large enough for use. This lightening of the crop encourages the remaining fruit to increase in size. If the smallest apples are left, the whole weight of fruit will be greater than if all the crop were picked at one operation. This applies in a lesser degree to mid-season cookers; but there is not much object in picking over late varieties.

Pears, with the exception of some of the earliest varieties, should not

TESTING AN APPLE BEFORE PICKING

Lift the fruit gently as shown. If the stalk parts readily from the branch the apple is fit for gathering, but if the stalk tears or splits (inset) the fruit is still immature.

be left to ripen fully on the tree. They are best picked when approaching maturity and stored until fit for use. Many people feel each specimen to see if it is soft. This method of testing only bruises the fruit. Picking should begin as soon as the first specimen begins to get soft just round the stem. Culinary pears do not ripen on the tree in this country. They may be picked in October and stored.

Storage Apples and pears require quite different conditions for storage. In the case of the latter it is a ripening process rather than true storing, and the fruits are best placed in a single layer on shelves, or in shallow trays, in a dry place. They should be examined from time to time and used as they ripen. Sometimes the ripening process may be hastened by bringing a few into a warm room.

Many people try to keep apples in the same way, but this does not prove satisfactory. Apples keep best in bulk, in a moist place, with a cool, even temperature. A frostproof shed with an earthen floor makes an excellent store, the earth floor keeping the atmosphere nicely moist. A cool cellar is probably the next best place, but anywhere where the atmosphere is moist and the temperature can be kept fairly even will do. The apples may with advantage be placed in boxes holding about a bushel. For the first week or so after the store is filled the ventilators must be kept wide open—this is while the fruit is 'sweating.' When the skins are dry again the store should be closed up and a steady temperature of round about 40° maintained.

CHAPTER THIRTY-NINE

Grape Vines

Among professional gardeners the cultivation of really good grapes is considered the great test of skill, and triumphs scored in the keen competition of the grape classes at the leading shows place the victors in the vanguard of their craft. Large numbers of amateur gardeners who own glasshouses have an urge to grow their own grapes. Many try, but not all succeed. Still, there can be no question about the achievement being worth the effort, for fresh-cut grapes are infinitely superior to bought produce.

The grape vine is a plant of marvellous vitality that will survive a great deal of maltreatment, but in order to obtain good economic results a great deal of that vitality has to be curtailed, or, more correctly, diverted from its natural outlet, which is production of abundance of branch and leaf, to the development of a limited number of bunches of fruit. It is in carrying out this intricate task of curtailment that the novice goes astray, and in a large proportion of cases of failure the fatal mistake was made at the very outset of the venture.

Preparing the Border The foundation of success rests in the making of the border in which a vine is to grow, and unless one is prepared to see that such foundation is well and truly laid, it is better to abandon the idea of growing grapes. Left to their own devices vine roots ramble far and wide, and it is an extremely difficult matter to regulate growth, because one can never be quite sure what unsuitable food material those wayward roots might find next. To obviate this difficulty the experienced vine grower constructs a tank-like pit with cemented sides and bottom and fills it with a prepared compost, thus making certain that the roots get just what he thinks best for them and no more. A study of the accompanying drawing will convey more clearly than words just how such a vine border should be constructed. Special note should be taken of the fact that gratings are provided at frequent intervals to allow an outlet for surplus moisture, and that the whole of the bottom is covered with at least 6 inches of rough rubble, preferably of a limy nature. A vine border can either be inside or outside the vinery, or indeed may even be partly in and partly out. The advantage of the inside border is that everything is under control, but against this can be urged the fact

Left: Drawing soil towards seedling peas as a protection against cold winds. *Right:* Staking peas with hazel branches, which should be in position early.

Mulching French beans with lawn mowings to conserve soil moisture.

Raising lettuces under cloches of the low barn type.

Earthing up broccoli after first spreading well-rotted dung round the plants.

that constant attention is required throughout the summer months and, if the amateur vine grower is likely to be away from home a good deal at that season, it is better for him to rely on an outside border which will not be entirely dependent on him for its water supply. The compost with which the border is filled should consist mainly of good fibrous turf, with a modest quantity of well-rotted farmyard or stable manure added and also some charcoal and sufficient sand to keep the soil open. Finally, it is an excellent plan to add a shovelful of ground bones to each

CONSTRUCTION OF A VINE BORDER

An outside border. The vine rods will be led into the vinery through suitable holes in the wall. (A) pre-pared soil over a layer of lime rubble (B), over a concrete base (C). (D) is the porous subsoil.

barrowload of prepared compost, as this will decompose very slowly and provide the vines with a steady supply of phosphates for years to come.

How Many Vines to Plant One vine can be made eventually to extend itself over an entire greenhouse of considerable size, but this is a matter of several years, during which time few grapes can be carried. The alternative is to plant sufficient vines to fill the roof space with rods at about 4 feet apart. Each vine may carry one rod or two rods as desired. Be content to plant all of one kind. Culture becomes complicated when several varieties are grown in one house.

How to Plant Start with good, strong, pot-grown vines, but, when planting, do not merely place the unbroken ball in the border and fill it in. To do this means that the original roots will for ever remain twisted in the compass occupied when restricted by the size of the pot. As these roots harden and thicken they will become so compressed that sap flow is impeded, and the plant will have to throw out entirely new roots from the base before the top growth can be adequately supported. Care

Q

must be exercised in removing the old soil and unravelling the roots. Breakage of the finer fibres is detrimental. Get the main roots spread out in a natural manner and as nearly horizontal as possible. The nearer the roots are to the surface the better, as long, of course, as they are completely covered.

Training   The main stem of the young vine should be tied up to the lowest wire under the roof, and cut off just beyond the next three buds. This allows for two laterals, one on either side, and a leader to continue upward growth. If two rods are required the vine is pruned to two buds above the wire and these are trained left and right until they are 4 feet apart and then are continued up the roof parallel to one another. All shoots appearing below the trellis are rubbed out. In subsequent winters such a vine will have the laterals pruned back to two buds or eyes to form spurs, and the leaders shortened again. Thus by slow degrees the vine will mount the roof clothed with spurs throughout its whole length.

Summer Care   During the summer the rods should make vigorous growth and, when the leading growths have each extended about 6 feet, their points should be pinched out. This will encourage the formation of laterals or side shoots, which should in turn have their points pinched out when they have made five leaves each. Watering will, of course, require regular attention, and it is important to remember that as the vine border is of considerable depth it will require a large volume of water to soak it right through. Surface sprinkling is worse than useless, and the best plan is to place the hose on the border in the morning connected to a tap turned sufficiently to give a modest flow and leave it in position for an hour or so. Such watering should be given as soon as the border shows signs of dryness on top.

Winter Treatment   By the end of October most of the foliage will have fallen from the vines, and ventilation should be given really freely until they are started into growth in late winter or early spring. This is important, as it gives the vines an adequate rest and prepares them for the effort of producing a few bunches of fruit during the following summer. As soon as possible after leaf-fall the vines must be pruned. The leading shoot of each is shortened according to its strength. If weakly, it must be cut back to within three buds of its base; if fairly sturdy, it may be left 2 feet in length, while very vigorous vines may have a young leading shoot 4 feet long after pruning. All laterals are cut back to two buds to encourage the formation of short spur growths from which future fruiting shoots will be produced. These spurs must be evenly spaced on both sides of the leading shoot and about 15 inches apart. If there are too many laterals some can be removed, but it is advisable not to do this until growth starts again in the spring. It will then be seen which laterals are making the sturdiest growths and the weakest can be rubbed out with finger and thumb.

Cleaning the Rods A new coat of bark grows on vine wood each year. At first it is very fine in texture and a light shade of brown, fitting very tightly to the wood, but as the rod gets older it becomes covered by loose, ragged, dry bark of a dark, dirty brown colour. This has finished its serviceability, and if left to encumber the rods it will simply collect dirt and afford shelter for mealy bug, aphis, red spider and the spores of various fungi that work mischief if allowed to develop. It will be found that by gripping the rod midway between spurs and working the hand forwards and backwards with a semi-rotary movement most of the outer coating of dead fibre will break away and fall in shreds. A few pieces will adhere to the spurs, but these can be pulled off with ease. Finish by brushing the rod with a moderately stiff but not too harsh brush, and painting it with Gishurst compound if any pests have been observed. Winter is the right time for this work, and it is usually most convenient to do it immediately after pruning, but, as already noted, young vines have no loose bark, and cleaning will not usually start until the second year, at earliest, after planting.

Two-year-old Rods From the second season onwards treatment continues unchanged, except for the fact that the leading shoots are allowed to continue their extension until the available space is filled, when they are stopped and thenceforward prevented from making any further growth.

Management of the Vinery The date of closing the vinery and so starting the vines into growth will depend upon whether artificial heat is available. If a temperature of 50° can be maintained easily the vines can be started in late February or early March, but in unheated structures it is folly to hurry matters overmuch. If a spell of warm, sunny weather is experienced early in March it is quite a simple matter to make the buds break by keeping the ventilators closed and so running up a fairly high temperature during the day, but elation at this achievement is likely to be short lived, for when a cold snap comes (and never a spring passes without one or more such sudden reversions to wintry conditions) it will be impossible to maintain growth, and the vines will probably suffer fairly seriously. In normal seasons and in the south and midlands it will be quite time enough to close the unheated vinery at the end of March, and a week or so later in the north. Moderate ventilation may be given during fine days from a little after sunrise until a couple of hours before sundown. Only the top ventilators should be used at this season. If air is admitted at the side of the house as well, it is extremely difficult to avoid cold draughts, and these encourage mildew. For the first week or so the rods should be syringed with tepid water every morning, but when shoots are about 3 to 4 inches in length only the floor and walls of the vinery should be wetted and not the foliage or rods.

Stopping The two buds left at the base of each lateral start into growth at this period, and it is very probable that a few other more weakly

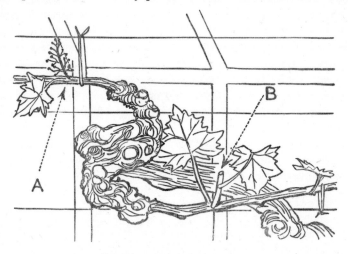

SUMMER STOPPING A GRAPE VINE

Two laterals are shown, one of which has formed a fruit truss (A), *while the other has thrown a sub-lateral which has been stopped* (B).

shoots may also appear from dormant buds which were not previously noticed. These latter must be rubbed out without delay, but the two strong growths may be retained until it is seen which is going to produce the better bunch. The less satisfactory of the pair can then be cut back. A week or so later than this the remaining lateral should be 'stopped'— that is, have its growing point pinched out—two leaves beyond the truss of flowers.

Exercise Great Care at Flowering Time The blossom period is a most important one, as it is essential to get the flowers properly fertilized.

For this a dry and warm atmosphere is needed. The owner of a heated greenhouse can attain this ideal fairly easily by ceasing to damp down (syringe) the house, giving a little extra ventilation and more boiler heat. But in the unheated structure it is necessary to strike a compromise. Damping down must be discontinued, and if the weather is warm and sunny the top ventilators may be thrown wide open for an hour or so around midday, but the house should be closed quite early in the afternoon, so that the thermometer may register 75° or more before nightfall. Should the outside atmosphere be wet, foggy, or cold, there is nothing for it but to keep the vinery closed. Damp air must not be admitted, or it will prevent the pollen from drying properly and being freely distributed from flower to flower.

As soon as the tiny berries form the temperature of the house may be allowed to fall a little with advantage. From early May onwards it is necessary to be very careful about ventilation early in the morning. If the sun is allowed to shine on the vinery for an hour or so before any air is admitted, leaves and berries are almost certain to be scalded. It is surprising how rapidly the temperature of a greenhouse rises on a bright morning.

Tying Laterals One very important matter that has not yet been referred to is the tying down of the laterals. These must not be allowed to press against the glass or they are almost certain to suffer injury. The process of tying down to the wires, about a foot from the glass, should be started early and done a little at a time, for the young growths are brittle and liable to snap off close to the spur if bent down too suddenly. First a strand of broad, soft raffia should be looped over the lateral a little more than halfway to its tip. Then the raffia is passed under the nearest wire, pulled gently so as to bend the lateral over, and tied into a bow. A day or so later the bow can be untied and the shoot pulled a little nearer to the wire, the process being continued, with the addition of further ties, until the lateral is in its proper position parallel to the roof, with the leaves clear of the glass.

Thinning the Bunches Most amateur gardeners err on the side of reserving too great a number of berries on the bunches, the general idea being that to cut away 60 or 75% of the berries is wasteful. The truth is, however, that even one-fourth of the berries of a well-set bunch will eventually attain a weight equal to that which is possible if the whole mass is left untouched, but there is this difference—the small number will develop into large, luscious fruits, whereas the greater number will be but rough skin and hard seeds. Nevertheless, it is advised that until some experience in grape thinning has been gained, the novice should go cautiously, at first cutting out only such berries as will obviously be crowded in the middle of the bunches, or so close together as to obstruct each other. It will probably be sufficient if at the first thinning about 50% of the berries are removed. As soon as possible a second start must be made, when careful observation will show where further removal will be necessary and advantageous.

Grapes Out-of-Doors Vines can also be grown in the open either with or without the aid of cloches. It is not possible to produce such fine bunches as under glass but, provided suitable varieties are chosen, fully ripened grapes of excellent quality can be produced.

The sytem of pruning is quite different from that used under glass. The young vine is cut back in winter to within a few inches of ground level. It is allowed to make two growths which are trained vertically. The following winter one of these growths is shortened a little and tied down horizontally about a foot above ground level. It is the cane that carries fruit the following summer. The other young growth is cut back to two growth buds (joints) and from these two more shoots are permitted to grow. They are trained vertically like the first two and are similarly treated the following winter when the fruiting cane is cut right out. If cloches are used, the horizontal fruiting cane is placed under the cloches and the vertical 'replacement' shoots are permitted to grow up through the top of the cloche. Rather tall cloches of the 'tomato' type minus the top pane of glass may be used.

The two varieties most suitable for eating are Pearl of Czarba and Ascot Citronelle. For wine making Madeleine Royale and Gamay Hâtif des Vosges are recommended.

CHAPTER FORTY

A Spraying Programme

I F the beginner happens to pick up a book devoted to the various pests
and diseases that may attack fruit trees, he will probably be dismayed
and bewildered by their number. He can, however, take immediate
comfort. There is no more necessity for him to familiarize himself with
the symptoms and appearance of all these foes than there is for him to
be conversant with the still more numerous ills from which human
beings may suffer.To follow the analogy a little further, the wise man
practises a regular course of hygiene which he knows will preserve him
from likelihood of infection by disease, and in exactly the same manner
the experienced fruit grower carries out certain routine precautions
season by season, not so much to rid his trees of foes as to prevent any
possibility of their getting a hold.

Winter Spraying The first thing is to make certain that there are no
eggs, scale insects, or larvae hidden in the bark and only waiting for
milder weather to become active and lay the foundation of a new
generation of pests. This is done, not by the old-fashioned method of
whitewashing the trunks, which has long since been proved useless, but
by spraying every part of the tree or bush with a good winter wash.
Many of these are now on the market and are offered by all dealers in
horticultural sundries in tins of convenient size with full instructions for
preparation. It only remains to mix them with water at the indicated
strength and apply them to the fruit trees with as much force as possible
and in the form of a fine drenching spray, the object being to make the
wash penetrate into the smallest crevices of the bark. January is the
best month for using tar oil washes, but there are other kinds, such as
DNC, which can be used as late as March. Fruits which should be
treated are apples, pears, plums, including damsons, cherries, peaches,
nectarines, apricots, all kinds of currants and gooseberries.

The next spraying will be required by peaches and nectarines at the
end of February. This time a fungicide known as lime sulphur is used as
a preventive of the leaf curl disease. Like the winter washes, it can be
purchased in various proprietary forms from horticultural sundriesmen
and is ready for mixing with water. The instructions on the container
will explain that the wash is to be used at various strengths according to

the season. For our present purpose it must be applied at the full winter strength, which is usually about 2½ pints of lime sulphur in 10 gallons of water, though this may vary a little with different brands according to the concentration of the fluid.

About three weeks later this same fungicide, but at double the

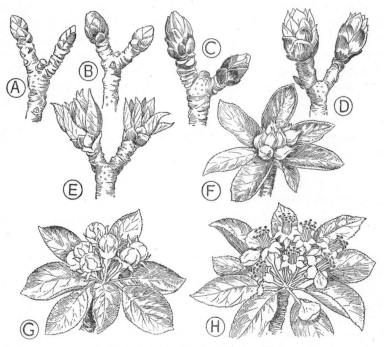

FRUIT BUD STAGES (APPLE)

The various stages of bud development at which spraying is carried out are (A) *dormant (winter);* (B) *swelling;* (C) *'green tip';* (D) *bursting;* (E) *'mouse ear';* (F) *'green cluster' or 'green bud';* (G) *pink bud;* (H) *petal fall.*

strength previously recommended, is applied to raspberries as a preventive of the cane spot disease. It should only be used if the disease has been observed.

Pre-Blossom Spraying   From the middle of March onwards comes the most important period in the fruit grower's calendar, for from then until about a fortnight after the fall of blossom is the best time to check attack of many of the worst pests and diseases. The fruit grower classifies the various stages of growth in apples, pears, and plums during this period by such terms as 'bud burst,' 'green bud,' 'pink bud' (of apples) or 'white bud' (of pears), 'full blossom,' and 'blossom fall,' and, as these terms are also generally employed by the manufacturers of fungicides and insecticides when giving instructions for their use, it is as well that the novice should clearly understand what they imply.

Bud burst is used to describe the period during which the buds are opening but before the tight green blossom clusters appear. If is often split into successive stages with such names as 'swelling,' 'green tip,' 'delayed dormant,' and 'mouse ear.' Green bud covers the next period of about a fortnight, when the first small leaflets unfold themselves, revealing the tightly closed flower buds within. This is followed by the pink bud or white bud stage, when the blossom buds themselves are swelling rapidly and showing the colour of the tightly folded petals within. This is followed by the period of full blossom, while blossom fall describes the period at which approximately three-quarters of the petals have fallen.

During the period of green bud apples and pears are sprayed with lime sulphur at the ordinary winter strength, with the object of combating one of the worst of all diseases, apple and pear scab. This is followed by a second application in the pink bud or white bud period, with the same object in view, and also to account for red spider that might have been missed by the tar oil wash. However, a much more effective control of red spider can be obtained by the use of chlorparacide in spring, according to manufacturer's instructions.

Plums and damsons do not require any spraying with lime sulphur, but should be treated at the white bud stage with a good insecticide to kill caterpillars.

Soft Fruit at Blossom Time Black currants will require treatment with lime sulphur about the first week in April (just before the blossoms expand) if they are showing signs of 'big bud.' This is caused by the presence of the black currant mite within the buds and is easy to identify, as the buds become very large and globular in shape and stand out prominently. The lime sulphur is used at double the ordinary winter strength; that is to say, about 5 pints in 10 gallons of water.

At exactly the same period gooseberries are treated with lime sulphur at the ordinary winter strength as a precaution against mildew, while during the blossom period raspberries, loganberries, and blackberries should be sprayed with a derris insecticide as a precautionary measure against the maggot which eats its way into the fruits. There are plenty of derris insecticides on the market now, some of which are mixed with water, while others are applied in the form of a dry dust. It is an advantage to mix a little soft soap with this spray to make it stick better. Some manufacturers anticipate this by supplying the derris ready mixed with soap.

Post-Blossom Sprays No further spraying is carried out during the blossom period, but at blossom fall the fruit grower must again get busy. Apples and pears will both require a third application of lime sulphur, but this time at the summer strength, which is only about 1 pint in 10 gallons of water. With it should be mixed an insecticide such as derris to account for caterpillars.

At exactly the same period of growth—though not necessarily at the same time, for they are usually a little earlier in dropping their blossom —cherries should be sprayed with a good insecticide such as DDT as a protection against caterpillars. Currants and gooseberries should receive the same treatment, while the last named should, in addition, be sprayed with lime sulphur at summer strength as a final preventive of mildew.

About ten days or a fortnight after blossom fall both apples and plums are sprayed with nicotine, this time against the sawfly, the larvae of which do a great deal of damage.

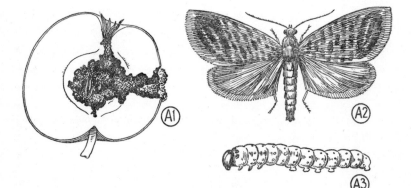

CODLIN MOTH
(A1) *The attack on the apple by the larva* (A3) *before it pupates, to emerge as an adult insect* (A2).

Summer Treatment About the middle of May the raspberries and loganberries may be given lime sulphur at about double ordinary summer strength as an additional precaution against cane spot disease, and in late June another application of derris as a precautionary measure against maggots in the fruit. At this time apples that have been attacked by codling moth maggots in previous years should be sprayed with lead arsenate or DDT. During June and July apples and pears may receive light sprayings against scab, particularly if brown spots are noted on the leaves and discoloured cracks and pustules on the fruits. For this summer treatment Bordeaux mixture is recommended for pears and also such apples as Newton Wonder, Stirling Castle, Lane's Prince Albert, Beauty of Bath, Rival and Lord Derby, which are damaged by sulphur.

Strawberries The only fruit of importance which has not so far been mentioned is the strawberry. The two foes most likely to give trouble in the ordinary way are mildew and mites, both of which can be controlled by spraying with winter strength lime sulphur in April. Also, for mildew, dust the plants thoroughly with flowers of sulphur just before the blossoms open.

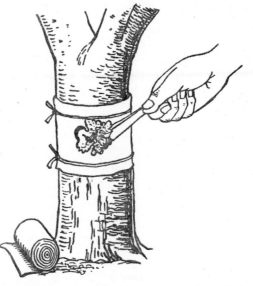

GREASEBANDING
Bands of greaseproof paper are tied well up the bole of the tree in autumn and covered with a special sticky compound to trap winter moth and woolly aphis.

Woolly Aphis A pest not readily controlled by spraying is woolly aphis (American blight) of apples. This is protected by its woolly covering, but it can be destroyed by brushing with methylated spirit occasionally during the summer. Greasebands placed in position in September and kept sticky until spring will catch many migrating insects.

V

THE VEGETABLE GARDEN

CHAPTER FORTY-ONE

Planning the Vegetable Garden

THE beginner who intends to include vegetable culture in his garden programme will do well to pay careful attention to the laying out of the plot in the first instance. In many gardens it is wise to plan the vegetable garden in close relation with the fruit garden, for shady walls can be utilized for some fruits, such as black currants and cherries, and on the other hand standard fruit trees can be used to provide the partial shade so essential for the maintenance of choice salads during the hottest summer weather. This attention to the fads and fancies of the different crops, and forethought in the planning of paths, etc., will make for high quality crops with the minimum of trouble.

Planning is Important Should the plot be encircled by a wall or close-boarded fence, the border at the foot of the wall facing south is just the place for the earliest crops of peas and potatoes. During the summer it is likely to be too dry for most purposes, but this disadvantage is far more than outweighed by the utility of early supplies of these essential vegetables. Similarly, a wall or fence with a north aspect should be used for fruit.

A border with an east aspect is a suitable place for semi-permanent crops, such as rhubarb and seakale. This border can be wider than any of the others—a necessary precaution, as, when these crops are being forced, it is necessary to cover the roots with earthenware pots or tubs, and to surround these in turn with straw or other littery material. This cannot be done conveniently on a narrow border, and it is a great nuisance if the straw, etc., continually slips out into the path.

A border with a south aspect can usually be divided into two sections, one partially shaded and the remaining one open to full sun. If the west end rather than the east is selected for the open portion, it will be sheltered to some extent from the early morning sun, and it is this that does far more harm to the tender young sprouts of early vegetables than frost itself. Frequently plants that have been frosted can be saved from all ill-effect by shading them with paper or tiffany for the first few hours of the day. If the frost is allowed to thaw out gradually, it does much less injury; it is the sudden transition that works the havoc.

This open portion is ideal for early peas and potatoes, which should have their relative positions changed annually, as each makes its own demands upon the food reserves of the soil.

Fruit in the Vegetable Garden If standard fruit trees are to be included in the vegetable garden, the best place to put them is in the main plot, but in such a position that they throw shade on to the south border. They then make it possible to use a portion of this plot during the heat of the summer when it would otherwise be useless. It is wise to keep the shaded portion solely for such summer salads as lettuces, radishes, young onions, endive, and chives.

Reserve Space for Seed Beds It is most economical to reserve a small bed in the main block solely for seed raising. This will be in use for the greater part of the year if a succession of greencrops is maintained. First sowings of cauliflower, broccoli, and Brussels sprouts will be made at the end of March and will be followed throughout the summer by colewort, kale, and other greenstuffs.

Asparagus An asparagus bed is worthy of very careful attention, for, if well made, it will last for many years. This is explained in detail in Chapter Forty-eight. A convenient width is 4 feet, with four rows of asparagus 10 inches apart running the length of the bed.

Rotational Cropping The main plot should be divided up into small sections for the various crops, such as peas, potatoes, onions, carrots, greenstuffs, beetroot, etc., according to the needs of the family. The actual positions and proportions of each are not arbitrarily fixed, and it is an advantage to shift the crops about each season, as already advised for the early vegetables in the south border. This practice is known as rotational cropping, and is of great value in economizing the natural food reserves of the soil and also in keeping down plant foes. One point of considerable importance is that all rows should run as nearly as possible north and south. Each will then get an equal amount of sun on both sides. If the rows run east and west, one side will be more or less permanently in shade, and the taller vegetables, such as peas and beans, may cast so much shade that the neighbouring crops will get a negligible amount of direct sunlight.

CHAPTER FORTY-TWO

Potatoes

ALMOST any soil will produce a crop of potatoes, but there is no getting away from the fact that a rather rich sandy loam is the most favourable medium. Nevertheless cold heavy ground can be improved immensely by digging in plenty of leaf-mould, or strawy manure in the autumn, together with bonfire ashes and sand. Chalky and very gritty soils are really the worst, as they encourage the development of common scab and misshapen tubers, troubles which, though they do not affect the quality of the crop, completely spoil its appearance.

Site The plot chosen for potatoes must always be fully in the open, while a sunny sheltered border is essential for the very early crops. The planting sets or 'seed' potatoes should be procured early so that they

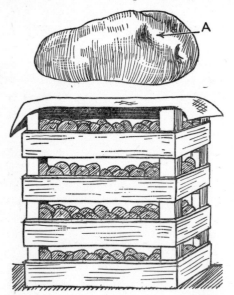

SPROUTING POTATOES

Place the tubers in shallow trays with the eyes (A) uppermost. Some protection such as sacking may be thrown over the trays in frosty weather.

may be sprouted, prior to planting. Scotch-grown 'seed' is usually considered the best, but there is no reason why one should not save one's own seed potatoes, at any rate for several successive years, unless, of course, disease has been very prevalent in the garden. At least six weeks is necessary for proper sprouting, and it is much better to allow a longer period. The tubers are stood with their eyed ends uppermost in shallow trays in a light but frostproof place. A north room will do very well, but it is a wise precaution to cover the potatoes with newspapers or sacking at night, especially when the weather is frosty. Tubers can also be sprouted in the greenhouse provided frost is excluded.

Early Varieties Planting of early varieties can start early in March if a sheltered border is available, and should be in full swing by the end of that month, maincrop and late varieties following a week or so later.

Planting The simplest method of planting is that shown in the sketch on page 256. Each row is marked in turn by a garden line, and the soil removed from one shallow trench is used to cover the tubers in the row

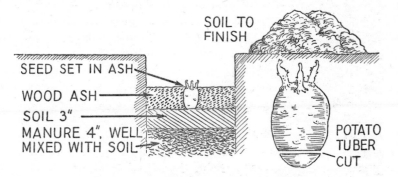

SOIL TO FINISH

SEED SET IN ASH

WOOD ASH

SOIL 3"

MANURE 4", WELL MIXED WITH SOIL

POTATO TUBER CUT

WHEN AND HOW TO PLANT POTATOES

The sprouted tubers (right) are placed rose end uppermost in ashes in prepared trenches. The ash is a preventive against scab and helps to keep the tubers clean.

previously planted. On lumpy ground or when planting for exhibition it is as well to place a couple of handfuls of leaf-mould or finely sifted compost round each tuber.

For early potatoes the rows should be 2 feet apart and the tubers 9 inches apart in the lines. For maincrop and late varieties these distances must be increased to at least 3 feet and 15 inches respectively. In all cases the tubers should be covered with about 3 inches of soil. When size of tuber rather than total weight of crop is the object, reduce the number of sprouts on each 'set' to two or at the most three, retaining the strongest.

Routine Work As soon as the shoots appear through the soil, hoe the surface between the rows and give a top dressing of a good potato fertilizer, which, if desired, may be prepared at home with four parts of superphosphate of lime, three parts of sulphate of ammonia, and two parts of sulphate of potash; this mixture is used at the rate of 5 oz. per sq. yard. Then pull the earth over the shoots with a draw hoe to protect them from frost and continue earthing up at intervals of a week or ten days until the soil is mounded into a series of wide, rather flat-topped ridges.

In the garden illustrated the west border is used as a frame yard for raising early vegetables and early seedlings. Marrows could be grown here on a hotbed, as it is a sheltered position which receives direct sun-

A GOOD METHOD OF PLANTING POTATOES

The soil removed from one row is being used to cover the tubers which have been planted in the previously made trench.

light for at least half the day. Early peas could be grown here, as in the south border. Nut bushes are used to enclose the rubbish dump.

Blight Spraying as a precautionary measure against potato blight should be carried out on all maincrop and late potatoes, as explained in Chapter Fifty.

Lifting Early potatoes are dug as soon as the tubers are large enough for use, but the maincrop and late varieties should be allowed to mature, and it is not usually wise to lift them until the haulm commences to die down. A fork should always be used for lifting, and there is no better type for this purpose than that which has round tines, as these do not readily bruise the tubers.

Storing Early potatoes should be used as dug, but maincrop and late varieties may be stored either in a cool shed or cellar or else in a clamp in the open. The clamp must always be made in a dry place, and it is advisable to spread plenty of dry straw on the ground first further to improve the drainage. The potatoes are then piled up in a conical heap and covered with a foot-thick thatch of straw, which is in turn protected by a deep layer of soil patted down smooth with the back of the spade to shoot off rain. Potatoes in clamps require ventilation, which is given by pulling a few wisps of straw out through the soil covering at intervals along the ridge of the clamp, so that they stick up, like so many chimneys, permitting escape of foul air.

CHAPTER FORTY-THREE

Peas and Beans

PEAS

CULINARY peas are of two types, round-seeded and wrinkled-seeded, the latter more familiarly known as marrowfat peas. From the garden standpoint only the second class is of much importance nowadays, for although the round-seeded peas were once grown for the earliest crop, they have now been replaced to a considerable extent even for this purpose by better-flavoured marrowfat kinds.

When to Sow for a Succession It is not wise policy to sow peas out of doors until the last week in March or even the first week in April in the north and midlands, but earlier crops can be obtained by sowing in a greenhouse or frame from the end of January onwards. It is best to make these indoor sowings in well-drained pots, placing three or four peas in each, so that they may be left to grow undisturbed until they can be planted out of doors, after proper hardening off, towards the end of April. For the earliest crops it is advisable to choose a dwarf variety, but for later use it is usually better to have a medium or tall pea, as in a general way varieties of these types crop more heavily than the dwarfs. In order to ensure a succession of peas throughout the summer, it is necessary to make sowings about once a fortnight until the first week in June. Naturally, for the first sowings early varieties are used, followed by mid-season and then late kinds, but the last sowings made towards the end of May and early in June should be of earlies again; late peas would take too long to mature at that season and would not be ready before the frosty weather of autumn.

Site Peas delight in an open sunny position and a deep, well-worked soil. It is far better to trench the whole plot throughout than to dig out a comparatively narrow trench for each row of peas, as is sometimes done. These narrow trenches are very liable to serve as drains in wet weather, collecting all the water from the surrounding soil and in consequence becoming very sour and cold themselves. If farmyard or stable manure is available it should be dug in freely, and if possible all preparatory work should be completed a month or six weeks before the peas are actually sown or planted.

When sowing out of doors or planting out the indoor-sown seedlings it is customary to arrange the plants in double rows about 9 inches or 1 foot apart, with at least 3 inches from plant to plant in the rows. The twin rows themselves should be spaced rather widely, and in no instance should be nearer together than the height of the variety when fully grown. For example, tall peas should be in double rows 5 feet apart, while medium peas may be 3 feet apart. It is quite an excellent plan to scoop out a flat-bottomed trench about 3 inches deep for each double line, planting or sowing on either side of this. If there are mice about it is advisable to shake the seeds—prior to sowing—in a tin containing a little red lead and paraffin.

Staking the Taller Varieties The medium and tall peas will require support, for which purpose there is nothing to surpass hazel branches.

TWO METHODS
OF SUPPORTING
RUNNER BEANS

On the left wires or strings are stretched from one end post to another, the upper ones being wider apart. Upright strings are then tied in position to each plant. On the right bean poles are driven firmly into the ground outside the plants and the poles whipped together at the top and firmed with a horizontal bar.

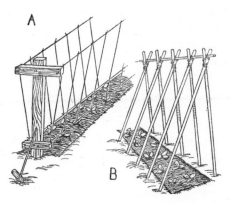

These should be arranged on either side of each row with the upper ends leaning a little outwards, not inwards, as one so commonly sees them, for the object is to spread out the growth as much as possible (see Chapter Twenty-one).

During the summer peas should be kept growing strongly, and will benefit from copious watering in dry weather, together with frequent feeding with weak liquid stimulants. For this latter purpose natural manures may be varied with a good compound garden fertilizer and an occasional dose of nitrate of soda dissolved in water at the rate of 1 oz. to 4 gallons.

BEANS

Beans are of three principal types—namely, broad beans, French or kidney beans, and runner beans. All are of the greatest importance from the standpoint of the amateur vegetable grower.

Sowing Autumn sowing of broad beans is not now practised as much as formerly, the earliest sowing usually being made in the greenhouse or frame in February. After proper hardening off, the plants from this sowing will be ready for planting out of doors early in April. The first outdoor sowing can be made about the end of March, followed by another for succession a fortnight or three weeks later. Dwarf kinds may be grown in rows 15 inches apart, but the more usual tall varieties will require twice that space, with 6 inches from plant to plant.

French or kidney beans and also runner beans are much more tender, and it is rarely wise to sow them out of doors, even in a sheltered sunny place, until the end of April; in the North it is better to wait until mid-May. Sowings in boxes under glass may be made two or three weeks earlier than this, but there is no point in planting seedlings out of doors until the end of May or early June, for they are liable to be killed by frost, even after hardening off.

Site With all types of bean a sunny position is desirable, and the soil can scarcely be too deeply worked or well manured, for they all delight in plenty of moisture and food material and are liable to become hard or stringy in dry, poor soils. Watering and feeding should follow similar lines to those indicated for peas. It is most important to pick the pods before they commence to ripen, as, if allowed to hang too long, the plants rapidly stop bearing. French and runner beans can be kept fresh for several days if they stand in a cool place with their stalks in about half an inch of water.

The ordinary French beans do not require any support and may be grown 9 inches apart in rows 2 feet apart. There are also varieties of French bean which climb like the runner beans, though not so strongly, and these should be planted in double rows a foot apart with at least 4 feet between the twin lines. A stout stick must be placed to each plant. Runner beans require even more space, and 8 feet is by no means an excessive distance to leave between the double lines, with the plants at foot intervals. A tip worth noting with all tall beans and peas is to arrange for the rows to run as nearly as possible north and south, so that each side gets an equal share of sunlight. Strong stakes at least 8 feet in length are necessary to support runner beans, and even these should be made secure at the top to another pole or wires strained between stouter uprights at each end of the row, for wind pressure when the beans are in full growth can be very great. Those who cannot obtain stakes may still grow runner beans by the simple expedient of constantly nipping out the points of the runners and so making the plants into big loose bushes, but when treated in this way the beans should be at least 3 feet apart each way.

Broad beans are liable to be badly attacked by black fly (aphis), and as a precautionary measure it is advisable to pinch out the growing point of each plant as soon as the lowermost pods are formed. A frequent cause of complaint with runner beans is that the flowers fall without producing any pods, but this can almost always be checked by adequate watering coupled with regular syringeing each evening during the flowering period with clear water.

Haricot beans such as Dwarf Dutch Brown and Comtesse de Chambord are grown in exactly the same way as dwarf French beans except that no pods are gathered green. Instead they are left to ripen, when the whole plant is pulled up and hung in a cool, dry place for a further few weeks. Then the beans are shelled out of the pods and stored for winter use. The crop is most profitable in mild districts.

CHAPTER FORTY-FOUR

Onions, Shallots, and Leeks

ONIONS

MARCH is the best month during which to sow the main onion crop; to start earlier is no advantage, as the seeds lie for a long time before germinating, and there is the risk of some of them perishing, while late sowing cuts the season of growth short and reduces the weight of the crop. The variety known as White Lisbon is sown in late August or early September to provide young onions in spring for use in salads. Growers of exhibition onions also used to practise autumn sowing in a sheltered border, planting out the seedlings in spring, but this practice is now on the wane, greenhouse sowing in January in a temperature of about 65° being adopted instead.

The onion needs really good soil, deeply dug and well manured, preferably with rotted farmyard or stable manure. Wood ashes can also be worked into the soil freely with advantage. A very firm bed is necessary to prevent the onions getting too thick at the neck, and to ensure this firmness a thorough treading must be given prior to sowing, choosing a day for the operation when the soil is in good condition—neither over-dry nor too wet. The position chosen for the bed must be open and sunny; incidentally, the onion provides an exception to the general rule of changing the positions of crops each season, for best results are usually obtained by preserving one plot for this vegetable and so gradually getting it into perfect condition.

Sowing When the surface soil has been broken down to a fine tilth with fork and rake, the drills should be made alongside a line, tightly stretched. These must not be more than $\frac{1}{2}$ inch in depth, and it is a great advantage to leave them exposed to the warming influence of the sun's rays for some hours before sowing the seed.

Some gardeners, instead of drawing drills, lay a straight, round rod, such as the handle of a rake or hoe, beside the line, thus making a firm, smooth groove for the seeds. This method has a decided advantage, in that the seeds can be seen more easily, and therefore the quantity sown is more readily regulated. Also the bottom of the drill is smoother and less liable to variation in depth.

The ordinary distance apart for the drills is 9 inches, but where big bulbs are desired it is best to allow a foot. To obtain good, well-formed, sound onions the sowing should be near the surface and as thin as possible. The seeds are then covered with specially prepared, finely sifted soil, which is smoothed down with a rake and firmed with the back of a spade.

Thinning should not be done all at once, and the thinnings can be used in salads. Final distance apart for the plants in the rows is from 6 to 9 inches, according to the size of the bulb desired. Chemical fertilizers, and particularly well-blended mixtures containing phosphates, potash, and nitrogen, can be used with great advantage in liquid form during the summer to stimulate growth, while the onion also responds to occasional top dressing of nitrate of soda, but the quantity should not exceed ¼ oz. per square yard each application. At all times the soil must be kept well hoed and free of weeds, and if mildew puts in an appearance the onions should be dusted with flowers of sulphur.

Ripening the Bulbs Towards the end of August, when growth is nearly completed, the tops are bent over to encourage final ripening off, and a

RIPENING ONIONS
The stems are bent over in August to encourage the bulbs to ripen.

week or so later the onions can be lifted carefully with a fork and laid out on the soil, or, better still, in a sunny frame, to dry. If they are to be stored for the winter, the best method is to plait them together into ropes in the manner practised by the vendors of onions who are so commonly seen hawking their produce.

SHALLOTS

The shallot is a close ally of the onion, but instead of being grown from seed it is propagated vegetatively by means of bulbs pressed into the soil in February 6 inches apart in rows 9 inches or 1 foot apart. A sunny site should be chosen and the site prepared exactly as for onions. Soon after midsummer growth will be completed, and each bulb produces a fine cluster, which should be lifted and ripened off as described for onions, the best being kept for use, the medium bulbs reserved for replanting the following season, and the smallest used for pickling.

LEEKS

The leek is one of the hardiest and most useful of vegetables for consumption during the early months of the year. It will grow in almost any soil, needs little attention, and even when planted on the poorest of land, where it rarely attains full size, the quality is of the best provided that the stems are suitably blanched to make them tender. The seeds should be sown in rows a foot apart as early in March as the weather will permit. Thin sowing is essential for securing nice sturdy plants.

The bed must be kept free from weeds by light hoeing, and the permanent site prepared for planting out in June. The plot should be well dug and manured, with the manure kept well down to induce deep rooting. The leeks should be spaced 9 inches apart in rows 18 inches distant. A good stout dibber can be used to make the holes, which should be roughly 6 inches in depth, and the plant dropped into each must reach to the bottom, when the surface soil should come to the base of the leaves. There is no need to push soil in round the plants; instead the watering-can is brought into use, and each plant is given a liberal quantity of water. This is sufficient to rinse enough soil on to the roots at the bottom of the hole to give the plant a start. Provided that the soil is in fairly good condition, the plants will eventually thicken in the stem sufficiently to fill the holes.

Leeks are sometimes grown in trenches in much the same manner as celery. This method is most useful on light sandy soils and also when growing for exhibition, but is not necessary for ordinary purposes if the soil is fairly rich.

Liquid manure may be applied occasionally between the rows during the growing season, and as the plants advance in growth they should be blanched. This may be done by drawing the soil up round the stems or by surrounding them with stout paper collars.

CHAPTER FORTY-FIVE

Cauliflowers, Broccoli, and other Green Crops

I F the cabbage family were to be excluded from the vegetable garden three parts of its most indispensable vegetables would be absent, for it includes varieties as different in appearance and use as the cabbage, savoy, Brussels sprout, cauliflower, broccoli, kale, turnip, and kohl-rabi.

Broccoli and Cauliflower These are two of the choicest and most appreciated of the group. The principal difference between them is that the latter has a more delicate flavour, but is less hardy than the former. Cauliflowers are available for use in spring, summer, and autumn, whereas broccoli are in season in autumn, winter, and spring.

Both thrive best in a rich, medium-heavy soil, though they may be grown in almost every garden after suitable preparation. The site should be well dug and manured as long as possible in advance, so that it may have time to settle thoroughly before planting. The practice of planting broccoli after early potatoes is economical of space, but is not calculated to produce the finest heads.

Sowing Seeds of cauliflower may be sown in a cold frame in September or in a warm greenhouse in February. Whichever plan is adopted, the seedlings must not be allowed to become drawn in the seed boxes. They should be pricked off as soon as possible and hardened off for planting out in April. Broccoli should be sown in a sheltered border outdoors from March to early May to provide a succession of plants, while in furtherance of this policy selection should be made from early mid-season and late varieties.

Protect the Curd In autumn and winter, when the white curds of cauliflowers and broccoli commence to form, it is a wise precaution to bend some of the larger leaves inwards to protect the hearts from frost, or alternatively to tie the leaves together in much the same manner as practised in blanching cos lettuces.

Brussels Sprouts These must have a long season of growth in order to give a good return. It does not pay to grow this vegetable on poor, shallow or very light soil. A good loam trenched 3 feet deep and liberally manured is ideal, and an open sunny position is another essential to really satisfactory results.

For an early-sown autumn crop seeds may be sown in warmth early in March. The seedlings are transplanted into deep trays as soon as possible and hardened off for planting out in May. For the general crop it is time enough to sow seeds at the end of March in a sheltered border outdoors.

A STURDY BROCCOLI PLANT
Note the compact ball of roots, the result of correct pricking out.

Cabbages in Variety These may be had for the table throughout the year. To achieve this end sowings should be made in spring and summer, and there must be a wise selection of varieties. A first sowing should be made in warmth in February followed by one outdoors towards the end of March, and another in the middle of April. Plants from these will be ready for their final quarters from late April to mid-summer, and will be available for the table from June to October. A May sowing will yield plants for use from November to January. The fourth and last sowing should be made during late July or early August to supply spring cabbage. As regards varieties, Primo is good for early summer, Winningstadt for early autumn use, Christmas Drumhead for late autumn and winter, and Flower of Spring or Harbinger for spring.

The red or pickling cabbage attains a great size, but is not a vegetable that need be largely grown. A few seeds sown early in August will supply sufficient plants.

The colewort, or collard, is most useful because of its compact habit and hardiness. Seeds sown in early June will yield plants that can be placed out permanently in July, 1 foot apart each way, and will be ready for kitchen use during the autumn and early winter.

The savoy cabbage is of similar growth to the ordinary white cabbage but has wrinkled foliage. The 'hearts' come in for use in autumn and are in best condition for eating directly after the first autumnal frosts. Seed must be sown outdoors during April and May and the seedlings planted out in June and July.

Kale The kales, or borecoles, are chiefly remarkable for their great hardiness, and they will survive the most severe winters when many other green crops are killed. There are numerous varieties, such as Asparagus Kale, which produces long, succulent shoots in spring;

PLANTING BRASSICAS
The young plants should be laid first along a garden line and then planted very firmly.

Cottagers' Kale, a most prolific kind with abundant crimped leaves; and the Curled Scotch Kale, in which the crimping is far more pronounced and gives the plants a distinctly ornamental appearance. Seeds of all these are sown out of doors in April and May.

Turnip and Kohl-rabi Finally, there are the root and stem vegetables, the turnip and kohl-rabi. The former is dealt with in Chapter Forty-seven. Kohl-rabi has something of the appearance of a turnip, but it is the stem, above ground, that becomes swollen. These stems are boiled like turnips and possess a distinctive, nutty flavour peculiarly their own. Seeds should be sown from April till June in a deeply dug plot. The seedlings should be thinned to 6 or 8 inches. The stems should not be allowed to get too big before the crop is lifted.

All members of the cabbage family repay good cultivation throughout. The extra labour involved in transplanting seedlings from the seed boxes or beds into nursery beds, in which they can be disposed a few inches apart each way, will be reflected in sturdier plants when the time arrives for final planting out. An occasional dressing during the summer of nitrate of soda at the rate of $\frac{1}{4}$ oz. per square yard gives a great stimulus to growth, while a thorough syringeing with salt water every other morning during June and early July will go far towards keeping caterpillars at bay.

CHAPTER FORTY-SIX

Summer Salads

EVEN in gardens too small to supply the family with the staple vegetables some attempt should be made to grow crops for summer salads, for these, by reason of their absolute freshness, can be far more delicious than the much-handled commercial crops.

Quick Development for Crispness In order to ensure fine, crisp salads of good flavour, most of the ingredients require to be grown quickly. Slow growth usually results in stringy tissues and a bitter taste. Quick development depends mainly upon three conditions—a richly nourished, moist, and warm soil. Stable manure, being warm, is the best for early crops, but for the hot period of summer cow manure, which is retentive of moisture, is more useful, especially on light soils, which, incidentally, if supplied with a liberal proportion of humus, suit most salad crops best. Hop manure is the best substitute for stable manure, but if the soil already contains plenty of humus any extra food material necessary can be supplied in the form of a good artificial fertilizer.

Lettuce This is one of the most important of salad crops, and will succeed in any rich soil, light or heavy, if it has been well worked to the depth of at least 1 foot. This is necessary to ensure a constant supply of water from below, and not because the lettuce is very deep rooting. In the absence of an abundant and uninterrupted supply of water, collar rot is almost certain to develop, in addition to the aforementioned toughness and bitterness. The long, or cos, lettuces are crisper than the round or cabbage varieties, especially if blanching is encouraged by tying the leaves loosely together with raffia.

It is a good plan to sow the seeds in boxes and to plant them out into the prepared bed as soon as they require pricking out. In this manner a small bed can be used to the maximum advantage. A small sowing should be made every six weeks till the beginning of August, the first outdoor sowing being made at the end of March in sheltered borders in warm districts. Where the seedlings can be given the protection of a cold frame or of cloches, the seed can be sown at the beginning of February and pricked out into similarly protected boxes. They must be kept growing steadily by keeping them in a good light and admitting air on all favourable occasions. Alternatively, the seeds can be sown in the bed. To save transplanting any seedlings, the seeds should be placed in groups of three at the required distances apart and thinned to one at each point when ready. Alternatively, the seeds can be sown in rows and the seedlings developing in the unwanted parts transplanted. These will be ready for use a little later than the undisturbed plants. The distance apart will vary with the varieties. Tom Thumb, a small lettuce, can be 6 inches apart in rows 9 inches distant. The medium-sized varieties, such as All-the-Year-Round and most of the cos lettuces, need 9 inches each way, while large cabbage lettuces may require to be 10 inches or even a foot apart. Small sowings may be made on odd pieces of ground, such as on the top of the ridges between the rows of celery.

BLANCHING COS LETTUCE
The heads are tied with raffia to protect the inner leaves from the light. The one on the left has been tied too low down and the one on the right is being done correctly.

The ground between lettuces must be kept well hoed or mulched with loose litter. The plants must never be short of water and benefit greatly by the frequent application of copious draughts of very weak liquid manure, sulphate of ammonia, or nitrate of soda. Slugs must be kept in check with soot or lime.

Endive Often treated only as a winter salad crop, endive can be grown equally successfully during the summer. The treatment is similar to that given to lettuces, with the exception that the plants must be blanched by covering them with flower-pots when they are well developed.

Radishes This crop may be grown in warm sheltered borders for early use and in cool, shady northern beds for main summer supplies. The early crop should be protected from late frosts by covering the plants with pea sticks and straw, but these materials must be removed whenever possible to keep the plants healthy. The seeds should be sown broadcast and thinly. They can then be pulled as soon as they are sufficiently grown without the necessity of thinning the bed. The soil should be well tilled and preferably one which has been manured thoroughly during the previous season, in which case only copious supplies of water will be needed. Sowings should be made once every three weeks from March until the middle of August if a constant supply is required. French Breakfast, Icicle, and the earliest Turnip Forcing varieties are reliable.

Mustard and Cress Both these can be grown out of doors under similar conditions to radishes. Cress takes a little longer to develop than mustard, and should therefore be sown about three days earlier. Successional sowings must be made once a fortnight to maintain a steady supply. To obtain a quick crop of these salads they should be sown in a frame or under cloches. An improvised frame of a box with the top replaced by a sheet of glass serves equally well. In such a structure the seed can be sown on the surface of the soil without the thin covering layer required in the open.

Spring Onions These may either be sown separately as a special salad crop, or the thinnings of the main onion crop may be used. If the crop is autumn sown, it will be found that the leaves are generally tough and the bases hot and strong, whereas onions raised in the spring under the protection of temporary or other frames will be infinitely better. The plants can be used while still very small; there is no need to wait till they reach the size of the autumn-sown thinnings. White Lisbon is the best variety. Perennial chives are often used in place of spring onions, and a few plants should always be grown in the bed allotted to herbs. The foliage may be cut to the ground level when gathering, for a new crop will soon push up.

The culture of tomatoes, cucumbers, and beetroot—all important constituents of summer salads—will be found in other chapters in this book. In addition to the afore-mentioned constituents of salads, peas, French and runner beans, and new potatoes are all frequently used cooked and allowed to become quite cold, while special cabbages and watercress form a valuable part of green salads. Young carrots can be used cooked or grated, and beetroot may also be grated and used raw instead of being boiled. Parsley, finely chopped, is also in demand.

CHAPTER FORTY-SEVEN

Root Crops

UNDER this heading are included carrots, parsnips, turnips, and beet. All these grow most satisfactorily in deeply dug soil that was well manured for the previous crop. If grown in shallow or stony ground or in contact with fresh, rank manure, the roots tend to fork.

Carrots When grown in England are almost always scarlet, though they may be short, medium, or long and stump-rooted or pointed, but white, purple, and lemon-coloured varieties are in common use on the Continent. Many amateurs grow only a main crop of carrots, but wherever brick pits or frames are available for forcing it is possible to

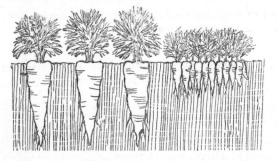

A LESSON IN THINNING CARROTS
The sketch shows the evils of overcrowding and the benefits which result from early and adequate thinning.

enjoy young carrots throughout the year. The ideal rooting medium for carrots is a deep sandy loam, or one of medium adhesiveness, brought to a fine tilth before the seeds are sown. Seeds of the carrot do not germinate freely in heavy cold soil, and where they have to be grown on such land should not be sown until at least a fortnight later than on sandy soil in the same district. Seeds of early varieties may be sown broadcast or left unthinned in drills and drawn for immediate use by successive thinnings along the rows. Such tender young carrots are much appreciated in salads. The later maincrop varieties should be sown in drills throughout April and May, though successional sowings for young roots may be made from February to September, provided the necessary temperature and protection can be given to both the early and late sowings. The maincrop sowings must be thinned as soon as possible,

272

Left: Hoeing between leeks to keep down weeds and maintain a dust mulch. *Right:* Lifting well-grown leeks as required for use.

Left: Removing off-shoots from celery prior to earthing up. *Right:* Earthing up celery to blanch the stems.

Young cucumber plants growing under glass being trained up short stakes to the supporting wires.

Left: Removing a side growth from the main stem of a tomato plant.   *Right:* Mulching tomato plants with well-rotted manure.

but not all in one operation, until the plants are left from 9 to 12 inches apart in the rows, which should be about a foot apart.

The soil between the rows must be kept hoed regularly throughout the summer, and the soil kept firm round the crowns to keep away the carrot fly. This firming is especially necessary after thinning. The fly may also be kept at bay by mixing a small quantity of paraffin with sand and sprinkling this between the rows once every fortnight throughout the summer. The young foliage of carrots is also liable to be attacked by greenflies.

Growing for Exhibition If carrots are to be grown for exhibition, or if the soil is in no way suited to their cultivation, the roots may be grown in holes filled with a specially prepared compost. The holes are made in the ordinary bed by means of a crowbar. They should be deeper than the depth to which the particular variety is expected to reach, and should be filled with a fine sandy compost. This can be made

STORING ROOT CROPS
Here matured carrots are being covered with dry soil layer upon layer. The whole is covered with soil and a straw 'chimney' is made for ventilation.

by mixing sand and sweet leaf-mould, and old potting soil from chrysanthemums, etc., may be added. Three or four seeds should be sown in the top of each hole and the strongest seedling only retained. By leaving a slight depression at the site of each hole surrounding cultivation can start at once.

Carrots should be grown as fast as possible, though this does not mean that they should be allowed to become drawn in the frames, for the best-flavoured roots without the least suspicion of stringiness are obtained in this manner. The soil between the plants may be dusted with soot and a good all-round fertilizer during showery weather, and during hot, dry spells should be well mulched to maintain the rate of growth.

In early autumn the main crop should be lifted carefully by means of a fork, care being taken that the roots are not bruised and damaged, and then stored in sand or ashes for winter use.

Parsnips In order to grow parsnips satisfactorily it is absolutely essential to allow them a long season of growth. The seeds should be

S

sown at least six weeks in advance of those of the main crop of carrots. The best soil is a light or sandy loam, and if there is lime or chalk below this so much the better. Cold retentive clay is not ideal for these roots, and on such a soil the method of individual holes, as recommended for carrots, should be employed.

If the soil is in need of manure, this must be applied not later than the autumn prior to sowing, and even then should be well rotted, for fresh manure causes not only forking, but also canker near the crown. Seed should be sown late in February and during the first two weeks of March, the exact date depending mainly upon correct soil condition at the time of planting. In addition to having the soil in a fine, crumbling condition it is wise to choose a still day, as the seeds are very light. The rows should be 18 inches apart and the seeds sown thinly and covered with an inch of soil. The seedlings must be thinned to 9 inches or more apart.

The Dutch hoe must be used freely all the summer to prevent the main bulk of the soil from becoming dry, for parsnips need an adequate water supply. Sulphate of potash is the only fertilizer that need be given. This should be applied at the rate of $\frac{1}{4}$ oz. per root once every week from the time that the crop is half-grown till it is almost mature.

Turnips By making successional sowings of turnips every three weeks from the first suitable days in March till the middle of September it is possible to have roots in good condition for the greater part of the year. Turnips succeed in most soils, if these are properly prepared. Ground in a low, moist situation is favourable for the production of good specimens during the summer period.

The seed should be sown an inch deep in drills which may be as close as 10 inches for the first sowings, but should be 15 inches apart for the later crops, to ensure that the foliage has plenty of room and does not become drawn. It will then be able to withstand cold weather much better. As cool and shady a place as possible should be chosen for the seed bed, and if the sun shines hotly before the final thinning the bed should be shaded. Thinning must take place when the first rough leaves appear, and is best done in the evening or after a shower.

The rows must be kept hoed, and in dry seasons the crop will have to be watered in the evening to keep the roots growing fast. In hot sun the roots not only grow slowly and thus become bitter, but they are very liable to attacks from the turnip fly. Soot, wood ashes, and a reliable fertilizer may be used occasionally.

Of the late-sown crop most of the plants will swell up before the winter, but the young growth of any which do not do so may be used in the spring as an addition to other winter greens.

Turnips are sufficiently hardy to remain in the ground during most winters, but it is advisable to lift a proportion of the well-formed roots and to store them in sand or ashes in a frostproof shed in case a very severe spell of weather is experienced.

Beetroot Beet do best on light sandy loam of good depth, but where this is not obtainable the next best in the form of well-trenched ground lightened with old mortar rubble and wood ashes must be employed. A plot just cleared of celery is ideal, for it will contain a certain amount of manure. Fresh manure is harmful.

The surface of the soil should be raked to a fine tilth in May, and the seeds sown in drills 2 inches deep. These require to be 12 inches apart. The seeds are best placed about 2 inches apart and later thinned to about 6 inches apart, only the strongest and best being kept. As birds often eat beet seedlings, it is advisable to protect them by means of black cotton stretched between twigs.

When lifting beet, great care must be taken to prevent damage to the skin and main roots, or bleeding will occur.

By careful stacking in sand, not ashes, beet may be stored during the winter. The roots must be placed upright and the leaves twisted or cut off.

CHAPTER FORTY-EIGHT

Miscellaneous Crops

I N this chapter a few vegetables are included which do not readily lend themselves to inclusion under any other grouping than a miscellaneous one. The first of these is asparagus, one of the real aristocrats of the vegetable garden. This and rhubarb are both reckoned among the most important permanent occupants of the vegetable garden—that is to say, plants which should remain undisturbed year after year. For this very reason it is more than usually necessary to prepare the soil thoroughly, for the results of careless work at the outset may prove a source of trouble.

Asparagus The asparagus bed must be in a sunny open position and, if the soil is naturally heavy, it should be lightened as much as possible by the addition of strawy stable manure, sand, dried seaweed, etc., and also by deep digging in the autumn. It is possible to raise asparagus from seed, but a far quicker method, and one to be recommended to the novice, is to purchase strong two- or three-year-old plants in April. The most convenient method of culture is to arrange these plants in beds 3 or 4 feet wide, in rows about 15 inches apart, with the same distance between the plants. A 2-foot alleyway should be allowed between each bed. The roots must be spread out carefully and covered with fine soil worked among them by hand and then made firm. The crowns or growing points of the plants should be 4 or 5 inches below the surface.

When to Cut It is a great mistake to cut asparagus from newly made beds or to continue cutting from established beds after the end of June. Even the second year after planting cutting should only be moderate as, if prolonged, it considerably weakens the crowns. Each spring asparagus beds may be top dressed with well-rotted manure, while immediately after cutting they will benefit from a top dressing of salt at the rate of 1 oz. per square yard.

Rhubarb This is not so particular as to soil or position, but the most satisfactory results are obtained in an open place in deeply dug and well-manured soil. The best time for planting is March, and no sticks should be pulled for the first year. Do not fall into the error of placing the crowns too close. They should be at least 3 feet apart. Forced

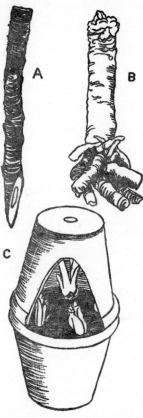

FORCING RHUBARB

Ordinary drain pipes will serve well for this purpose if covered with earthenware flower pots.

CULTURE OF SEAKALE

(A) *Suitable thong or root cutting for planting out.* (B) *a sturdy crown lifted for forcing;* (C) *forcing crowns potted up and covered to ensure proper blanching.*

rhubarb is always much appreciated, and may be readily obtained by covering well-established crowns in November with old barrels, drain pipes, or special forcing pots surrounded by dead leaves or other dry litter. If drain pipes are used the tops must be suitably covered to exclude all light. The object of the dry litter is to maintain an equable temperature, and so encourage steady growth.

Seakale Forced in much the same manner as rhubarb and, like it, seakale is a permanent crop. It is propagated by means of thongs, which are nothing more nor less than root cuttings 5 or 6 inches in length inserted during late March out of doors in the position in which they are to grow. This should be an open sunny plot of well-drained ground which has been deeply dug and given a good dressing of rotted dung during the preceding winter. The rows of root cuttings must be 18 inches apart with a foot from plant to plant. The cuttings themselves may be dropped into suitable holes made with a dibber, and it is an excellent plan to place a little sharp sand or ashes round each to give it a start. During the summer, feeding with liquid manure, watering during the dry weather and regular hoeing are the cultural items necessary, and by the autumn the plants should be strong enough for forcing, either in the manner already described for rhubarb or by lifting the roots and arranging them close together in large pots filled with sandy soil and then introducing them to a warm greenhouse. During the forcing period the crowns must be kept in total darkness, as, unless properly blanched, the seakale is bitter.

Summer Spinach Summer spinach thrives in any reasonably well-worked soil, and should be sown at fortnightly intervals for succession from February until June. It is advisable to make the later sowings in a semi-shaded position, as, for example, near standard fruit trees, for the plants are apt to run to seed if they are in a very hot place. The rows may be about 5 inches apart, and seedlings should be thinned out to 2 or 3 inches apart when large enough to handle. There is also a 'winter' or prickly spinach, which should be sown early in August to stand the winter, while the perpetual spinach or spinach beet is sown about the middle of March and again in August, in rows 1 foot apart, seedlings being allowed at least 6 inches each in the rows.

Marrow and Cucumber The vegetable marrow and ridge cucumber are worth growing well, but it is a mistake to place the plants on raised mounds, as one so frequently sees them grown. No vegetables have greater appreciation of ample moisture than these, and perched up on a heap of soil it is extremely difficult to keep them adequately watered. A far better system is to dig out a wide hole some 2 feet deep and fill this to within 3 inches of soil level with old turves, grass side downwards, and a liberal quantity of decayed manure or vegetable refuse. If the young plants are set out on this, 3 feet apart for bush marrows and 5 feet for all trailing kinds, they will get plenty of nourishment, and it will be a simple matter to soak them adequately from time to time. Seeds may be sown singly in 3-inch pots early in May and germinated in a frame or greenhouse, or may be sown directly in the outdoor bed at the end of the month. It is not wise to plant cucumbers or marrows out until the first week in June, because they are very tender. The runners of the trailers should have their points pinched out when they reach the limits of the bed. This will encourage the formation of side growths which bear more satisfactorily. Always cut marrows while they are still quite young unless required for jam.

Celery Here is a most attractive vegetable to grow, for it provides a real test of cultural skill, and, incidentally, in producing good celery one goes a long way towards permanently improving the quality of the soil, for which reason many experienced gardeners shift the position of their celery trenches each year, so that, little by little, the whole vegetable plot obtains the benefit. The best time to sow seed is in March, and it should be accommodated in boxes or pans either in a frame (preferably on a mild hotbed) or else in the greenhouse. Sow thinly and prick out into a compost containing plenty of leaf-mould as soon as the seedlings can be handled.

Meanwhile, the trenches should be prepared in a sunny position out of doors. For this purpose the soil must be taken out to a depth of 3 feet, and each trench for a single row of plants should be fully 15 inches in width. If two or more trenches are to be made they should be spaced at 3-foot intervals to allow for easy earthing up later on. All the soil is thrown out and is then returned a little at a time together with well-rotted farmyard or stable manure in almost equal bulk. Soil and manure must be thoroughly mixed together, while the final 6 inches should be soil only. The trench is only filled to within about 6 inches of ground level, and the plants are set out in the centre of this prepared trench in early June. They should be a foot apart in the rows.

Celery must be kept freely watered during the summer, and from time to time should be syringed with soot water or one of the special leaf-miner insecticides to ward off the celery fly. All side growths at the base of each main stick must be removed, as they detract from the shapeliness and value of the plant. Blanching should not be commenced until the plants are fully developed. It is achieved either by placing brown-paper collars round the stems and tying with raffia or more usually by drawing the soil around them, so forming a ridge right up to the base of the foliage. About six weeks is usually necessary for complete blanching. The celery can be left in the ridges during the winter and dug as required, but should be protected with dry straw in very cold or wet weather.

Artichokes These are of two kinds, globe and Jerusalem, but we are only concerned with the latter variety here, as the globe artichoke is almost exclusively a connoisseur's vegetable, and it is not often attempted by the beginner. Jerusalem artichokes are exceptionally easy to grow and may well be relegated to the more unfavourable parts of the vegetable garden, as they are well able to look after themselves. Tubers should be obtained and planted in March. They should be arranged about 15 inches apart in rows 3 feet apart, as growth is very vigorous. Lift in autumn as required.

Mushrooms This crop is really outside the scope of this elementary book as it requires highly specialized treatment. Intending growers should certainly study a good handbook devoted to the culture of mushrooms. All that can be said here is that mushroom cultivation is quite within the scope of the amateur provided he will take the trouble to master the peculiar requirements of the crop. Though fresh manure was at one time regarded as essential it has now been found possible to grow mushrooms on compost made from straw or chaff treated with chemicals. One or two firms specialize in the production of such preparations and are ready to furnish full particulars regarding their use to all interested persons.

Herbs Lastly, there are those two important garnishing and flavouring vegetables, parsley and mint. The former, strange to say, does best in rather poor soil, and so no great preparation is necessary beyond the usual digging and the breaking down of the surface to a fine tilth. It is best to make several sowings at short intervals, the first some time in March and the last about the second week in June for a winter supply. The only attention necessary is thorough watering should the weather happen to be dry. Mint can be purchased as plants, which should be placed out of doors during April in well-dug soil; once established it will grow almost anywhere, but is sometimes a little slow about making a start. It can be propagated very easily by means of short lengths of root lined out in boxes of sandy soil in late winter and started into growth in a sheltered place or, best of all, in a cold frame.

CHAPTER FORTY-NINE

Tomatoes, Cucumbers
and Melons

TOMATOES

WITHOUT doubt the tomato is the amateur greenhouse owner's favourite summer crop, though it must be confessed that his success with it is by no means always on a par with his enthusiasm. The fact of the matter is that, though tomatoes will drag out some kind of existence and even produce a modest crop under very unfavourable conditions, a fair amount of skill is necessary to attain really satisfactory results.

Tomatoes under Glass The common causes of failure under glass are starting too early with insufficient artificial heat to maintain steady growth, irregular and inadequate watering during the summer months and insufficient ventilation. It must be understood that the tomato almost more than any other greenhouse plant delights in a warm, rather dry atmosphere. As it also requires abundant moisture in the soil, the necessity for free ventilation and sufficient fire heat to keep the air warm yet circulating during cold weather becomes apparent.

Though professional growers continue to have tomatoes practically throughout the year, it is better for beginners to confine themselves to a summer crop from seeds sown in March if a heated house is available. A temperature of 55 to 60° is required for germination. There is no necessity to place the seed pans or boxes in a close frame, as a very damp atmosphere is not desirable, but it is wise to cover each box with a sheet of glass, removing this when the seedlings appear.

Prick out the seedlings into deeper boxes as soon as they have formed their first pair of rough leaves, and then, two or three weeks later, pot them up singly into 2½-inch pots provided with plenty of drainage material.

During these early stages a compost containing a fair proportion of leaf-mould and peat should be used, and it is a wise precaution to sterilize it a week or so before use by placing it in a bucket and standing this in a copper of boiling water for about an hour.

Planting in Permanent Quarters   On no account must the young plants be permitted to become overcrowded, for once they get thin and drawn it is a bad lookout for the crop. By early May the plants should be large enough for the final move, either direct into the greenhouse border or into large pots or boxes. Orange boxes serve very well, one plant being placed in each compartment. The compost should be mainly good fibrous loam, with the addition of some bonfire ashes if available, and bonemeal at the rate of one 5-inch potful per bushel. A little well-rotted manure can also be added, but not too much at the outset. It is necessary to plant very firmly, and if the tomatoes are set out directly in the greenhouse border it is all to the good if this is not above a foot in depth with a good drainage layer of slates beneath, as then feeding and

PLANTING A TOMATO IN A GREENHOUSE BORDER

The young plants are removed from the pots and put straight into the previously prepared border, and staked.

watering will be more directly under control. Rows of plants must be at least 2 feet apart, with a foot between the plants in the rows.

Tomatoes are trained to a single stem each, all side shoots being pinched out as soon as they are noted. Usually a short bamboo cane is placed to support the base of the plant, and then a length of soft twine is stretched between two hooks in such a way that the main shoot may be trained along this right up to the apex of the greenhouse. When this is reached the growing point is pinched out.

Management during Growing Season Watering must be carefully attended to throughout, a safe rule being to give sufficient to soak the soil right through and then no more until it commences to show signs of drying out on the surface. Pots may, of course, be tapped as explained in earlier chapters.

In the spring, ventilation should only be given during the day, but as the weather gets warmer the ventilators must be left open a little throughout the night and particular care taken to admit plenty of air early in the morning as soon as direct sunlight first reaches the glass.

Feeding should start when the first truss of flowers is set and the tiny fruits can be seen. A good proprietary tomato fertilizer may be used, or the mixture recommended for potatoes in Chapter Forty-two, in which case it should be dissolved in water at the rate of ½ oz. per gallon and applied freely once a week instead of ordinary water. A few weeks later white rootlets will probably appear on the surface of the soil, an indication that a top dressing of rotted stable or farmyard manure, dried and passed through a very coarse-meshed sieve, may be given with advantage.

It is usually advisable to assist fertilization of the flowers, especially early in the summer, and to this end the plants should be gently jarred, preferably about midday when the sun is shining, so that pollen is scattered freely.

Towards the end of the summer some of the lower leaves should be removed to allow light and air to penetrate more freely and so encourage ripening of the fruits. If the plants carry a very heavy crop it may even be necessary to pick the fruits as soon as they start to colour, finishing the ripening process in a sunny window so as to give the remaining fruits a better chance.

The Unheated House In cold houses it is not advisable to attempt to raise tomatoes from seed. Instead plants, properly hardened off, should be purchased about the second week in May, subsequent treatment following the same general lines as in heated greenhouses, except that less ventilation should be given for the first week or so until danger of frost is past.

Tomatoes Outdoors Tomatoes can also be grown outdoors though it is always something of a gamble as to how much ripe fruit is gathered. Principles of cultivation are the same as under glass but there are differences in detail. Seed should not be sown until mid-March, indeed it may under favourable conditions be delayed until early April. The seedlings should be potted on as for greenhouse work and should be well hardened off in a frame during May. They should not be planted outdoors until June unless some protection (as with cloches) can be given. The position chosen should be sheltered but sunny and the soil should be prepared as in glasshouse culture. Each plant should be tied to a strong stake or cane and should be stopped, *i.e.*, the top should be removed, when four trusses of flowers have been produced. Water will be needed in dry weather and the plants should be fed in the same way as glasshouse tomatoes. The Amateur is a good early ripening variety for outdoor culture.

CUCUMBERS

Cucumbers under Glass Cucumbers are by no means so popular with the amateur, probably partly because they are less in demand for table purposes and in part due to the fact that the cucumber is not such an

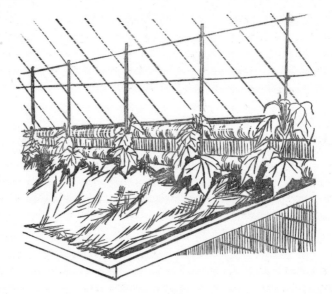

CUCUMBERS

Mounds of compost are built up over galvanized sheets placed on the rafter to ensure free drainage.

easy plant to manage as the tomato. Even more than the tomato it demands a house to itself, because it requires a comparatively high temperature and an exceedingly moist atmosphere. Trade growers usually cultivate cucumbers in forcing-houses, the floors of which are below ground level, but equally good crops can be produced in an ordinary greenhouse provided it is adequately warmed. Ridge cucumbers are dealt with on page 278.

The best time to start is March unless the house has little artificial heat, when it is advisable to defer seed sowing until early May. A temperature of 60 to 65° is essential for satisfactory germination. The seeds should be sown singly in 3-inch pots filled with a compost containing plenty of leaf-mould or peat, and it is advisable to germinate in a close box, but a day or so after the seedlings appear the pots can be removed to the greenhouse staging. A suitably moist atmosphere is maintained by thoroughly wetting the paths and staging at least twice a day, at the same time syringeing the plants with tepid water. The roots must also be kept well supplied with tepid water.

When preparing the beds, drainage is an important item, and a glance at the illustration on page 284 will indicate more clearly than many words just what is required. The compost is of good fibrous loam, with plenty of well-rotted stable or farmyard manure and a good sprinkling of bonemeal. This should be spread to a depth of 4 or 5 inches all over the staging or floor, while mounds, each composed of about a bushel of compost, should be made about 3 feet apart for the plants. As soon as these have made two pairs of rough leaves each they should be set out, one on the top of each mound.

The main stem of each cucumber is trained up the roof of the house on wires suitably placed, while, contrary to the practice with tomatoes, side shoots (except for a few right at the bottom of each plant) are retained and trained horizontally. It is on these side growths that the flowers and fruits appear, and each is stopped as soon as two tiny fruits have been formed on it or it has grown so far as to interfere with the neighbouring plants.

A temperature of 65° without direct sun heat is maintained, and the house is lightly shaded to prevent leaf scorching. Water must be given freely and damping down continued. After a week or so white rootlets will commence to appear on the surface of the compost, and this is a signal for top dressing with about 2 inches of good loam, leaf-mould, and well-rotted short strawy manure, the dressing being repeated later if the roots come to the surface again.

Throughout, ventilation must be given very carefully, for a dry atmosphere is not required and cold draughts must be avoided. Nevertheless, a little air should be admitted on fine days, or disease may take hold of the plants. Cucumbers should always be cut as soon as they attain a useful size, for if allowed to hang too long the crop will suffer and the cucumbers may commence to rot at the end.

MELONS

The culture of melons is practically identical with that of the greenhouse cucumber. Indeed, there are only two points of real difference. One is that pinching is rather more severe with the melon. True the fruits are produced on laterals, but these should be stopped just beyond the first leaf following the tiny fruit, and no secondary side shoots should be permitted to form; thus each plant is restricted to a central stem with short fruit-bearing laterals. Melons can be spaced as closely as 2 feet.

The second point of cultural difference is that the flowers of melons must be fertilized by hand, and this is done by pushing the pollen flowers (which are usually borne in clusters) into the centres of the fruit-bearing flowers, which are borne singly, each showing the young melon on the foot stalk. Restrict each plant to four female flowers and fertilize these all on one day.

CHAPTER FIFTY

Keeping Crops Clean

ANY of the foes that attack crops in the vegetable garden are either identical with or else very similar to those that do damage in the flower and fruit gardens, and the general principles covering the control of these pests and diseases have already been fully dealt with in Chapters Twenty-five and Forty. There are, however, just a few instances of enemies more or less peculiar to these crops.

Potato Disorders For example, the potato is frequently attacked by potato blight, which usually makes its appearance about July, causing dark discolorations on the foliage which rapidly gain in size, eventually causing it to wither and die. In time the disease passes to the tubers as well, making them unfit for storing, and in bad cases causing complete loss of crop. Fortunately, though this disease cannot be easily cured, it can be readily prevented. The early potato crop usually escapes the disease, as it is lifted before the blight makes its appearance, but all maincrop and late potatoes should be sprayed as a matter of course early in July with ordinary Bordeaux mixture, which should be applied as a fine spray to both the under and upper surfaces of the leaves. It is a wise precaution to repeat the application towards the end of the month.

The potato tubers themselves suffer from three distinct troubles, two of which are known as scab, thus causing some confusion, while the third is termed wart disease. The common scab disease only affects the skin, causing roughness, and is usually due to young tubers having come into contact with harsh soil, cinder ashes, grit, or lime. It does not do much damage, though it spoils the appearance of the tubers for exhibition. What is known as corky scab is a much more destructive disease, causing deep rusty pits in mild cases, while in bad ones the tubers appear as though eaten by rats. It is not advisable to grow potatoes for several years on ground that has been infected with this disease, and even then it should be given a dressing of flowers of sulphur at the rate of $2\frac{1}{2}$ oz. per square yard a week or so prior to planting.

Wart disease is far and away the most serious of the three, and if an attack occurs it is necessary to notify the Ministry of Agriculture. The disease causes large wart-like eruptions, which may eventually cover the whole tuber, and the spores which spread from it remain in the soil, affecting it for a long while. Fortunately there are a number of varieties of potatoes which are immune to this disease, and these should be planted in all districts in which the wart disease is known to be present.

WART DISEASE
Large crusty wart-like growths appear on the potato.

Seedsmen nearly always state in their catalogues which varieties are immune, while lists of immune varieties are published annually by the Ministry of Agriculture.

Enemies of the Brassicas   Cabbages, and the various other allied crops such as broccoli, kale, and brussels sprouts, are all subject to a few special pests and diseases, most important among which are club root and cabbage root fly. The former is caused by a fungus which infects the roots, causing them to swell up and gradually decay, with a peculiarly unpleasant smell. Once the disease has got a hold there is nothing for it but to pull up the plants and burn them. There are, however, one or two proprietary preparations on the market which can be used to prevent the spread of this disease. Most of these have to be used on the seed bed, as it is while the plants are still quite small that they usually become infected. Autumn or early spring application of air-slaked lime at the rate of 1 lb. per square yard will check the disease.

The damage caused by the cabbage gall weevil is often mistaken for club root, for this pest also causes swellings, but on the base of the stem, not on the roots. The true nature of the foe can, however, be ascertained if one of the lumps is cut through with a sharp knife, for if the gall weevil is responsible a small white grub will be found curled up within. The pest is not usually a very serious one, though it occasionally checks growth severely. It is easily controlled by removing the galls when planting seedlings.

The cabbage root fly lays its eggs in the soil near the stem of the plants, and the small white larvae soon eat their way into the roots, causing them to decay, and the plants to turn a leaden colour. The most effective preventive is to sprinkle 4% calomel dust in a thin band on the surface soil around each seedling in early May and repeat two or three times until late June.

Seedlings of the cabbage family including turnips are sometimes

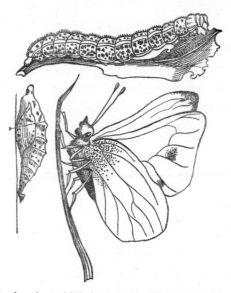

THE SMALL WHITE CABBAGE BUTTERFLY

This or other caterpillars attacking vegetable crops should be kept in check by hand picking and spraying with salt water.

badly holed by the turnip flea beetle, which is very small and jumps when disturbed. A complete cure can be effected by dusting with DDT.

Carrot Fly A fly similar to the cabbage root fly attacks carrots, and the maggots bore into the soft parts of the roots. If this pest is known to be prevalent, the plot reserved for carrots should be dressed in autumn with naphthalene at the rate of 6 oz. per square yard. As an additional precaution fine sand saturated with paraffin oil should be scattered over the surface of the soil immediately after the young carrots have been thinned out for the first time. A barrowload of sand is treated with about a quart of paraffin oil.

Celery Leaf Miner Celery is attacked by a leaf-mining maggot which causes similar damage to that done by the marguerite fly maggot, and can be kept in check by similar means. See Chapter Twenty-five.

T

Pea and Bean Weevil This pest eats the margins of the leaves of peas and broad beans so that they have a scalloped appearance. Two separate species, both grey in colour and about ¼ inch long, produce similar damage and the remedy is the same for both. Complete control can be obtained by dusting the foliage with DDT or gamma-BHC insecticide in spring and early summer when the damage is likely to be greatest.

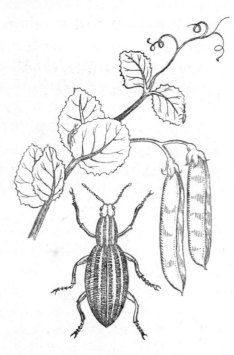

PEA AND BEAN
WEEVIL

This destructive pest and all other biting insects can be controlled by the use of a non-poisonous insecticide such as derris.

Thrips These are very active, tiny pests (rarely exceeding one-eighth of an inch in length) which commonly attack peas. They cause silvery streaks on the foliage, stems, and pods, often accompanied by considerable distortion. They can be kept in check by spraying with a good insecticide, preferably nicotine, but this must not be used on pods which are swelling.

Tomato Ailments Tomatoes, both under glass and out of doors, are subject to various troubles. Probably the commonest is the light brown leaf-mould, well described by its name. This is usually encouraged by inadequate ventilation and too damp an atmosphere, and improvement of these conditions affords the best method of controlling the disease.

If the tomatoes are crowded towards the end of the summer it is some-times advisable to remove some of the lower leaves to let in the light and air and then to spray with colloidal sulphur. Similar remarks apply to the mildew that attacks cucumbers, particularly under glass.

Tomato stem rot cannot be cured once it has made its appearance, and the plants should be immediately removed and burnt. Subsequently the soil should be sterilized with formaldehyde, as described in Chapter Thirty-four.

Stripe disease is quite distinct from stem rot, the symptoms being vertical brownish streaks on the stems, yellow patches on the foliage and distortion of the young leading shoot. The disease is encouraged by soft, sappy growth, and can be checked by dissolving sulphate of potash in water at the rate of $\frac{1}{4}$ oz. per gallon and applying 1 pint of this solution once a week to the soil round each plant.

Various troubles affect the fruits of tomatoes, the commonest being known as blossom end rot on account of dark discolorations always appearing at the 'eye' or blossom end of the fruit. This is not a disease in the true sense of the word, for it is almost always traceable to under-watering a few weeks previously. If tomatoes are allowed to go really short of water even for a few hours when the weather is hot, blossom end rot is almost certain to make its appearance, though probably not for five or six weeks.

White fly, often a serious pest in tomato houses, is controlled by fumigating with tetrachlorethane, as described in Chapter Forty.

Take Care with Sprays Very poisonous sprays should never be used in the vegetable garden on account of danger to human beings. Caterpillars and similar leaf-biting pests can often be kept in check by hand picking. When this is no longer practicable spraying with a non-poisonous insecticide such as derris should be adopted.

Virus Diseases One group of diseases not yet referred to are those caused by viruses. Almost all plants are liable to attack, potatoes and tomatoes being frequent victims. Common symptoms are stunted growth and deformed, mottled foliage, and all such plants should be burnt or the advice of an expert sought.

Index